D0893306

Eng

Ideology and Jewish Identity
in Israeli and American Literature

EDITED BY

Emily Miller Budick

STATE UNIVERSITY OF NEW YORK PRESS

Published by
State University of New York Press, Albany

For information, address State University of New York Press,
90 State Street, Suite 700, Albany, NY 12207

Production by Diane Ganeles
Marketing by Michael Campochiaro

Library of Congress Cataloging-in-Publication Data

Ideology and Jewish identity in Israeli and American literature
    p. cm.
    Includes bibliographical references and index.
    ISBN 0-7914-5067-8 (alk. paper)—ISBN 0-7914-5068-6 (pbk. : alk. paper)
    1. Israeli fiction—History and criticism. 2. American fiction—Jewish authors—History
and criticism. 3. American fiction—20th century—History and criticism. 4. Jews in
literature. 5. Group identity in literature.

PJ5029 I34 2001
892.4'360935203924—dc21   00-051017

10 9 8 7 6 5 4 3 2 1

For Professor Gershon Shaked,
in gratitude and affection

Contents

Preface

From the winter of 1996 through the spring of 1997, the Center for Literary Studies at the Hebrew University conducted a research seminar entitled "Narratives of Self-definition in Israeli and Jewish American Fiction." The following chapters are the product of that venture, in which a series of sterling academics and writers, from Israel, the United States, and Germany (some of them represented here, some of them not), presented papers on the subject of Jewish identity in fiction and poetry over the last fifty years.

The occasion of the seminar series was the retirement of Professor Gershon Shaked of the Department of Hebrew Literature. Conceived in his honor, the project also proceeded in the spirit of his work. It reflected not only his considerable achievement as a scholar of Jewish, and, in particular, Israeli literature, but his own deep commitment to the Jewish people as a viable, creative cultural entity. The author of numerous scholarly volumes, including the comprehensive five-volume history of Hebrew fiction from 1881 to the present (published in a one-volume English translation abridgment by Indiana University Press [2000]), Shaked is a vital, integral part of the story of Hebrew literature that he has told and taught. An immigrant to Israel from Vienna, he arrived in Israel in 1939 at the age of ten, one of many European refugees already stung by the events gathering into a catastrophe beyond anyone's imagining. There he not only underwent the transformation from German-speaking diaspora Jew to Hebrew-speaking Israeli, but began the series of intellectual moves that would make the subject of his life's work the literary tradition of which he now found himself a part. He received his undergraduate and graduate degrees at The Hebrew University and by 1959 he had already taken up a teaching position there. Both at Israeli institutions and abroad, as a visiting scholar, lecturer, and teacher, Gershon Shaked has molded many of today's most prominent scholars of Hebrew and Jewish literature. The many honors that he has received over the years, including the prestigious Bialik Literary Award and the Israel Prize, barely mark his importance on the scene of Israeli literary culture. On behalf of the many of us in his debt, this volume is dedicated to our teacher, colleague, and friend, Gershon Shaked.

As with any collective undertaking, there are more people to thank than the space of a mere inscription in a book allows. Though I have edited this book on my own (and am therefore responsible for whatever errors inhere), I conducted the research project jointly with Yigal Schwartz now of the Hebrew Literature Department of Ben-Gurion University, himself a student of Gershon Shaked. Yigal did more than define and organize the Hebrew literature program. He educated his co-director of the project in contemporary Israeli culture, bringing her into a world of vibrant literary discourse she had heretofore only barely, fleetingly glimpsed. My debt to Yigal is enormous, and these scant words of acknowlegment will never match the generosity, intelligence, and cheerfulness of his partnership.

The seminar series was funded primarily by the Shirley Collier Fund of the Literary Center of the Hebrew University. The center's director, Sanford Budick, who would in any case have offered assistance to the project, found himself of necessity wedded to it in a somewhat closer, more intimate relation. My special thanks to him alongside my acknowledgment of the moneys that permitted this project to go forward, not only from the center but from the Annenberg Budget of the Department of American Studies of The Hebrew University and The Franz Rosenzweig Center for German–Jewish Literature and Culture (then directed by Gabriel Motzkin), both of which helped bring in foreign participants from the field of American and European Jewish literature.

We appreciate permission to reprint materials that appeared elsewhere, namely, portions of essays by Hana Wirth-Nesher (in Michael Galinsky et al., *Insider/Outsider: American Jews and Multiculturalism* © 1998 by University of California Press); Ruth Wisse (in Wisse, *The Modern Jewish Canon* [New York: Free Press, 2000]); and Gershon Shaked (in *Modern Hebrew Fiction* trans. Yael Lotan, ed. Emily Miller Budick [Bloomington: Indiana University Press, 2000]).

The following permissions to reprint copyrighted material are also gratefully acknowledged: from the Jewish Publication Society for permission to reprint in Chapter Twelve excerpts from "Draft of a Reparations Agreement," "Tower of Babel," and "Footprints" by Dan Pagis (as translated by Stephen Mitchell); from ACUM-Israel, for permission to reprint in Chapter Twelve lines from "Because I'm Around" by Nathan Zach, © Nathan Zach c/o ACUM-Israel and in Chapter Eleven "Kappela Kolot" by Avot Yeshurun © Avot Yeshurun c/o ACUM-Israel.

Four gifted research assistants helped the project along at various stages: Janine Woolfson, Yael Shapira, Hava Burshtein-Rothenberg, and Zoe Bienstock. To them, much appreciation and thanks.

Finally, I cannot refrain from thanking my daughters Rachel and Ayelet, who not only provided counsel and comfort but who, in many ways, constitute the very reason for this project, which very literally bridges my own American Jewish roots and their native *Israeliuth* [Israeliness]. This expansion of the family definition of Jewish culture was helped along as well by the addition of my sons-in-law Shaul and Yuval and my grandsons Hananel and Mica, to whom I would most especially like to communicate my debt of gratitude, for letting me share in their somewhat different Jewish origins.

Introduction

This book stages a dialogue between Israeli and American Jewish authors, scholars, and intellectuals. It is a dialogue that has only very recently begun to emerge, and it concerns the issue of Jewish self-definition as expressed in literary texts. Indeed, an aspect of Jewish self-definition that emerges, powerfully if obliquely, from between the lines of the last fifty years of Israeli and American Jewish fiction is the mutual disinclination of writers and intellectuals from the world's two major communities of Jews to relate seriously to the experience of the other—as if these two populations of Jews had nothing whatsoever to do with one another, at least within the realm of literary fiction.[1]

This Israeli American failure-to-engage on the literary level could seem to be a nonissue. After all, we do not expect British writers to write about France or French writers to write about Russia. Yet Jewish Americans and Israelis share a several-thousands-year-old history, which is quite literally genetic. Most of the populations of Israel and America are only one or two generations removed (if that) from their joint ancestry. They are the individuals and their descendants, who fled Europe for the States and Palestine in the first half of the twentieth century (both preceding and following the Second World War). Or they are the remnant of those who perished there, who might be expected to feel a special interest in, and ugency to, describe the other survivor population of their shared ancestry. Finally, over all of the preceding centuries of their dispersion Jews retained a remarkable sense of unity and peoplehood, such that other ethnic groups have sought to emulate them. This transnational identification of Jews with other Jews also continues to characterize much of world Jewry on the popular, institutional level. It occupies almost all other groups of Jewish writers (i.e., writers of historical, philosophical, and theological texts). And not so very long ago it was expressed nowhere

1

more powerfully than in the burgeoning canon of Hebrew and Yiddish writing, out of which both Jewish American and Israeli fiction developed. Yet, with a few notable exceptions, Jewish American and Israeli literature have developed in some significant isolation from one another.

I submit that this disinclination of Israeli and American Jewish fictional narratives to gravitate toward the other, which makes the experience of the one seem to be somehow irrelevant to the experience of the other, tells us as much about processes of Jewish self-definition over this period—at least for creative writers—as the narratives themselves. Indeed, it goes to the heart of one major paradox of Jewish identity in the contemporary world, which extends well beyond the narrow confines of literary production. This paradox immediately comes into view when one considers the fact that almost none of the narratives discussed in this book imagines religion, Judaism, as the organizing feature of contemporary Jewish identity. This is the case, despite the fact that religious issues flit in and out of some of the narratives discussed here, and even though some of the critics represented in this book are themselves religious and strive for religious meanings. It also stands in direct contradiction to the trend of the last decade or so for writers to take more seriously Judaism as a religion as opposed to a cultural or historical identity—a trend that emerges precisely because of the lack of concern with religion in previous narratives (Hana Wirth-Nesher, in her chapter, deals with the use of religious ritual in contemporary American Jewish writing). This skirting of the issue of religion may either seem to be surprising or inevitable, depending on how one images the relationship between secular literature and theology. In the case of modern Jewish literature, however, this fact of the exclusion of religious identity points to a major feature of the literature's history: that secular Jewish writing came into being expressly as a rejection of Jewish orthodoxy, at least in its institutionalized forms. This feature of its origins, I maintain, produced both the distinctive aspects of contemporary Jewish self-definition *and* the divide, such as it is, between the two secular, intellectual communities. I say *such as it is* since Jewish American and Israeli literature, despite their lack of direct reference to one another, may not be as different as one might at first imagine.

What then does constitute the bases of Jewish self-definition in modern Jewish literature? As a recently published volume of essays entitled *What Is Jewish Literature?* (edited by Hana Wirth-Nesher) has made abundantly clear, there are many ways of defining this body of texts, not all of which are mutually compatible, and many of which raise questions concerning the possibility or even desirability of answering the question at all.[2] Jewish literature has been many things to many people, especially after its break in the nineteenth century with the tradition of religious writing that preceded it. What critics do seem agreed about, however, is that Jewish literature presents certain unique problems of definition. While the concept of a Jewish literature is modeled on the idea of a national literature (American literature or French literature), Jewish literature cannot be defined in exactly the same ways, since until 1948 the Jews did not constitute a nation as such; and even after 1948 a large segment of the world's Jewish population continued to exist as a nonnational entity. I want to suggest that, while Jewish literature does not, until after the founding of the State of Israel, or, in relation to non-Israeli writers, till the present time, present the same possibilities of national definition as other literatures, nonetheless one powerful strand of continuity among Jewish literary texts of at least the last century is the desire for nationhood and the grappling with its implications. This is as true, I suggest, for American Jews as for Israelis, even if the way in which national identity is conceptualized and expressed differs in the two literatures. Indeed, what thinking about both literatures in terms of each other and an idea of nationhood may afford is the opportunity to see how the Israeli American Jewish difference is more in the local details of the text than in their themes, structures, or self-definitions.

In other words, while the establishment of the State of Israel in 1948 surely produced a major shift in Jewish reality, which bore on nothing more powerfully than on the creation of Jewish literature, it may still be the case that, from the same perspective of Jewish national self-definition, the emigration of the Jews to the United States was no less significant. It was the Enlightenment, with its promise of reason as the controlling factor in human history and the evolution of culture, which permitted European Jewry to emerge from the *shtetl* and from traditional religious orthodoxy and to imagine the possibility of a Jewish life on other, secular and national, terms. And it was the failure of that promise, the failure of the European nations to grant full cultural as well as political citizenship to its Jews, which thwarted the assimilation of secular Jewry into European culture.

This produced two determinative consequences for the future of Jewish secular culture. One was the massive immigration to the

United States, where, one might say, the promises of the Enlightenment were finally, largely, fulfilled and the goals of assimilation achieved. The other was the inception of the idea of *a Jewish national* culture. As originally conceived, this culture was not to be geographically located. Rather, it was imagined that such a Jewish national culture could exist dispersed throughout Europe, not wholly identified with any particular European nation.[3] When this option proved to be untenable, most dramatically, of course, during the Holocaust, but, increasingly all through the early twentieth century in the form of pogroms and other violence perpetrated against the Jews, Zionism completed the logic of the secular, nationalist thrust of the culture. In establishing a Jewish state in a national homeland, Zionism might either have continued to fulfill the logic of a transnational culture, responsible not to a single community of Jews (now located in Palestine/Israel) but to world Jewry (a point powerfully elucidated in Eliezer Schweid's chapter). Or it might avail itself of its new condition of, if not real security (since there was still the continuing threat to its existence), at least, the lack of persecution within the national entity, finally to make good on the promises of the Enlightenment. It might, in other words, produce a national culture completely parallel to that of the European nations that had refused to receive them (in language as much as in any other area of endeavor, as the chapters by the poet, novelist, and literary critic Yitzhak Laor as well as by Nili Rachel Scharf Gold, make abundantly clear).

The thrust toward nationhood as part and parcel of the attempt by Jews to constitute themselves as a group on something other than religious terms is not itself difficult to understand. Aside from the simple political protection statehood might provide the Jews (either within the European nations or in America or in Israel), national identity answered to the possibility of a rational, secular culture like that which characterized other peoples, such as the Germans or the Poles or the Russians. It also corresponded to a fundamental structure of their own identity as Jews, as expressed within the institutional forms and religious logic of Judaism. Perhaps one of the most fundamental aspects of Judaism distinguishing it from other faiths is its emphasis on practical performance, on the mitzvoth, which are not, as they are commonly misunderstood to be in American Yiddishized jargon, "good deeds," but rather the commandments that regulate Jewish ritual practice. For this reason Jewish learning is largely centered on the halakah—the body of Jewish law compiled in the *Mishnah* and the *Gemara* (collectively referred to as the *Talmud*), which itself forms the dominant mode of commentary on the *Torah* (the Five Books of Moses). In other words, as a religion, Judaism is less defined by abstract theological argumentation centered on issues of belief, than by the interpretation and codification of a body of law, a set of rules and regulations by which observant Jewish life is to be governed. *We will do and we will hear*, it is written in the *Torah*. Practice, in traditional Judaism, precedes understanding; doing comes before theory.

To be sure, nonreligious, secular Jews in the United States and Israel share history, culture, and family, the significance of which is not to be underestimated. This is especially the case after the decimation of European Jewry during the *Shoah* (the Holocaust), which exerted a powerful pressure on the world's remaining Jews to preserve their identity as Jews, at least nominally (a subject in my own chapter). And yet what seems to emerge from many of the major texts of Jewish literature, both in America and Israel over the last fifty years, which constitutes a basic definitional feature of their Jewish identity and which, perhaps, forms their link with their religious backgrounds, is a commitment to acting in the world and thereby enacting one's identity as a Jew (rather than, simply, as an ethical human being) through political, moral, and social action.

Since it is the insistence on the letter of the law (rather than on its spirit) that largely differentiates Judaism from Christianity, the Jews' insistence on doing rather than believing may be something of a defensive posture. Confronted with centuries of anti-Semitism, Jews may have clung all the more fiercely to the legal construction of their faith. Whether or not this is the case, it is certainly understandable that, after the Enlightenment, when Jews were allowed greater access to the instruments of sociopolitical power in their respective countries of residence and yet were still prevented from fully integrating into their host nations, they should have joined themselves to various movements of social reform (e.g., socialism and communism) which seemed to many Jews not only a way of securing their political rights within their host countries but nothing less than a secularized version of the essential ambience of their faith. The following statement by Irving Howe can be taken, I think, to apply equally to Israeli as to American aspirations, concerning not only socialism but other forms of social activism, such as the civil rights movement in the United States or the kibbutz movement in Israel:

[F]or many immigrant Jews, [socialism] was not merely politics or
an idea, it was an encompassing culture, a style of perceiving and
judging through which to structure their lives. . . . Only radicalism seemed to offer the prospect of coherence, only radicalism
could provide a unified view of the world. . . . Comparisons between radical politics and religious practice are likely to be
glib . . . yet in thinking back to these years I'm forced to recognize,
not very comfortably, that there were *some* parallels between the
two. Everything seemed to fall into place: ordered meaning, a
world grasped through theory, a life shaped by purpose. Is that
not the essence of conversion? . . . Unacknowledged motives were
also at work, having less to do with Marxist strategy than our
own confused and unexamined feelings about Jewish origins.[4]

What I want to suggest concerning Jewish American and Israeli writing of the last fifty years, which seems to me to be a
principle argument emerging from the chapters in this book, is
that it may be this *shared* commitment to *doing* in the world in a
very concrete, literal, ethical, and political way (both within and
outside the context of religious life) which, ironically, produces the
presumably *different* allegiances claimed by Israeli and American
Jewish writers in the second half of the twentieth century and
which accounts for the failure of each group to find much personal
relevance in the experience of the other group. Both Israeli and
American Jews have discovered, each in their respective places, the
same possibility for secular, ethical enactment in the world and for
the production of a society based on such principles of moral behavior that might seem, in form and content both, to be Jewish.

To be sure, the assimilation of the Jewish writer into a non-
Jewish culture such as America does, of course, provide the possibility (e.g., for a writer like Norman Mailer) to completely leave
behind his Jewish identity—something that is not possible in the
same way in a self-designated Jewish country. But what is the
difference, really, between the insistence of American Jewish authors (e.g., Bernard Malamud and Saul Bellow) that they write as
Americans, even when they continue to write about Jews and even
when they continue to transport into their fiction elements of a
Jewish (Yiddish) literary tradition, and the practice of Israeli writers, who, in their concern with the realities of nation-building and
social reorganization, may feel that the history or content of Jewish
life is quite secondary to such national interests? How different, in
other words, is the Jewish self-definition of the American writer for
whom Jewishness is the ethnic component of her Americanism

(parallel to being an African American or an Italian American) and the Israeli writer for whom ethnicity or hyphenated identity isn't an issue or even an option, but for whom Jewishness is an historical background and *Yisraeliuth* (Israeli identity, i.e, becoming an Israeli as opposed to being only or merely Jewish) exactly the raison d'être for the existence of a Jewish state? The activities of the Jewish characters in American and Israeli fiction may not be the same activities. But in both cases the literary tradition imagines Jewishness as an aspect of something more vital and important than religious identity: the evolution of a social, cultural, ethical position for the Jew in the modern world. Even in the American tradition, where there is certainly much more possibility, and indeed incidence, of Jews interacting with non-Jews, the primary focus of the fiction is on the internal dynamics of Jewish community life. Neither field of literary investigation, in other words, is necessarily more inherently, definitively Jewish than the other.

At the beginning of the century, and well into the 1950s, both Jewish American and Hebrew, Israeli literature shared a somewhat different relation to Jewish origins and peoplehood. This is the subject of the chapter that leads off this book. As Eliezer Schweid puts it, the idea of Zionist or Israeli Jewish identity was not, in the pre-State period, or even directly following independence in 1948, meant to substitute for what the writers understood to be Jewish identity. Indeed, Zionism was imagined as a tool for the preservation of that identity. It was only in the decade following statehood that a radical transformation in Jewish self-definition repositioned the literature. In the very intensity of the literature's focus on the specificity of Jewish identity in the land of Israel, *Yisraeliuth* came to displace earlier goals and self-understandings. This construction of *Yisraeliuth* is the subject of A. B. Yehoshua's chapter as well, as he charts the development of his own generation of Israeli authors—the *Dor Hamedinah* or "State Generation" writers—who continue to this day to dominate the stage of Israeli culture; indeed, who are primarily responsible, in Yehoshua's astute interpretation, for constructing Israeli culture as it now exists. As Gershon Shaked both places this generation in the context of what it resists, and charts the literary development that subsequently resists this resistance, modern Hebrew literature represents a series of responses to an earlier, pre-State metaplot, which was ideology-driven, and that imagined Israel not only as the fulfillment in the land of Jewish culture and history, but as wrenching the new Jew, the Israeli, free of all the constraints and dysfunctions of the past.

Taking up the causes of ethnic and gender difference, and further straining against the goals of national consolidation and historical fulfillment, the contemporary writers discussed by Shaked produce a contemporary literature that further differentiates itself from the literary trends that have preceded it.

Before examining how Americanization equally served the twin goals of normalization and Jewish self-realization in American Jewish writing, and in order to make Schweid's, Yehoshua's, and Shaked's descriptions more comprehensible, let me fill in some more of the context of pre-State and post-State Hebrew writing, which only after 1948 becomes Israeli literature per se. Though there is also secular literature written in the Hebrew language in the nineteenth century, modern Hebrew literature can be dated from 1881. As Gershon Shaked tells the story of Hebrew fiction in his five-volume history, most of this first generation of writers (from the 1880s to the 1920s), lived in the diaspora (though there also exists a corresponding community of authors within *Eretz Yisrael*—"the Land of Israel"—as well), and they wrote in Yiddish as well as in Hebrew, often translating their own writings from Yiddish to Hebrew. The diaspora writers include such figures as Mendele Mokher Seforim, David Frishmann, Micha Yosef Berdyczewski, and Avraham Laib Ben-Avigdor; the Palestinian authors were Y. Barzilai-Eisenstadt and M. Smilansky. A second generation of writers, most of whom were born in the diaspora but eventually moved to Palestine, appeared on the scene at the beginning of the twentieth century. It was this group of authors that effected the shift in the center of Hebrew writing from Europe to Palestine, setting the ground for what would eventually become Israeli rather than merely Hebrew writing. The key figures here were Haim Nahman Bialik and Yosef Haim Brenner. Others included Yitzhak Dov Berkowitz, Gershon Shoffman, Uri Nissan Gnessin, Jacob Steinberg, Elisheva Bikhovsky, and Devorah Baron. Writers of this generation whose literary careers began in Palestine rather than in the diaspora were Shlomo Zemach, Aharon Reuveni, Dov Kimhi, Lev Arieh Arieli-Orloff, Shmuel Yosef Agnon, and the native-born Yehuda Burla and Yitzhak Shami. A third generation of authors appears at the end of World War I, most of whom arrived in Israel with the third and fourth *aliyoth,* were deeply influenced by the Zionist movement, and were products of the two world wars and the Holocaust (writers, e.g., Nathan Bistritski, Aharon Ever-Hadani, Yitzhak Shenhar, Yehoshua Bar-Yosef, Yaacov Horowitz, and Haim Hazaz). The fourth generation is the one most familiar to most of us today, containing some of the best of the Israeli writers, many of whom are still active on the scene of Israeli culture, and who are predominantly native born (S. Yizhar, Benjamin Tammuz, Moshe Shami, Yonat and Alexander Sened, Yehuda Amicahi, Pinchas Sadeh, Aharon Appelfeld, Amalia Kahana-Carmon, Yoram Kaniuk, Amos Oz, A. B. Yehoshua, and Yehoshua Kenaz).[5] This tradition of writers, needless to say, wrote as varied a panorama of texts as any literary tradition. Yet themes of Jewish persecution and the internal disruption of Jewish communal and cultural life punctuate the early texts in this tradition, gradually yielding in the 1930s and 1940s to more Israel-focused and often idealized portraits of the newly emerging Zionist entity, which are, once national autonomy is secured and a truly national life ensues, gradually displaced by the internal self-critique that most of us recognize as literature itself. Wolfgang Iser's concluding chapter bears very heavily on this idea of literature and on its special relevance to Jewish literary history.

As Shimon Halkin (who introduced Hebrew literary studies to Israel in the 1950s) tells the story of modern Hebrew literature—that is, not Israeli literature, but literature written in Hebrew, initially outside the geographic and political boundaries that generally define literary nationality—the objective of the literature had, indeed, as Schweid also argues, been to preserve an idea of *Jewish* as opposed to some other nationally determined, local identity (e.g., Polish or Russian or even Israeli): "From its very beginnings," writes Halkin, "Hebrew literature tended to evaluate the changes taking place in the emancipated Jewish life, not in terms of the Jew is one country or another, but in terms of Jewry as a whole. . . . Hebrew writers believed and insisted that the Jew, bound as he was to seek a better and richer life and greatly changed in the pursuit of it, must still preserve his historic Jewish identity."[6] This international quality of the literature is reflected in its publication in international journals, written both in local, national languages and (increasingly) in Yiddish and Hebrew. This turn-of-the-century and early twentieth-century European Jewish literature, Gershon Shaked makes us aware, wholly reflected the forces of Enlightenment and secularization that characterized the authors' world and which, in the first instance, had enabled the production of a modern, secular, Jewish literature. Nonetheless, despite the rebellion against traditional religious orthodoxy, such that the literary foundations of contemporary Hebrew literature can be said to be, by definition, nonreligious, perhaps even antireligious, and despite the powerful pull toward assimilation, still the literature preserved much of the ambience of traditional, which is to say religious, Jewish life.

In other words, early twentieth-century European Jewish literature, written in Hebrew in Europe—the writings of Mendele Mokher Seforim, Frischmann, Peretz, Berdyczewski, and Feierberg—was not simply Jewish in terms of theme and character. It was densely Jewish, in terms of its fields of allusion, ambience, and intertextuality. Even more importantly, perhaps, it was Jewish in terms of language, whether that language was Yiddish or Hebrew (many of these writers wrote in both languages). Indeed, for the writer of Hebrew literature, writing in Hebrew was both an act of recognition, registering the continuing segregation of the Jews from European culture, and it was a solution to the problem of Jewish secular life, especially when the possibilities of conducting such a life in Europe began to disappear.[7] I emphasize the matter of language, since, if there is a major difference between Jewish American and Israeli fiction it is the difference produced by language (relevant here are, again, the chapters by Laor and Gold, as well as Ruth Wisse's chapter on Glatstein and Agnon).

Yet this difference may not work exactly as we might imagine—as we will see. As Robert Alter points out, the use of the Hebrew language had specifically nationalist objectives, which inevitably, perhaps necessarily, produced the desire for statehood. To quote Alter: "Hebrew was associated with Jewish political autonomy, and the awareness of this association played a crucial role in Hebrew literature long before, and beyond, the emergence of political Zionism. For if Jews were to create a culture like others, not dominated by a clerical establishment and not defined exclusively in religious terms, the great historical model had been cast in Hebrew of the soil of ancient Palestine." And Alter cites the Israeli critic Dov Sadan to make the point that "there was a kind of imaginative logic which produced a compelling movement from literature to politics: after writers had succeeded in creating an *as if* reality in Hebrew, the conditions of consciousness had been established in their readers for seeking to build an actual Hebrew reality, with all the requisite social institutions and political apparatus, in the real geography of this world."[8]

For Halkin, Alter, Shaked, Schweid, and others, the move toward a national literature, in a national homeland, written in the language of the Jews, was meant to concretize Jewish identity and to establish its separate but equal status among those of other peoples and nations. It was meant to normalize Jewish existence on secular terms, without sacrificing specifically Jewish identity in the process: "The social significance of Hebrew literature," Halkin explains,

> does not possess the glamour of a universal doctrine; but its revo-
> lutionary character, paradoxically enough, lies precisely in its
> stubborn refusal to identify the Jewish question with the social
> struggles of universal man. While it recognizes that Jewish his-
> tory is an integral part of human history, Hebrew literature does
> not regard the anomalies of Jewish life in the modern world as
> mere symptoms of the general maladjustments of human society;
> and consequently it does not see the cure of the anomalies as
> wholly dependent upon the cure of general social ills. Rightly
> interpreted, therefore, the revolutionary character of modern
> Hebrew literature is to be found in its tireless insistence first of
> all upon our will to survive as a people even in the most ideal
> world-order to be achieved by mankind; and conversely, upon the
> impossibility of such survival, even in the most conceivable ideal
> state of human society, unless we ourselves normalize our group
> existence by acquiring those characteristics of healthy group liv-
> ing of which we are deprived by the extraterritorial nature of our
> people. It is specifically since its emergence from the ghetto, dur-
> ing a century and a half of actual or nominal emancipation, that
> Jewry has tended to become more disintegrated, more character-
> less than ever before its long history. And while it has constantly
> reaffirmed the will of the Jewish people to persist, Hebrew litera-
> ture as been calling upon Jewry to face squarely its own extinc-
> tion unless it measures up to the formidable task of re-establishing
> itself as a normally functioning national organism.[9]

For Halkin a major difference between the Israeli (Zionist) Jewish experience and the diaspora Jewish experience was to be summed up in just this difference between the universal and the particular. It was contained in the difference between Jewish history and culture as models, one might even say as allegories or parables, for the world (almost in parallel with Christianity's allegorization of the Scriptures), and Jewish history and culture as expressions of the specific density and depth of the life of a defined group of people, the Jews, even if this life, like all human lives, contains something in it for others to learn.

Thus, explains Moshe Shamir, one of the major modern writers of Israeli realist fiction (a subject in Schweid's chapter):

> the decisive, exciting, fateful problems of our lives are those in-
> herent in the life and growth of the State of Israel. This life does,

of course, rise on Jewish historical foundations . . . but the first
and foremost meaning of our Jewish historical liberty, as we see
it, is, *Jews*—Jewish men and women; Jews who come to this country and who live in it, their experiences and their relationships
with one another, their children, their education, their future,
their security. . . . No author in the world, no philosopher, has ever
had a wider horizon or a more far-reaching vista than that opening up and available to the eye from as high as the height of a
man standing on the ground. Moses brought the tidings of redemption to humanity because he redeemed one nation in one
given hour. But even the decision to redeem that one nation did
not come about on an abstract level, but rather on a personal one.
He saw an Egyptian beating a Hebrew. And then he saw a Hebrew beating a Hebrew. That was the problem he wanted to solve.
Who knows better than an artist or a writer that anything universally and generally applicable is a function of matters personal
and private?[10]

Though for Shamir, the problem that the Jewish author had to
solve might be said to be double—the Egyptian beating the Hebrew and the Hebrew beating the Hebrew—what emerges powerfully from Shamir's formulation is that for the *Israeli* author the
problem might increasingly move in the direction of the second of
these two conditions. In other words, and in contrast to what
might be understood as the major tradition of diaspora Jewish
writing, which dealt with Jewish historical foundations, that is,
the Egyptian beating the Hebrew, Israeli fiction held out the
possibility of concentrating on the Hebrew beating the Hebrew.
Indeed, the contemporary corpus of Hebrew literary texts, while
hardly forgetting the threats against the survival of the state, do
focus on the interpersonal relations between Jews on the very
private, domestic level (the aforementioned Oz, Kenaz, Kahane-
Carmon, Yehoshua, and the somewhat younger David Grossman
and Meir Shalev, whom Shaked discusses in his chapter, all write
this kind of fiction). For the Jewish writer of Hebrew Israeli literature, writing such literature was already a fulfillment of the conditions of both personal Jewish identity and artistic production:
"Being an Israeli Jew is not a matter of consciousness for me,"
explains another Israeli writer, Aharon Megged, "nor is it a problem. It is life itself."[11]

How different is this from the self-understanding of American
Jewish writers like Bernard Malamud, Saul Bellow, Cynthia Ozick,
and Philip Roth—to cite the four major figures in this tradition? As

Morris Dickstein, in his chapter, describes Jewish American narratives of self-definition over the last fifty years in the United States, the trajectory of the tradition quite parallels what Schweid describes in relation to Israeli literature. At first dwelling on the immigrant experience and on the early years of Jewish American adaptation and assimilation, American Jewish fiction (quite in parallel with Hebrew literature during the first decades of its immigration to *Eretz Yisrael*) told a story that was recognizably, perhaps even quintessentially, Jewish: the story of persecution, immigration, and assimilation. But as the Jews in America achieved the goals of integration, they, like their Israeli counterparts, were confronted by a new Jewish reality. This new condition released them from the necessity for special pleading. It permitted them to write a literature which, if not exactly freed from the pressures of the Jewish past, was nonetheless far less compelled by them.

As Dickstein demonstrates, the subject of American Jewish writing becomes, increasingly and self-consciously, the subject of American Jewry itself, as having an independent identity, history, and literary tradition, with specifically American, but no less importantly Jewish, bases. Indeed, as H. M. Daleski notes in his chapter on Philip Roth, for a Jewish American writer like Roth, Jewish American culture might, for all its apparent lack of Jewish density and content, seem to Jewish Americans more fully to express Jewish culture than Israeli culture, which, in its drive to consolidate a new secular, national, Jew (an Israeli) may have rejected much of those historical circumstances that had given rise to contemporary Jewish experience in both places. Thus Roth's definition in *Operation Shylock: A Confession* of the diasporist as "a Jew for whom *authenticity* as a Jew means living in the Diaspora, for whom the Diaspora is the normal condition and Zionism is the abnormality—a Diasporist is a Jew who believes that the only Jews who matter are the Jews of the Diaspora, that the only Jews who survive are the Jews of the Diaspora, that the only Jews who *are* Jews are the Jews of the Diaspora."[12] In America, rather than in Israel, the Jewish writer may finally have realized the goals of the Enlightenment and achieved national normalization *without* the sacrifice of a strong national Jewish character. In other words, for many Jews, the immigration to the United States represented exactly the fulfillment of, rather than a detour from, the Jews' philosophical, ethical, and political goals. It is this universal humanism that is the subject of my own chapter and that constitutes the backdrop for Michael P. Kramer's.

Philip Roth once had the following rather cynical remark to make concerning American Jewish identity (which Kramer discusses in his chapter):

> There does not seem to me a complex of values or aspirations or beliefs that continue to connect one Jew to another in our country, but rather an ancient and powerful disbelief . . . the rejection of the myth of Jesus as Christ. . . . The result is that we are bound together, I to my fellow Jews, in a relationship that is peculiarly enervating and unviable. Our rejection, our abhorrence finally, of the Christian fantasy leads us to proclaim to the world that we are Jews still—alone, however, what have we to proclaim to one another?

For those who are skeptical of a viable *Jewish* existence in America, Roth's definition serves perfectly to convey the potentially negative valence of American Jewish identity. Such Jewish identity as persists, some would maintain, is simply the defiance of non-Jewish culture (so well expressed in Roth's own novel *The Counterlife*), the Jew's final resistance, especially after the extermination of the six million Jewish victims of the Holocaust, to allowing the Jew to disappear from the face of world culture. Hence, Roth says the following of Nathan Zuckerman's mother in the second of the Zuckerman novels: "[H]er first time in the hospital, the doctors diagnosed a minor stroke . . . four months later . . . she was able to recognize her neurologist when he came by the room, but when he asked if she could write her name for him on a piece of paper, she took the pen from his hand and instead of 'Selma' wrote the word 'Holocaust,' perfectly spelled. . . . She had a tumor in her head the size of a lemon, and it seemed to have forced out everything except the one word. That it couldn't dislodge."[13] For the Jewish American writer, identity had very much to do with Jewish catastrophe, in particular the *Shoah*.

For this reason, perhaps, as David G. Roskies claims in his chapter on Yiddish and American Jewish writing (Wirth-Nesher's piece produces interesting confirmation of this in her differently focused project), Yiddish signals nostalgia for, and an identification with, a dead Jewish past rather than the building stones of a new Jewish present. To give up Jewish identity is for many American Jews unthinkable. But to live in the present the Jewish experience of the past is equally unimaginable. Thus does Jewish American fiction express Jewishness as little more than ethnic inflection, which merely pays lip service to Jewish identity—in the form of embracing such popular forms, Roskies suggests, as klezmer.

But the situation of the Jewish American writer is hardly so simple or defensive, and as emerges from Wirth-Nesher's chapter, even what might seem to us a mode of Jewish mourning for an unrecoverable past such as both Dickstein and Roskies describe might constitute the basis for a new resurgence of Jewish creativity. For most Jewish Americans, America represented far more than a permanent or even creative solution to the problem of historical anti-Semitism. It represented a nationalism that at least seemed to be founded on a commitment finally to resolving, for all peoples and for all segments of the population (and not only the Jews), the racism, classicism, and power politics that had disfigured European civilization. For the Jews, then, America would do more than finally permit what European culture had never quite allowed (as became horrifically clear in the years during and following the Second World War). It promised as well to do this within a context of universal humanism with which the Jews of Europe were quite familiar (as the example of Hannah Arendt makes so clear) *and* to do it in a nation that had, from its inception, defined itself as a *promised land*, the *Israel* of the modern world. This metaphor of America as Israel has a long life in the United States, originating in the biblical discourse of the Puritan settlers of New England (how uncannily similar the origins of American and Israeli tropes of nationhood), who described their passage as an Exodus from a British Egypt, themselves the Israelites led by their Moseses and Joshuas over an ocean described as a desert, and arriving in a place that was Canaan itself. Not accidentally, then, or haphazardly, did a black writer like Claude Brown entitle his text *Manchild in the Promised Land* or the Jewish Mary Antin entitle her 1912 autobiography *The Promised Land*. For Antin, as for many immigrant Jews, it was as if America was there, waiting in readiness, for the chosen people to take up their places and help this promised land make good on its original intentions. America was not only a possible home for Jews; it was the only and perfect home—even after 1948.

In this new Israel American Jewish intellectuals pursued a familiar path in modern Jewish history, a path that would also be taken, with similar consequences, in the other promised land to which their brethren ascended: they became political activists. In this way, they defended themselves against discriminatory practice and exclusion. Equally important, perhaps even more important as Jews begin to move into positions of power within American society, they defined their position as Jews within American culture as having to do with the protection of minority rights for all Americans—thus making Jewish Americans more American than the Americans themselves. If, on the one hand, Jewish Americans felt their identity as Jews to derive from the circumstances of Jewish history, in particular the Holocaust, so much so that a critic has recently argued that certain Jewish American intellectuals use the Holocaust for the purposes of constructing their ethnic identity,[14] on the other hand, American Jewish intellectuals pursued that definition in terms of large, universally defined moral issues, which Jewish history might be thought to embody and the Jew specially endowed or empowered to enact. For a good number of Jewish American intellectuals, the commitment to social causes became the indivisible expression of both their Americanism and their Jewishness. To bring Roth and Howe into relation to one another, one might say that, if, on some level, Jewish Americans preserved their Jewishness out of an abhorrence of conversion to Christianity, they discovered in America a way of converting without converting, to pick up the key metaphor in Michael Kramer's chapter. They realized their Jewishness in their conversion to a social activism which, in the particular ethnic context of America, could become an expression rather than a repudiation of their Jewish identity (see, again, my chapter).

Implicit, then, in the Jewish American writer's self-definition was both the adoption of America as Israel and, just as important, the rejection of any other Israel, as of any other nation, as either a safe refuge or a homeland for Jews. Whatever it may look like from outside the United States, for Jewish Americans their experience in America was not an erosion or an obliteration of their Jewishness but a pouring of their Jewishness into an Americanness that was already Hebraic, as if America (almost in parallel with the antitypical relationship between Christianity and Judaism) were the fulfillment of Jewish history, which retrospectively could be cast as something of a moral allegory. Nor was this position simply a withdrawal for Jewish Americans from enacting their presence in the world. In a symposium held in Israel in 1963, in which Jewish American and Israeli intellectuals did address each other (and from which I've taken some of my other quotations in this chapter), Max

Lerner, a Brandeis University sociologist and intellectual, observed that American Jews had found satisfaction in America because

> we have had a share in the creation of the selfhood of the American nation, a rather important share.... One of the reasons we feel at home in it is that the first immigrants who came to America were people of the Book.... The Jewish immigration helped Americans to remember the life of the mind. In that sense, we American Jews have a natural sense of belonging. We also have a natural sense of belonging in another sense: we have helped to shape the great American revolutionary tradition.... We in America who are Jews are willing and even avid participants in [the struggles of America] because there is something about that struggle in terms of the passion for justice, in the passion for equality, the passion for expression, which gives us a feeling not only of belonging but of fulfilling ourselves.[15]

How superfluous, then, was Israel for American Jewish intellectuals, who had found in America a way of realizing their most fundamental, moral and historical, sense of themselves as Jews; and how threatening: since for Jewish Americans, America was not merely the place in which the Jew might fully experience both her religious *and* secular self, but, in a remarkably literal sense, America *was* Israel; it *was* the promised land. Even if its language was English and not Hebrew, it was, for its Jewish population, no less a Jewish Israel than the new nation in Palestine—at least for the founding fathers and mothers of the literature and for the intellectual tradition. For the question that Dickstein raises at the end of his chapter, which is the question raised by Roskies and Ruth Wisse as well, and to which Wirth-Nesher provides something of an answer, is the question whether Jewish fiction as such has any future in the United States. And it is here that the fact that America is (as Wirth-Nesher points out) an English-speaking promised land becomes critically important, though, as with many of the other differences between Israeli and American Jewish writing, this difference may also not be as absolute as we at first imagine.

For Ruth Wisse, in her chapter concerning the Yiddish and Yiddish/Hebrew writers Glatstein and Agnon, language determines literary and national/cultural fortunes. From the beginnings of modern Hebrew literature, and especially in the period preceding its relocation to *Eretz Yisrael* (the land of Israel), language marked the difference between a Jewish literature which, written in one national vernacular or another, would eventually disappear as

Jewish literature, and that literature that would persist as quintessentially and irrevocably Jewish. Saul Bellow records the following conversation with S. Y. Agnon, when the latter asked Bellow if his books had been translated into Hebrew: "If they had not been, I had better see to it immediately, because, he said, they would survive only in the Holy Tongue. . . . I cited Heinrich Heine as an example of a poet who had done rather well in German. 'Ah,' said Mr. Agnon, 'we have him beautifully translated into Hebrew. He is safe.' "[16]

As Wisse puts the situation in relation to Glatstein's hero: "Yash is as free as any Jew has ever been, the modern man free of Jewish observance, free from persecution, free to travel the world, and in this book, even freed temporarily from daily routine." Yet this freedom also "divested [him] of power, community, and God." Thus while "the Yiddish writer [in America] balances on the horizontal tightrope between Gentile history and the Jewish experience of it, the Hebrew traveler [i.e., Agnon] stands on a vertical axis, between a weakened Almighty and a demoralized people." And in the end, it is Agnon who, to quote his own view of the matter, remains safely within the ongoing life of Jewish literary history.

From the beginning, then, the decision of Jewish writers to write in Hebrew represented a political, ideological decision, in many ways akin to other ideological features of the budding literature (see again Schweid). As Gershon Shaked has demonstrated in his book on Hebrew fiction, an excerpt of which appears as a chapter in this volume, from the beginning of its sojourn in *Eretz Yisrael* (the Land of Israel), Hebrew literature was characterized by an essential tension, which produced at least two distinct literary tendencies as well as literary texts divided against themselves. On the one hand, the writers of early twentieth-century Hebrew literature (e.g., Yoseph Haim Brenner or U. N. Gnessin) desired what all writers of literature desire: the possibility of producing literary works expressive of the range of human circumstance and feeling, quite irrespective of any political function that the literature might perform. On the other hand, the writers, many of whom settled in Israel for ideological reasons or who, if native born, were educated to this ideology (Smilansky or Shami), recognized that the situation of the Jew in the modern world, including Palestine and later the nascent state, demanded of its writers a literature that would further the prospects of Jewish survival, individually and nationally. From the late 1950s on, as the literature matured and as political circumstance changed, the fiction began more and more to concern itself with the internal dynamics of Israeli culture (the Hebrew beating the Hebrew). The ideological sway of the literature diminished and other subjects (the Holocaust and the cultural life of European Jewry) and other types of characters (European refugees, Sephardic immigrants, and women) emerged, including those events and individuals that might be thought to harp back to the Old World experience that the new life in Israel was supposed to supersede.

In this movement of Hebrew literature into self-determined and aesthetically governed subjects of its own, language may have remained the last bastion of the literature's ideological underpinnings, remaining largely under the sway of the same principles of composition that accompanied modern Hebrew literature into birth. This is Laor's contention in his chapter. Unlike an Agnon, who managed to keep alive in his language multiple traditions (religious and nonreligious), such that his language emerges both as literary and as Jewish in the most profound ways (it is useful to refer to Ruth Wisse's chapter again in this context), the contemporary Israeli writer, Laor suggests, evidences vestiges of the ideological commitments of the past at the expense of writing vital, literarily powerful prose. By dictating the use of a preordained standard of language, imposed from outside the culture, and preceding it into being, the Hebrew writer writes in a language not the nation's own. Nili Rachel Scharf Gold, in her chapter, gets at some of the same problems of language as ideology, as she recovers the repressed resonances of the German mother tongue in the language of Natan Zach, Yehuda Amichai, Yoel Hoffman, and Dan Pagis. So doing, she throws into even greater emphasis the relationship between the expectations of the new society (the designs of *Yisraeliuth*) and the historical circumstances of individual lives, which, even when conditioned by as tragic a fact as the Holocaust, are not so easily set aside. Gold also suggests the emergence, or, perhaps more precisely, the reemergence, within Hebrew literature of subjects not ideologically, Zionistically, determined, stories personal and private but also public and historical that cut across ideologies and reframe the very meaning of a Hebrew literature. As is confirmed by the emergence both of *Yisraeliuth* and a new respect for the diaspora origins of many of Israel's population, Hebrew literature may, like its American cousin, be beginning to imagine the ethnic difference among the citizens of the Jewish state, the double consciousness that is part and parcel of hyphenated identity, which is to say *all* identity, in the contemporary world. The final poem quoted in Laor's chapter moves toward a similar position.

Though the chapters that are included in this book focus on narratives of self-definition in the two major Jewish communities today, it is virtually impossible to understand contemporary American and Israeli Jewish writing without some sense of its prehistory, particularly in the German-speaking world. Therefore, this book concludes its own collective and international narrative of Jewish self-definition with a chapter that deals with German and Austrian Jewry in the prewar period. Wolfgang Iser reaches back to the moment of the inception of the Jewish secular culture that comes to take up its separate existences in the United States and Palestine/Israel. He describes the origins of the Jewish double consciousness that is probably more familiar to those of us who deal with American Jewish identity formation than the Israeli example. Iser's chapter unfolds on several levels. It takes its inception from the end of a process: namely, the compilation of the Hebrew literary canon as put together by Gershon Shaked, the inheritor of Shimon Halkin's mantle as a leading critic of Hebrew literature in Israel and a major force (as attested to by his frequent appearance in many of these chapters) in the construction of contemporary Hebrew culture. By thinking through Shaked's earlier work on Franz Kafka and Joseph Roth, Iser illuminates both the critical role played by the *condition juive* in the construction of modernism itself and the implications for Jewish artists, not to mention Jewish critics like Shaked himself, of the superimposition of statelessness on the internal alienation from Judaism that this nonnational position produced. The dynamic of "dual identity" that Iser figures forth in his discussion of Kafka, Roth, and Shaked, who is himself an Austrian Holocaust refugee to Israel, culminates in a view of Jewish literature and literary criticism, both in the diaspora and among those Israelis who take their place in Israeli culture as inheritors of this diaspora experience, as "an adumbration of what lies buried" in the "mutilated life."

This subject of what lies buried in the mutilated life, we might feel, is not only the subject of literature itself, but the subject that once again brings together the Egyptian beating the Hebrew and the Hebrew beating the Hebrew: the subject of a people which, even when it wasn't a nation, existed within the context of other nations, and which, when it became a nation or a part of another nation (as in the United States), pursued the path of culture to all its destructive, self-destructive, and, finally, hopeful and promising extremes. It is this story which, as much as any other story, Jewish literature of the last fifty years tells. It is the story that emerges from within the narratives of Jewish self-definition in Israel and the United States that are the subjects of the following chapters. And it is the story that emerges individually and collectively through the chapters themselves, which are, each of them, also narratives of self-definition.

Notes

1. This American Jewish lack of interest in Israel has been the subject of a recent book by Andrew Furman, *Israel Through the Jewish-American Imagination: A Survey of Jewish-American Literature on Israel 1928–1995* (Albany: State University of New York Press, 1997), which does, nonetheless, cite and discuss those American Jewish works of fiction that have concerned themselves with Israel. His list of texts can now be supplemented by recent works of fiction by such younger authors as Allegra Goodman, Rebecca Goldstein, and Ayreh Lev Stollman. The subject also concerns Alvin Rosenfeld in his article "Promised Land(s): Zion, America, and the American Jewish Writers," *Jewish Social Studies* 3:3 (1997): 111–132. An occasion in which American and Israeli writers did confront each other is summarized in the articles in *The Writer in the Jewish Community: An Israeli-North American Dialogue,* eds. Richard Siegel and Tamar Sofer (New Jersey: Farleigh Dickinson University Press, 1993), while Naomi Sokoloff has edited a recent issue of *Shofar* (winter 1998) dealing with *Israel and America: Cross-Cultural Encounters and the Literary Imagination.* There have, of course, also been studies of Jewish fiction that cite both Israeli and American examples.

2. *What Is Jewish Literature,* ed. Hana Wirth-Nesher (Philadelphia: Jewish Publication Society, 1994).

3. Gershon Shaked, *HaSipporet Haivrit 1880–1990* [Hebrew Fiction 1880–1980] (Israel: Hakibbutz Hameuchad and Keter Publishing Houses, 1977–2000). 5 vols. [Hebrew] Abridged and translated as *Modern Hebrew Fiction,* trans. Yael Lotan, ed. Emily Miller Budick (Bloomington: Indiana University Press, 2001).

4. Irving Howe, *A Margin of Hope: An Intellectual Autobiography* (San Diego: Harcourt, 1982), pp. 11–14 and 47.

5. Taken from the introduction to Shaked, *Modern Hebrew Fiction.*

6. Simon Halkin, *Modern Hebrew Literature from the Enlightenment to the Birth of the State of Israel: Trends and Values* (New York: Schocken, 1970, first published 1950), pp. 19–20.

7. See again Shaked *Modern Hebrew Fiction.*

8. See Robert Alter, *The Invention of Hebrew Prose* (Seattle and London: University of Washington Press, 1988), pp. 12 and 71.

9. Halkin, *Modern Hebrew Literature,* pp. 102–103.

10. *Congress Bi-Weekly* 30:12 (September 16, 1963): 50.

11. Ibid., p. 4.

12. *Operation Shylock: A Confession* (London: Jonathan Cape, 1993), pp. 170–171.

13. *Zuckerman Unbound,* in *Zuckerman Bound* (New York: Farrar, 1985), pp. 447–448.

14. Walter Benn Michaels, " 'You who was never there': Slavery and the New Historicism, Deconstruction and the Holocaust," *Narrative* 4 (1) 1996: 1–16.

15. *Congress Bi-Weekly,* p. 19.

16. "On Jewish Storytelling," in *What Is Jewish Literature?* p. 18.

CHAPTER ONE

The Construction and Deconstruction
of Jewish Zionist Identity

Eliezer Schweid

Zionist identity in its various manifestations has been one of the most striking registers of general changes in Jewish self-definition during the modern period. Confronting the national and social movements that shaped Western culture during the nineteenth and the first half of the twentieth centuries, Zionism put forward the need to create, parallel to other peoples, a secular-nationalist Jewish identity that could also serve as an all-encompassing cultural alternative to traditional Jewish identity defined through religion. Each of the factions that comprised the Zionist movement, including religious Zionism, proposed a model for this national culture, which it sought to realize in *Eretz Yisrael*, the "Land of Israel." The tense confrontations, both among these different models, on the one hand, and, on the other, between them and traditional religious culture, shaped the complex features of this emergent *Eretz Yisraeli* identity. This identity developed and maintained itself until the establishment of the State of Israel, persisting well into the first decade after nationhood. It was thereafter swept away by the various social transformations that overtook the new nation, including the waves of mass immigration and the establishment of the national polity. The earlier *Eretz-Yisraeli* Hebrew culture served as the basis for the as yet inchoate identity of *Yisraeliuth* ["Israeliness"], which quickly began to display its difference from traditional "Hebraism" in all respects, except, perhaps, for the linguistic one. This was particularly true in regard to the manner in which *Yisraeliuth* understood and presented its Jewishness.

❖   ❖   ❖

A precise description of the development and breakdown of Jewish-Zionist identity in *Eretz Yisrael* requires that we draw a distinction between two historical moments. On the one hand, we have the formative stage of Zionism and its literature in the diaspora, as it developed in anticipation of settlement in the Land of Israel (both in *Eretz Yisrael* itself and abroad) as a project of exile. On the other hand, there is that stage during which Zionism, taking root in the Land, began to create its own perspective on the Jewish people and its culture. During the first stage, Zionism as such was not understood as a substitute for Jewish identity. Indeed, Judaism was seen as the common denominator that had united the Jewish people throughout its generations, notwithstanding the disputes within it. In this view, Zionism represented a small contemporary avant-garde within the larger definition of the people. Judaism was the broader entity, which subsumed Zionism within it. It served as the fructifying soil, and it was inconceivable that it be defined as a subset within Zionism, but rather had to be understood as preceding and generating it.

Zionism, of course, had its own definition of the Judaism from which it had sprung. It perceived Judaism as, from its very inception and in its essence, a national culture, which united both religious and folk elements. The motivation for Zionism, therefore, was anchored in the less theological and more down-to-earth strata within Judaism, which Zionism sought to renew and to develop. However, Zionism as such did not seek to express the entirety of Judaism. Rather it endeavored to express only its ideological aspects and practical dimensions and to implement those institutions whose task it would be to realize these dimensions. Zionism aimed at establishing for the Jewish people a civil, universal base, derived from Western culture, so that it might develop a national "culture" derived both from the sources of historical Judaism (in particular those that related to the connection of the people to the Land of Israel) and also from the foundations of modern Western culture.

In order to understand the development of Jewish identity in *Eretz Yisrael,* it is important to emphasize this fact: that not a single one of the great Zionist thinkers or ideologues, such as Ahad Ha-Am, H. N. Bialik, A. D. Gordon, M. J. Berdyczewski, Jacob Klatzkin,Yehezkel Kaufmann, Ze'ev Jabotinsky, or Joseph Klausner, perceived Zionism as Jewish identity per se. Zionism was only a tool for the creation of a modern national framework, intended to unite within itself the entire people and to link this people to the sweep of its historical experience. The definition implied in the concept, so widespread today, of "Jewish-Zionist identity," according to which Zionism is the secular alternative to the religious or ethnic definition, is the explicit result of the second stage in the development of Zionist-Jewish identity, when the project of settlement in *Eretz Yisrael* was realized. It originated in the message or vision conveyed to their offspring by the parents who negated existence in the exile: that their children would be part of a new and different definition of Judaism. But this only became an existential reality in the activity of those children who grew up in Israel and whose Jewishness thus came to be identified with Zionist realization in the Land. The parents, even if they wished to free themselves from the pain involved in their heritage, still carried it within them. They defined their Jewishness by means of it. In fact, their very motivation to negate the exile and to free their children of its burdens stemmed from this Jewish self-definition, which was inseparable from the *Galut* (Exile) experience.

In addition, the generation of the *Tzabars* (native-born Israelis) did not receive its Jewish cultural heritage directly, via its original sources (with the exception of the Bible). Rather, they inherited it primarily by means of modern Hebrew literature. In particular they took their idea of Jewish culture from the writings of the Enlightenment and Zionist renascence authors such as J. L. Gordon, Abraham Mapu, Peretz Smolenskin, Mendele Mokher Seforim, H. N. Bialik, U. N. Gnessin, the poetess Rahel, and Hayyim Hazzaz. They also received their cultural vision through the literature of the third aliyah authors, in particular Avraham Shlonsky, Nathan Alterman, and Leah Goldberg, all of whom tended to negate the experience of the exile. In order to soften this negation somewhat, authors like Y. L. Peretz, Shalom Aleichem, and S. Y. Agnon were added to the Hebrew literary canon. But this attitude of negation nonetheless dominated.

Thus, the past that constituted the background of the new culture was identified with the revolution that pushed forward to negate the past, while the present was already the beginning of a different future, one that focused upon the values and contents of Zionist realization. These included knowledge of the concrete landscape of the Land of Israel: of its flora and fauna and of the historical, archaeological legacy hidden therein. Also incorporated within this realization was the revival of the Hebrew language as an autochthonous (i.e, native) national language, an earthly mother tongue. For this reason, the *tanach* (the Old Testament) represented the present and immediate expression of the people's history, connecting the contemporary population to its concrete surroundings. From this followed personal commitment to settlement, to physical labor and to the building of a new society, and to defending the Land, even with one's life. There also followed a series of rituals that helped define and shape this emergent Zionist self-identity: hiking through the Land and celebrating the seasons and the harvest and the Haganah and its commander educators, who were entrusted with the national defense. All of these constituted the cultural components of Jewish-Zionist identity for the native-born generation. They were helped along by a partisan, youth-movement system of education, which fostered the dominant ideology and put it into action through the various pioneering movements, Betar, and the scouting organizations, which quickly followed in their wake.

Indeed, the difference between the Zionist perspective of those who lived outside the Land of Israel and those who grew up and were educated there can be brought into focus by means of a comparison between the messages of the Zionist youth movements in the *Golah* (Exile) and those of parallel movements in *Eretz Yisrael*. In *Eretz Yisrael* the youth were granted considerable freedom for independent expression. The focus, tending toward fanaticism, was upon the present and the future, rejecting the past, and emphasizing self-realization in a double sense: realization of the individual person and realization of the Zionist dream through the personal commitment of each person. The central emphasis on the values of the geographic and linguistic homeland (the exclusivity of Hebrew as a mother tongue) placed the identity-formative messages of the majority of the *Eretz Yisrael* youth movements (with the possible exception of Gordonia) on the edge of Canaanism. That is, it put them on the verge of a decision to cut themselves off completely from the inherited Jewish identity in order to infuse themselves with exclusively autochthonous values.

But only on the verge. For simultaneous with this thrust toward Canaanism, the Zionist youth movements displayed a strong revulsion against taking the final, ultimate step of completely cutting themselves off from Jewish history and Jewishness. This in turn produced a hostility towards the Canaanism they themselves desired. What led to this revulsion rooted in attraction was the mind-set of the parent generation, who could not completely disconnect themselves from their exilic origin, however much they wished to. Furthermore, the community in the Land (the *Yishuv*) was still a minority. It did not yet enjoy national autonomy and therefore still depended upon the people in the exile for its very existence. The elementary fact of dependence upon the people in the exile proclaimed itself from all of the life circumstances of the *Eretz Yisrael Yishuv,* from its weakness and isolation to the growing opposition to its survival by the Arab populations, the mandatory rulers, and even Jewish residents of the *Yishuv.* This feeling of dependence reached its peak during the years of the Second World War and the Holocaust. It is not surprising, therefore, that the parents who wished to negate the experience of exile also wished, and generally speaking also succeeded, in conveying the ambivalence of that desire. On the one hand, they believed that only the Land of Israel solved the problem of the Jews. On the other hand, they continued to feel responsible to the Jewish people, whose survival and whose relation to the Land of Israel were both the condition for Zionist realization and also the condition of their own independent future. For this reason, even among the native-born generation, Jewishness was preserved as a framework of connections that imposed responsibility and commitment to a shared Jewish destiny.

This sense of Jewishness did not transcend Zionism. Rather it was derived from within it. Even among the native-born generation Jewishness as separate from Zionism was preserved as a consciousness of a shared destiny—in both directions. Indeed, one might say that the *Eretz Yisraeli* youth movements created a relationship of commitment to the Jewish people only insofar as a corresponding commitment to the Zionist enterprise was expected on the part of diaspora Jews. Those segments of the people that did not identify with Zionism, and even more so those who opposed it, were seen as outside the connection of belonging. The reaction of *Eretz Yisraeli* youth to the Holocaust, both in terms of their positive involvement in helping save the remnant, and in terms of the human estrangement they sometimes demonstrated toward the refugees, may also be explained in terms of this same attitude. The *Yishuv* felt responsible for the destiny of their fellow Jews insofar as they were seen as future partners in the enterprise. But it no longer participated in a general feeling of Jewish identification, which was the precondition for a feeling of deep participation in the unique sufferings of their people.

The transformation from the Zionism of the parents' generation, based upon an a priori Jewish identity, to a Zionism that incorporated Judaism within itself as subordinate to Zionist identity, received its fundamental expression in the *Tzabar* (native-born Israeli) literature, which first emerged as a clearly defined literary entity during the years surrounding the Second World War and the War of Independence. This literature posited as its goal the realization of an *Eretz Yisraeli* Zionist identity. At its best, it engaged in the heroic struggle to express and to affirm that realization, or, at least, to embody the inner struggle for such realization, in the experiences and activities of the first generation. This is the generation whose values had been formed by the youth movements and that had been entrusted with the task of continuing and completing the project of pioneering settlement, but who soon found their central and unique task in war: first in the Second World War, in acts of rescue and illegal immigration, and then in the defensive wars that established independence and maintained it. For generations of native-born Israelis *(Tzabarim)* the war for the Land of Israel became their basic experience, the literary expression of which crystallized their Jewish-Zionist identity. S. Yizhar and Moshe Shamir stand at the head of this generation and exemplify its basic ethos.

S. Yizhar preceded all the major writers, both in terms of his actual literary production and also in terms of his experience in the Land. His rootedness in Zionism predated the period during which war became the axis of self-realization. His first and primary experience was the pre-State *Yishuv,* with its values of Land and the commitment to the Hebrew language. True, in retrospect, the war became for him, too, the great test. Nonetheless, when he turned to it in his novellas *Hirbat Hiza* [Story of Hirbet Hiza] and *Ha-Shavuy* [The Captive], as well as in his great epic, *Yemei Tziklag* [The Days of Ziklag], his earlier background persisted, albeit charged with ethical and existential problematics. The war experience came to challenge his own and his heroes' idea of an uncomplicated native-born self-identity. Yizhar's characters struggle to affirm this identity, but they do not succeed in giving it any strong basis. Nor do they discover any way to transform or deepen it. Hence, the struggle itself becomes the expression of such identity as they wish to assert.

Yizhar's literary talent, which was not narrative but descriptive-lyrical, lent itself to expressing the experiential elements of his native-born Zionist background. He created a colorful epic that embodied within itself a journey of double-rootedness: rootedness in the Land of Israel as an old-new homeland, and rootedness in the Hebrew language as an old-new language. At its best, S. Yizhar's fiction is a story of the love affair between the Hebrew language and the Land where Hebrew was born. His aim is to uncover the spiritual depths of the Land through the religious depths of the language, which is at one and the same time a biblical and a modern language. Internalizing the words of the poet Tchernichowsky, which hold that a human being is no more than the image of his homeland, Yizhar sought to expose the depths and fullness of the language through the qualities of the landscape.

The literary challenge Yizhar's generation had inherited as a mission, which was also the horizon of their personal identity, was thus to become rooted in the landscape. They would realize this goal by means of the sensuousness of the Hebrew language. It is the spiritual life of the Hebrew language, in its flowing and inexhaustible color, which they would live, through the infinitely unique, equally sensory experience of landscape itself. All of Yizhar's works tell this love story of language and scenery. Beyond any narrative or thematic content, their ultimate artistic and meta-artistic purpose is this expression of the linguistic experience of a people intermingling with a landscape that is its own mirror. The Zionist significance of this love story stands out particularly in the earliest stories, such as "Efraim Hozer la-Aspeset" [Ephraim Returns to the Alfalfa] and, even more strongly, in the novella *Pa'atei ha-Negev* [The Far Reaches of the Negev]. In these early works there isn't yet that doubt regarding the Zionist ethos that troubles his later works.

It is particularly interesting to note Yizhar's choice of the Negev as a site for revealing the scenic-linguistic richness of the Land, which was hidden behind what had seemed to the generation of the immigrants (who unconsciously sought in the Land of Israel the scenery of their European birthplaces) desolation. The parent generation preferred the verdant and water-filled Galilee. The Negev elicited feelings of alienation and estrangement. Thus, in *Pa'atei ha-Negev,* the young author, who has rebelled against his parents in order to continue their enterprise in his own native-born way, encounters in the Negev nothing less than an image of his own unique destiny. From his point of view, the virgin, open, limitless spaces of the desert, the blooming abundance hidden in the depths of the soil, and the astounding richness of visible life that was manifest only to the discerning eye—these, and specifically these, are for him the true expressions of the Land of Israel. Similarly, the new Hebrew language is the true Hebrew; it was, so-to-speak, only born from the Bible in order to realize itself in its ability to decipher this scenery. For this reason, the encounter between the renewed Hebrew language and the uninhabited Negev staged the true encounter between the son of the Land and the son of the language, who is the hero himself.

With the writing of the novellas *Hirbat Hizah* and *HaShavuy,* the war penetrated into the very heart of Yizhar's epic of scenaric-linguistic Zionist realization. In these works he continued his love story of self, language, and landscape, particularly in the Negev, which he celebrated in *Yemei Tziklag* and in his other writings. But the war for the conquest and acquisition of the land could not but evoke a deep moral and existential crisis, so much so that the Zionist realization seemed beyond the power of the narrator and his heroes (who directly stand for the author as well). Is the scenery of the Land of Israel really the scenery of a homeland? If it is decreed that the native-born Jew must fight for it against those whom he always saw, like himself, or perhaps even more so, as inseparably part of the ancient landscape, and whom he therefore strove to emulate, can he really be said to be the reflection of that landscape?

Beyond the ethical questions raised by war, it was this existential trauma which upset his identity to the very core. It was incapable of resolution without his altering his identity, which seemed to be likewise impossible. Who, then, is the Jewish hero, for that is how he must identify himself in contrast with the true hero of the *Eretz Yisrael* landscape, whom he must unwillingly fight and even defeat? From whence did he come? From where does he derive the feeling of primeval certitude that the Land in which he, albeit not his parents, was born, is in fact his homeland?

If there is any source for an answer to these questions, it is in the Hebrew language that established the primeval connection to the land or, to be more precise, in that Hebrew literature—namely, the Bible and the modern literature that derived from it—that transmitted that language and renewed it in its full authenticity and vitality. Yizhar's heroes do not themselves arrive at this answer. The same books that would have opened to them the sources of their language are closed to them because of their Jewish content, rooted in the exilic heritage that connected his parents to a homeland from which they struggled to be free. In casting off their heritage, the parents, upon arriving in the promised land, threw off as well the traditional sources of the literature that they themselves had created. The sacred books of the Torah were placed in a corner and not taught to their children. From this point on, all of Yizhar's stories express inner struggle centered around two axes of ethical-existential crisis: the relationship to the Arab inhabitants of the Land and to their nationality, and the relation to the religious sources that the preceding Hebrew literary tradition both documented and concealed. This futile struggling and the wish to determine the relation to the Land were not, however, the rejection of native-born Zionist identity. Rather they were its confirmation and perpetuation. Thus the author agonizes over this identity, denies it, cries out against it, and criticizes it, but he returns to it over and over again with the inexhaustible love expressed in the linguistic-scenaric lyricism of his prose.

Moshe Shamir's narrative talent tends more toward the dramatic than to the descriptive. The subject that constitutes the axis of his plots, particularly in the early novels, is the education and development of the native-born *Tzabar*. It is thus only natural that the experience of the war for the Land of Israel should lie in the center of the plot that documents the devotion to the Zionist realization. Eventually Shamir expanded the canvas of his dramatic work from the biographical-historical present to the distant historical past (i.e., the period of Alexander Yannai and thereafter of King David). He also expanded his undertaking in the direction of the more recent past (Zionist history of the beginning of the century), endeavoring to uncover the roots that were concealed to him when he wrote the biographical novels that first secured him stature and fame (in particular *Hu Halakh Basadot* [He Walked in the Fields] and *Pirkei Elik* [Chapters of Elik]). Nonetheless, even in these later works, Shamir remained close to the native-born and fighting *Eretz-Yisraeli* personality and to the immediate historical background from which his own Zionism developed.

That is to say, the effort to place and to justify the figure of the *Tzabar* as a Zionist hero lies in the center of his narrative enterprise. In the early novels the native hero, characterized by his lack of historical memory and particularly by his lack of propensity toward reflection of any sort, stands at the height of the great historical drama: the war for the Land itself. The battle's present is his own biographical present. Unlike Yizhar's heroes, he identifies with the battle and discovers there both himself and his personal destiny, even though, like Yizhar's heroes, his do not initiate it, nor do his heroes understand either their national purpose or its significance.

In the biographical novels Shamir's *Tzabar* heroes do not bear any relation to their parents' past. The parents bequeath to them their war without passing on the lessons of their lives. True, it may be that Elik's birth "from the sea" (as the novel puts it) incorporates the idea of an exilic "there" from which his parents came. Indeed, it is clear that the historical drama in which he finds himself is rooted in something whose source is beyond the present and over the sea. But this fact, while known to him, does not interest him. He does not examine it. His identity is founded, not only on the Zionist imperative that was communicated to him by his parents but on the example of their lives. These he accepts and enacts unquestioningly, so as to prove himself and validate his own being.

Thus the hero fulfills his parents' expectations of him, albeit not for their reasons, which are never made quite conscious to him. He desires the war, not for the redemption of his people, but in order to realize his own native-born identity, in order to produce a new beginning such as his parents also desired. This alone he received from them, and thus his heroic personality becomes completely egocentric. He is proud and confident, completely naive and at peace with himself, but with himself alone. War, maturation, and victory—these are his personal goals, through which he evidences to himself those traits that identify him as native-born, as opposed to his foreign-born parents.

Victory in war thus confirms his nobility, but its tragic consequences are not long in coming. There quickly emerges an unavoidable conflict between the hero and his parents, and the confrontation between the parents' aspirations and his purely external and superficial realization of them soon takes the form of a contradiction between his own inner self and his idealized self-image. It becomes clear to him that from those same fonts of egocentricity and naïveté from which his victory as war hero is derived also originate his personal failures in love, in creating connections with others, and in establishing a family. In other words, in the depths of that selfsame mission of national redemption that he took upon himself without understanding its sources and motivations originate both his personal failings and his inadequacy before the mission he attempts to perform.

In this way, Shamir's heroes and Yizhar's converge in their suffering. However, in the continuation of his work, at the center of which lies the historical drama of the people and not only its hero who fails in his very victory, Shamir uncovers the historical backgrounds of the failure of his native-born protagonist. By returning to the sources themselves, he deepens the challenge of reflective self-understanding, and expands the horizons of his native-born protagonists' identity-crisis. Did, then, the crisis of identity experienced by Shamir's characters lead to their exchanging their native-born Zionistic identity for a broader and deeper Jewish identity, such as characterized Jews earlier on? Did they discover the broad historical background that united them with their people and their Jewish inheritance?

There is no unequivocal answer to these questions. As a writer, Shamir clearly tended toward a recovery of the Jewish origins, both in his novels and in his theoretical and scholarly works. As he became more and more critical of his native-born heroes, he came to identify more strongly with the idea of the *Whole Land of Israel,* which becomes linked as well to his identification with religious Zionism. Unlike Yizhar, Shamir became more and more conscious of the Jewish depths that were hidden from the eyes of his native-born heroes. He confronted, not only the sources of Zionism, which were buried within Jewish culture, but also the ideological disputes that broke out because of the secular nature of that culture, which depreciated the spiritual, religious nature of Judaism. In other words, he discovered the dimensions of Judaism that transcended Zionist identity and that had once constituted part of the frame for Zionism itself.

Already in *Melekh Basar v'Dam* [King of Flesh and Blood], he presented the conflict between Judaism and Jewish secularism by staging the confrontation between the Hasmonean king, whose worldview and ethics were explicitly Hellenistic and earthly, and the Sages, who represented the prophetic sources of Judaism. The Sages were not, of course, in opposition to national-earthly independence. But they refused to sacrifice their ethical-religious principles for its sake, and they preferred religious principles above power-oriented attainment as an end in itself. In thus displaying his understanding of the clash of worlds, Shamir may or may not have been striving toward a synthesis. Either way, he was unable to find the personality who would embody such a synthesis. Furthermore, if he were asked who the hero was who could drive forward the ongoing historical drama, the answer would still be the naive, egocentric, native-born hero, whose nature and function are expressed in warfare, and who sees the realization of his native-born identity in the very fact of victory (the acquisition of rule and the application of power). This is the case notwithstanding the fact that at the end of his path, when he must confront the failures that await him after his victory, he well understands where he erred, yet could not behave differently.

The heroes by whose means Shamir advances his dramatic axis are thus unable to cross the boundary between a native-born

Zionism, born out of a sealike present and lacking in past and future, and the world of the Sages, who have a past and future but no present. The positive attitude displayed by Shamir toward the ethical and religious contents of the Jewish tradition is only possible for him from within his Zionist viewpoint, such that, in the final analysis, the ethical-religious contents of Judaism are important to him only as a necessary complement to Zionism, and not as an end in themselves. This means that his fiction itself, and not only its protagonists, fails to cross the borderline of Zionism. The author only gazes over this border and longs for understanding the connection between the two Jewish identities, which are drawn one toward the other and need one another for the sake of Jewish survival.

In considering the transition from the first *Tzabar* generation to the two generations that followed it, it is worthwhile taking at least a glance at the interesting testimony of Aharon Megged. While he belongs to the first *Tzabar* generation, the beginning of his work reflects the transition that took place between the period of the *Yishuv* and that of the State. Moreover, his manner of relating to the issue of Jewish identity and Zionism is distinctly different from that of his predecessors, possibly because, notwithstanding his upbringing and education as a *Tzabar,* he was not (like Elik) born "from the sea," but rather came from the diaspora as a child. His identity, in other words, had roots in the exile, and the Zionism that he seems to have received from his parents also contains a more significant amount of traditional Jewish heritage, a fact that stands out most strongly in his later writing.

Megged's first novel, *Hedvah v'Ani* [Hedvah and I], which established his reputation as a writer, is at first glance an expression of loyalty to Jewish-Zionist *Eretz-Yisraeli* identity following the creation of the State and the War of Independence. Its uniqueness lies in the sharply critical gaze with which it examines the transformation that took place among members of the *Tzabar* generation after the creation of the State—that is, at the moment when the process of emptying their identity of its value contents first began, when Zionism began to be placed within quotation marks and became a form of ideological identity that had little in common with a way of life or a living culture. Megged's penetrating diagnosis was that in the course of this process the *Tzabar* betrayed himself and lost his own "I." His hero's desertion of the kibbutz, which was still considered the focus of settlement and self-realization in the Land of Israel, and his moving to the city for the sake of a career in government bureaucracy, were not only a betrayal of his Zionist values, but also a betrayal of himself.

On the face of it, this is the moral implied by the narrative weave of this novel, which documents the milieu of an older Israeli society that exploited the merits of its past activities for the sake of materialism and power. The message seems to be a mocking rebuke, a warning, to the generation that is on the verge of missing the challenge of its life. It must return to earlier values so as to save its own identity and return to the path of self-realization. However, a deeper examination reveals that Megged's critique is rooted in a prior and more basic criticism of the hero. If the protagonist has become an antihero merely by descending from one stage onto another, if he dissolves so easily in the face of power and materialistic desire, such that there is nothing left of his identity aside from its frayed external symbols (the Tembel [idiot] hat and the short trousers), then there could not, from the outset, have been much internal personal substance behind the exterior expression. It becomes clear that *Tzabar* identity was nothing more than the outer garment of a puerile society whose pioneering and fighting uniforms set it apart and identified it so long as it functioned as a group and elicited respect from the public it served. Even then, this group identity concealed a lack of self-definition that became obvious when serving the collectivity was no longer considered as an ideal.

Megged's first novel does not explain the cause of the weakness of the *Tzabar* personality, its failure to be accepted, and its susceptibility of being betrayed the moment it encounters life outside the domains of its group's activity. But every line of Megged's subsequent novels, written to document the entire period of the establishment of the State, reveals this explanation from different angles and perspectives. Like previous authors, Megged's plots are explorations of Israeli society through the examination of the relations of fathers and sons. This plotting of the story not only places Megged's work in the tradition of Hebrew literature from Mendele Mokher Seforim to Shmuel Yosef Agnon; it also conveys the historical drama of Zionism not only from within the Zionist narrative itself, but also in the broader context of the history of the Jewish people. In particular, Megged adopts Agnon's historiographical position, as expressed in *Oreah Noteh Lalun* [A Lodger for the Night] and *Temol Shilshom* [Only Yesterday]. In this narrative of Jewish history, sin and punishment descend from generation to generation and the destiny of the sons atones for the sins of their parents only by their own becoming the victims of that same sin, which is revealed in their natural yet erroneous behavior.

This theme stands out in particular in Megged's last novel, *'Avel* [Injustice]. This is not the best of Megged's works in terms of its narrative construction, but it has a clearly defined historiographical position that relates explicitly and directly both to his previous works and to the perceptions of both Yosef Haim Brenner and Agnon regarding the place and function of Zionism in the history of the Jewish people. Brenner represented the extreme of the desire to negate the exile and sever connections with the Jewish heritage. Megged shares with Agnon an ironic stance in relation to the idea that Jewish identity had been established anew in the Land of Israel and in the Hebrew language and in adopting a secular culture that comes entirely from outside Jewish history. Thus, Megged identified with Agnon's insight into Brenner's view: that the Jewish religion in all its variations has utterly lost its credibility.

There were real justifications for Brenner's rebellion. Indeed, his rebellion embodied within itself more Jewish authenticity than the Orthodox zealotry that opposed it, for he wished, with utter good faith, to renew an authentic Jewish culture. But the attempt to redeem Jewish self-identity from the falsification and distortion of the exile was transformed in Brenner's writings into a new distortion. It became its own variety of assimilation and denial, which betrayed an authentic existential Jewishness and thus subverted the meaning of the rebel against exile. These consequences of the Brenner position are necessarily revealed for Megged in the next generation, in the lives of the sons who inherit nothing but a negative position against their own sources. Thus, the so-called redemption contains within itself a further reincarnation of a sinful alienation. Thus Zionism strives for redemption but actually moves back into self-negation and Exile.

In *'Avel*, Aharon Megged continues the dialectic first initiated by Agnon concerning the generation that had received the heritage of Brenner. These sons would seem to have no escape from their destiny, as even the choices open to Brenner have been denied them. They miss the significance of their own Zionist self-realization at the very moment that they give their lives for it. Indeed, in the poem that Megged attributes to an imaginary poet Assaf Hagoel in the book by that name—*Assaf Hagoel* [Assaf the Redeemer]—who represents the generation that carried on the War of Independence, it becomes a major uncertainty in which direction the warriors are heading. Moving southward, are they going deeper into the Land of Israel, in an effort to discover the source of its significance in the life of the Jewish people? Are they expressing their longing for the Sinai that is the source of the people's ancient covenant? Or are they instead exiting the Land altogether, repudiating the covenant of their ancestors and returning to Egypt? Are they turning (and returning) toward the task of redeeming Jewish life? Or are they committing spiritual suicide? The answer given in the course of the story is almost unequivocal. The distortion of the wonderful and mysterious poetic work of Assaf Hagoel by a young poet of the second generation, who originally hid it away, reveals the text's own point of view concerning the inheritors. The forger is indeed the spiritual son of the original author, because in his striving for assimilation, he enacts the negation of the Zionist enterprise.

Like Agnon, Megged attempted to help facilitate the dialectical continuation of Jewish-Zionist identity by means of returning Zionism to the diaspora and reconnecting it to its Jewish heritage. He thus gives his hero an illegitimate son from a mother who (both reflecting and posing a contrast to his unfaithful wife), takes that son back to the diaspora to raise him there as Jew. But can a faithfulness to Jewishness that originates in betrayal to the motherland correct what was distorted by the original betrayal that compels it? Is this not simply a further round of the same sin and the same failure? Thus the "injustice" that was done to Assaf Hagoel by the forger who hid his original work and distorted its meaning is fundamentally identical to the betrayal that he himself has caused. It stems from the attempts of a man who loved and married an unfaithful wife who could not bear him children, to hide behind a glorious messianic pseudonym. He himself already exhibited the tendency to self-negation, exile, and death, which the next generation inherits.

The hero and his work were both born out of the sin of Zionist parents and teachers who betrayed their Jewishness, and this sin is continued by the betrayal of the poet himself of his own life goal, which is the realization of Zionism. The only ray of hope left at the end of the novel is the abandoned synagogue from the days of his childhood to which the narrator, who identifies with his hero, returns at the end of writing his story, in order to prove to himself that the roots of his Zionist identity are planted in this place of Jewish worship, just as the roots of the identity of the "lodger for the night" in Agnon's story were implanted in the *beit midrash* (house of study). But the author who sent the son of his hero into the exile in order for him to become reconnected to his Jewishness knows full well that he himself cannot return to the synagogue whose worshipers abandoned it already in their own Land, and that certainly his sons, who worry about him as their biological father but are completely estranged from his spiritual, Zionistic values, also cannot do this, since he has failed to pass onto them, not only his Jewishness, but also his Zionism.

In the works of the two outstanding authors of the second generation of *Eretz-Yisraeli/Tzabar* literature, Amos Oz and A. B. Yehoshua, the motif of Zionism's self-betrayal undergoes a further dialectical turn, arriving at a playing out, which is also its conclusion. The historical background for this turnabout is that selfsame transition from the period of the *Yishuv* to that of the State that also posed sharp questions for the first generation. The biographical starting points for Oz and Yehoshua are found in the same historical continuum of the history of Zionist realization in Israel as those of Yizhar, Shamir, and Megged. The difference between them lies primarily in the difference in their ages, which brought them into the historical continuum at a later stage, precisely at the point of demarcation between one period and another.

The final years of the period of the *Yishuv,* the years of the Second World War and the Holocaust and of the War of Independence, passed over Oz and Yehoshua as children, youth, and young adults. They grew up in the Zionist movement, entering into their period of literary productivity at the end of the 1950s and the beginning of the 1960s. The project of Zionist realization received at that time a tremendous push in terms of the scope of *aliyah* and settlement, the consolidation of the economy, the strengthening of the military, and the support of the entire Jewish people in the diaspora. The members of this *Tzabar* generation, in other words, grew into adulthood during a period of extreme hopefulness that, after what was doubtless the most difficult period in the history of the *Yishuv* and in the history of Zionist realization, they would be the generation that would finally live beyond conflict. They would be the generation that would arrive at the promised land and see the light; they would build and create and not need to go out to war.

But in the course of their entering into responsibility for the new reality that was imposed upon them, they also saw everything that their predecessors, particularly Yizhar and Megged, had seen: the grave implications of the problem of the Arab refugees, in whose homes and villages Jewish immigrants had settled in their stead; the problems of absorbing the mass *aliyah,* with all of the injustices this involved for the immigrants; the cracks that began to be seen in the ethos of Zionist realization of the old *Yishuv,* whose sons and warriors now assumed positions of leadership, and, above all else, the endless wars, the need to sacrifice life in order to defend the State arising over and over again from a cycle of enmity that seemed to have no cure.

Only one substantive thing had changed in this cycle of hatred, and it became the greatest challenge of all for the continuity of Zionist realization. Against the background of the Holocaust and the mobilization of all the Arab peoples against it, the State of Israel had seen itself—with objective justice—as David fighting Goliath. But being educated in his own state, the second generation *Tzabar* began to feel as the stronger of the two antagonists. When he confronted his primary defeated enemy, the Palestinian people, he saw in them the same misfortune and injustice that he had experienced as a child during the War of Independence. Was he then a Jewish Goliath to a Palestinian David?

The basis was created here for a double identity: identification with the Zionist realization and identification with its victims. The realization of Zionism was the hope, the salvation, and the great refuge. It was the field of activity and creativity and self-realization. At the same time it was the source of injustice to the defeated-undefeated enemy, which continued to confront it exactly as it had in the past. As in the past, the Zionist realization demanded blood sacrifices of its young sons and of its enemies in order to exist. It both gave life and took it. True, it did not choose this. Nevertheless, it was responsible for this, and over the course of time there began to be felt the suspicion that the unavoidable necessity in whose name it spoke was not always such in fact. The *Tzabar* of this generation identified not only with himself but also with the enemy who was like himself, in whom he saw his own image, not in opposition to his identification with Zionism but, on the contrary, literally from within it.

We thus have a dialectical imbroglio of affirmation of Zionist identity together with its interrogation, of challenging Zionist identity while confirming it. That Jewish Zionist identity remains valid is an undeniable fact. This statement is explicit and definite in the political rhetoric of Oz and Yehoshua. But even on the ideological plane this is a fact that is not easy to admit, and even more so to embrace fully. The careful reader will find that the affirmation of Zionist identity is based more upon the negation of the exile than on the positive reaffirmation of the reality of Zionist realization in the Land of Israel. Both Oz and Yehoshua see the reality of realization as the consequence of an ancient sin, the sin of a people who willingly abandoned their land, who adhered to exile because of some perverse character trait that deviated from the normal identity of other native-born peoples, and who tarried in returning to it, doing so only when they were persecuted to within an inch of their life and found no other refuge, only to find to their misfortune that the refuge had meanwhile been occupied by another people and was no longer empty. Moreover, even now the majority of the people holds fast to its exile and does not let go. Once more it refuses, to invoke a midrashic context, to "go up as a wall," that is, to take upon itself the task of returning as a people intact to Zion.

Zionist identity is thus expressed in a feeling of great oppressiveness and guilt. It is true that it was not the members of this generation who perpetrated the injustice, but they were the ones who inherited and perpetuated it. Therefore, Oz and Yehoshua feel an obligation to apologize before their conscience and before their Palestinian enemies-judges. They explain and justify their Zionist identity with difficulty, as an unavoidable necessity brought about by the catastrophe that befell their people. In order to legitimate the Zionist enterprise, they call upon their people to quickly complete its delivery from exile and thereby to give it their definite seal of approval. Otherwise that part of the people that has returned to its Land will become cut off and separate. It will define its Zionist, native-born identity as transcending exilic Jewish experience, indeed as transcending even Zionism, which only has significance so long as the people in the Land carries responsibility also for the people in the diaspora.

This ideological tangle, filled with ambivalence to the point of internal contradiction, is well reflected in the literary work of Oz and Yehoshua, where greater attention is paid to the psychological and spiritual side of Zionist self-contradiction. It is expressed in the characters' internal anguish, in their hidden wishes to break free and to escape from the limitations of a failed native-born identity to "another place": to Greece and Italy in Oz's *Hamatzav Hashelishi* [The Third State] or to India or England in Yehoshua's *Hashivah Mehodu* [*Open Heart*]. The literary work documents its Jewish-Zionist identity and that of its creators with the same absolute matter-of-factness that is demonstrated by journalistic writing. We have here a continuity based upon choice and identification, even innocent love. The native-born works of Oz and Yehoshua even have a tradition of native literature upon which to base themselves and from which to draw. For this reason, the *Eretz Yisraeli* motifs in their work resonate more fully and achieve greater complexity and cultural depth than those of their predecessors. But it is precisely because of this background that the internal complexity in the depths of their Jewish-Zionist self-identity seems to be deeper and sharper. Likewise, the internal struggle with the Jewish heritage that has been swallowed up within the native-born-Zionist identity also becomes more focused and self-conscious. It is viewed with an insight, not only into the depths of their own lives, but also into the depths of the lives of their parents. Even as these parents concealed their heritage, they also exposed it, albeit unknowingly, in a degree that was sufficient for the sons to discover what had been hidden from them.

Empathy thereby turns into critical irony. Suddenly it becomes clear that the parents gave their children far more than they imagined or intended to transmit. Was it possible that in the depth of longing for "another place"—to invoke the title of one of Oz's books—in the dream to free themselves in fact or by means of literary expression from the travails of an identity that was caught between doubled feelings of guilt, there is expressed that same obsessive Jewish attachment to exile discerned by Yehoshua in the Jewish soul itself? Is it possible that the *Tzabar* heroes inherited this, too, from their parents, alongside the negation of the exile and the yearning for a native-Zionist identity?

It may be that all this was unconscious. But this confusion is expressed directly even beyond the complex relations of Oz's and Yehoshua's heroes to their parents, who are both admirable and contemptible in their eyes, simultaneously ludicrous and authoritative, both internalized and rejected. The parents negated the exile while realizing its aspirations. Firmly recognizing the justice of their struggle for settlement in their own country, they sinned, in their children's eyes, against their own ideals. From their point of view, it was they who saved their children from the exile and gave them a whole and healthy, earthy native-born identity. From their perspective, they had borne them above the stormy waves of the sea of their national destiny, which had threatened to swallow them up, so that they might merit to live happily in their homeland. They sacrificed their very lives for their children. But in so doing, they subjugated their children to the burden of their vision of redemption. They imposed upon them their identity and literally bound them as sacrifices in the ongoing war for the refuge that they, in their great guilt, had so much delayed coming to.

This fraught ambivalence in the relations of fathers and their sons, who, like Oz and Yehoshua, represent the native-born State Generation *(Dor Hamedinah),* placed at the very heart of the Jewish-Zionist identity the same myth of pre-Zionist exilic Jewish identity from which Zionism consciously sought to free itself, but to which it returned out of the dialectical logic of historical destiny. This was none other than the myth of the binding of Isaac. The intention on the parts of the writers was, of course, not to affirm but to negate this myth. It was the final effort of the "generation of Isaac" to throw off its hands the bindings, to knock the knife out of the hands of their fathers, who had in their own day been bound by their fathers, to come down from the altar and to free the ram from the thicket, so that they could live their own native-born lives, for themselves and not for their fathers or their ancestors. They wanted their lives for themselves, truly only for themselves, as was the intended meaning of their native-born identity. And yet they remain bound.

If this analysis penetrates to a truth in the works of Oz and Yehoshua, then this is both the happy and sad ending, the empathetic and ironic conclusion, of the entire story of the construction and deconstruction of Jewish-Zionist identity. Another ending which screams out from despair and frustration and failure, is heard from another great work—perhaps the most significant literary work written by the native-born generation in Israel—Ya'akov Shabtai's *Zikhron Devarim* [Past Continuous], which documents with painstaking, Brennerian exactitude the wilting, dying, and death of the ethos of Zionist realization. Shabtai's novel records the complete disintegration of the personality that despaired of Jewish-Zionist identity and longed for another, which it found neither below, nor above, nor beyond the artificial heritage that it received. Thus this personality sets upon the different path of ethical and spiritual suicide. Yet such a work as Shabtai's is already beyond this story of the Zionist realization of Jewish identity. Perhaps it is the beginning of another story altogether.

Meanwhile, several other stories of Jewish identity have begun to develop, among the new groups of immigrants that have gathered in the Land of Israel, within religious Zionism, from anti-Zionist and a-Zionist ultra-Orthodox Jewry, and through the experience of the third and fourth generation of natives of the country, whose Israeli identity was nourished by the reality of the State and has a different beginning. If Zionism continues to be an important factor in guiding the activities of Jews in *Eretz Yisrael*—and it seems to me that it will indeed continue to be significant as a program and as a policy for the Jewish people also in future generations—it certainly will not be a form of identity that defines Jewishness within itself. Rather it will serve a very wide variety of understandings of Jewish identity that will be anchored in the sources, including the Hebrew literature of *Eretz Yisrael* that I have discussed here.

Translated by Jonathan Chipman

CHAPTER TWO

Hebrew Literature and *Dor Hamedinah*: Portrait of a Literary Generation

A. B. Yehoshua

I am not a literary scholar, even though I do teach literature at the university. I see myself as a reasonably good interpreter of literary texts, but not as a person who has the comprehensive knowledge or the credentials that give him the right to make sweeping statements concerning literary process or the identity and defining characteristics of different literary generations. For this reason, if I venture to bestow on the *Dor Hamedinah*, "State Generation," writers (i.e., the writers who wrote after the establishment of the State of Israel) a certificate of identity, I do so only on the authority of a writer who belongs to that generation of authors and not as a scholarly researcher.

Even so, I do not intend merely to provide personal testimony. Rather I want to try to adduce from the works of the writers themselves general characteristics. I believe that, notwithstanding some qualifications, one can say there is in this generation as a whole— in their writings, their artistry, their politics, and their life experience generally—a defining coherence. And despite the fact that literary work springs from the depths of individual experience, from the psyche and soul of the author, nonetheless the work of art is also tied to, and nourished by, the spirit and events of its age. By the same token, the work of art stands in constant interaction with the other works being produced simultaneously with it.

When we speak of *Dor Hamedinah* we are talking of a generation that has functioned for some forty years, and that still exists today, overlapping with at least three other generations. My own first stories I published in *Masah* magazine more than forty years ago, in 1957 to be exact; and I remember Aharon Appelfeld that very same year reading his stories "Ashan" [Smoke] and "Bertha,"

A. B. Yehoshua

in a student literary club. Amos Oz read me his first story a year or two later, and in *Keshet* magazine we found a beautiful story by one "Avi Otniel." When I asked Aharon Amir who this person was he told me about a young man named Yehoshua Kenaz who lived in Paris. I remember that during those same years I went to the General Staff Headquarters to meet with a major by the name of Yitzhak Orpaz who wanted to discuss my story "The Evening Express of Yatu" with me, and also to tell me about a story he was writing. Yoram Kaniuk returned to the country at that time, and Dan Miron wrote an enthusiastic article on his book *Hayored Lemalah* [The One Descending Upwards] and solemnly warned all of us that this was the real thing. In the university library Appelfeld introduced me, enthusiastically, to Amaliah Kahane Carmon, and we both congratulated her on her wonderful story "Im Na Matzati Chen" [If I Had But Found Favor], which was published in the distinguished journal *Amoth*. To these names it is possible to add, of course, also Ben Ner, Dan Tzalka, and Ya'acov Shabtai (*z"l*) who began to write a few years later.

Thus, together we began, each one of us, to undergo his or her own individual processes of development. And accompanying us on our way were several literary critics, academics, whose opinions were very important, at least to me. These were still the days when academics were treated with respect and were invested with wide-sweeping spiritual authority. (This was before the expansion and banalization of the university. The general population in Israel at the end of the fifties was one and a half million. The student body numbered six thousand. Today, while the general population has only quadrupled the number of students has increased twentyfold.) When I recall these literary critics, I think first and foremost of Gershon Shaked, Gabriel Moked, Dan Miron, Eddy Zemach, and Menahem Brinker, who guided us, each in his own way, with deep interest, and, I repeat, their opinions mattered greatly, at least to me. Especially profound was the connection between many of us writers and Gershon Shaked and Gabriel Moked, whose literary judgment was more balanced than that of others, and their caprices more measured.

If I were asked to give a concise definition of the identity of the *Dor Hamedinah* writers, as I see them, I would express it thus: *Yisraeliuth* (Israeliness) as the totality of Jewish identity. Similarly, if I had to examine my own work from its point of origin— the quintessentially Agnon-inspired, surrealistic short story "Mot Hazaken" [Death of an Old Man], which was published in 1957—

up to and including my last novel published forty years later (*Maasah El Tom Haelef* [Journey to the End of the Millennium]), I would say that, despite the oddness of the beginning and of the (hopefully temporary) end of that trajectory, it is still possible to see the path from "Mot Hazaken" to *Maasah El Tom Haelef* as an organic progression. Even though it was difficult to guess that the somnambulant and abstract style of writing that characterized "Mot Hazaken," detached from time and place, would arrive in the end at a dense mimetic prose depicting Jewish existence at the heart of the Middle Ages, quite devoid of connection to the Land of Israel, nonetheless it seems to me that if one attends carefully to the point of view that accompanies both works, the development of the one from the other wasn't impossible to predict.

In the story "Mot Hazaken," Mrs. Ashtor, who represents the nation's forces of vitality, physical sturdiness, and self-confidence, buries her ageless but ancient old boarder, who embodies, if you will, that Jewishness that is faulted with being inert, senseless, and without purpose. But the exhausted narrator, who cooperates with the charismatic and energetic Mrs. Ashtor, comprehends (albeit only after the funeral) that, on the contrary, hastening death by means of burying the living is dangerous, not least of all to him. Sooner or later, he knows, that strange creature, Mrs. Ashtor, whose charisma so sways him, will also get rid of him. Thus, during those years when we, together with others, were fanatically establishing an Israeli identity, it wasn't just that we didn't see any conflict between that identity and either Jewish identity or Jewish culture, but, rather, that we saw Israeli identity as absorbing and assimilating Jewishness within itself and taking upon itself responsibility for its every detail. This was the point that I ceaselessly returned to and emphasized in a thousand lectures and tens of articles: *Yisraeliuth* as *identity,* not *citizenship* in which the Israeli Arab minority also participated, but complete Jewish identity. This is an idea, to which, for the last thirty years, I have not stopped returning. It aroused more than a little wonder and opposition on the parts of many. But now, when one sees how a third of the Israeli government dons beards and *peoth* (earlocks), one has to admit that there was in fact truth in my words, even when the Israeli government went around in open-necked, khaki-colored shirts.

First in poetry, then in fiction and drama, and perhaps also in film, *Dor Hamedinah* (and I very much like that label and am pleased to belong to it), assisted, along with many others, in shaping and consolidating an Israeli identity, and I want to put before you several features that characterize that generation. These characteristics can help us define this generation of writers, not only in and of itself, but also in its distinction from the adjacent generations: the one that preceded it, that is, the generation of the War of Independence, and the two generations that have come afterward. And just as a process of self-definition helped us differentiate between ourselves and these other generations, facilitating the construction of our identity as a generation unto itself, so, perhaps, these principles may assist the generation who has succeeded us in consolidating its own generational identity in opposition to ours. (I am referring here to the generation of the 1980s and 1990s, as described in Gadi Taub's excellent book, *The Dejected Revolution.*)

First. We were the generation that internalized with utter clarity the transition from *Eretz Yisrael* (the Land of Israel) to Israel. This was highly significant, since it provided us with a clear consciousness of boundaries, and it provided the security that comes with knowing borders. If I had to define Zionism in a single word I would say: *boundaries.* We were the generation, the only generation, I would almost say, in the two-thousand-year history of Israel till then, which possessed a clear consciousness of the physical boundaries of our country. It was we who understood what existed within the area of its authority and responsibility and what not. And this greatly facilitated our consolidating our identity as a generational unit. Parenthetically I want to remark that, in my opinion, the cornerstone in the foundation of *Yisraeliuth,* nourishing and fortifying it, remains this consciousness of boundaries, which crystallized in particular between 1956 and 1967. In my opinion we do not fully take the measure of the persistent damage attendant upon the last thirty years of people growing up and residing here who do not know and cannot agree on final territorial boundaries or, similarly, the demographic borders of the country or its capital. This I think is also the reason why many have been seduced into exchanging their primary and organic consciousness of their national identity for a partial consciousness based on ethnic, cultural, and political affiliations.

One of the clearest examples of the literary benefits facilitated by such knowledge of boundaries was the possibility it afforded of dealing with the image of the Israeli Arab in fiction. I remember a visit I made as a boy, with my father, to a village in the Galilee, when he served as the head of the Moslem and Druze Division in the Ministry of Religion during the early 1950s. It was then that I first understood the feeling of belonging to the same institutional framework that turned the Arabs toward us; this feeling allowed me, some twenty years later, to enter into the souls of Arab characters, for example, Naim (in *Hame'ahev* [The Lover]), and to set them naturally within the weave of the novel. They were, for all their national and religious differences, and despite their enmity and grievances, ours. And what determined their belonging to Israeli identity was the clear-cut nature of territorial borders.

These boundaries also preserved the security of the individual, and one of the things that distinguished our generation from others was a further loosening of the ties that bound together the collectivity. It was as if defined territorial borders also strengthened and consolidated the boundaries of self. On the one hand, the events of the 1950s and 1960s were, relatively speaking, less momentous than earlier disturbances and dangers. Therefore, they didn't require our experiencing them from within the consolidated front of the collectivity (see, e.g.; Yizhar's *Yamei Ziklag* [The Days of Ziklag] which is narrated in a kind of collective stream of consciousness). On the other hand, the solitary hero was able to exceed many more rules of behavior without endangering himself or the framework in which he operated, since, for us, the country was already a determined reality. And this is what you won't find in Yizhar or Shamir or Megged. It is not even to be found in Leibovitz, who always spoke about the government as a pragmatic instrument of governance and not as an ideal or essential expression of the communal life in which might reside the potential for actually realizing good and evil.

And from here follows the second point: we took a positive but also a realistic stand in relation to the creation of the State, with none of the romanticism that characterized the previous generation. This generation, the generation of the War of Independence, had already absorbed a rhetoric of disillusion, as evidenced by Aharon Megged's *Hedva V'Ani* [Hedva and I] or even in the long monologues of the young men in *Yamei Ziklag* [Days of Ziklag] or in *Haheshbon V'HaNefesh* [The Reckoning and the Soul] by Haim Bartov, in which the hero goes to Paris to bewail the newly established State, or in Matti Megged's *Hamigdalor* [The Lighthouse]. I could cite other examples. We didn't expect too much of the State because we didn't give birth to it. For this reason we also weren't too disappointed in it. But we could also criticize its existence without fearing that our criticism would destroy it. Amos Oz's critique of the kibbutz, for example, was far more subjective and

personal than it was ideological-Zionistic, as had been the case in
the writings of generation preceding us, for example in the works
of Nathan Shaham. Similarly, I was able to write a surrealistic
story in the voice of the last commanding officer of a group of
reservists who spend their reserve duty in a kind of lazy stupor,
because I believed, not only that the War of Independence was a
just war (I still believe this), but also that the State was essentially
finished with war, so that it was possible finally to surrender to
passivity and slumber rather than go on chasing around all over
the landscape.

Thus we were freed in a certain way from the weighty perspective of the collectivity, which had provided intimacy but that had
also loomed omnipotent. We discovered our individuality, which
was vital to constructing a personal style of authorship, even while
this individuality remained contingent, anchored. Ours was a soli-
tariness that remained tethered to the strong, prior collectivity
that we ourselves had experienced as a guiding light during the
1940s. (This accounts for some of our problems in naming our
heroes.) Even if we eventually chose to separate ourselves from
that collectivity, in the final analysis we treated it with respect. We
also felt a sense of responsibility. The concept of responsibility did
not abandon us.

This individualism displaced politics and ideology, which began to grow dim in the 1950s and the beginning of the 1960s. And
when the Six Day War arrived on the scene at the end of the 1960s,
with the burdensome ideological and political questions it stirred
up, our generation, which was already a full decade into its literary
career, was able to absorb this renewed occurrence of the ideological-
political within its already established personal-literary identity.
From this point of view, we did not develop like the previous
generation, which set out on its way with a weight of ideological
questions. And we didn't emerge like the generations after us, who
were born into the political reality of occupation, a burning, all-
encompassing reality, demanding, exhausting, and easily exploited,
sometimes also a riddle so convoluted as to force one to flee it.
Because there remained a steadfast foundation of solidarity and
identification, the political-ideological breathed the spirit of life into
our writing at a certain stage without too quickly exhausting it.

And from this follows my third point. The transition from a
Land-of-Israel identity to Israeli identity as such (*Yisraeliuth*) destroyed the romantic option provided by Canaanism, which to a
certain degree had permeated the consciousness of earlier genera-

tions. The large waves of *aliyah* that inundated the nation, even if they were beyond our literary range, provided clear and definitive evidence that neither we nor our fathers were born either from the sea or from the fields of Philistia. Behind the Canaanitic pronunciation of Jonathan Ratosh and Aharon Amir (the founding fathers of Canaanism) stood Jewish forefathers from Eastern Europe, who, when you thought about it, were also not so different from those who immigrated from Morocco or from Libya, whose pronunciation of the letters *ayin* and *chet* was also much more authentic. Canaanism is an excellent spice with which to freshen and sharpen the flavor of Zionism, but only when applied cautiously and with moderation. Discarding the Canaanitic option also allowed us to relate to Judaism more maturely, with less anger and with less hypocrisy. And that in my opinion greatly facilitated the absorption of Judaism into Israeli identity.

And from here I arrive at another point: the relationship to religion and the religious that characterized our generation of writers. In the 1950s and 1960s the atmosphere was not saturated with the same harsh enmity to religion and the religious that would be found in the generation or generations following us. At the same time there wasn't the same absolute avoidance of religious elements, as in the writings of the War of Independence generation. Take, for example, the kind of deep evasion of this subject in *Yamei Ziklag*, which is probably our most illustrative document, both subjectively and sociologically, concerning the spirit of the War of Independence generation.

Our own lack of hostility to religion permitted many of us to integrate into our writings, in a limited but significant way, traditional elements that had been central both to our peoplehood and to our culture, and to do so in a richer and more honest way than had heretofore been possible. Think for example of the stories of Amalia Kahane Carmon, "Naama Sasson Koteveth Shirim" [Na'ama Sasson Writes Poems] or "Im Na Mazati Chen." Thus we were able, here and there, to incorporate religious people and religious ritual within the weave of the fiction, enriching, diversifying, and also perhaps deepening, it. I think of Orpaz's story, "Tomozhenna Street," and others, and of course the powerful religious characters in the later novels of Appelfeld. *The Last Jew* of Kaniuk provides further evidence of this pattern. In my own fiction as well, in *Mar Mani* [Mr. Mani] and *Maasah El Tom Haelef*, I was able, as a secular agnostic, to enter, without difficulty, into the souls and spiritual world of rabbis and religious Jews, and, without first getting into the tiresome debate for and against religion, to place them tenably at the forefront of the story. Indeed, there was during this period a feeling, which afterward revealed itself to be minor and fleeting, that secularism or secular nationalism had won such a resounding victory over the religious and over religion, that it was possible to add here and there a few bizarre religious details, slightly decayed, a bit crazy, in order to enrich the mix of the story. Yehoshua Kenaz once told me that his mother, who was herself the daughter of a rabbi, had told him: pay careful attention to the religious in your midst; in few years they will no longer exist. They do not seem to me, in the meantime, to have, in the least, disappeared from our world. Still, the panic-stricken representations of many of my friends today concerning the increasing demonic strength of the religious seem to me an exaggeration at best.

In the 1950s and 1960s, in any event, we experienced the religious, in every way, as a world disappearing and in decline, and for that reason not threatening. And therefore their incorporation as an element within our *Yisraeliuth* became more possible. These were also the good days of Agnon's "Edo and Enam," of Kabbalah and Jewish mysticism. Through the writings of Agnon, Gershom Shalom, and Yeshaya Tishbi, we felt that we had gained the possession of treasures with which to spice and perfect our literary feast.

And this brings me to another point; our feeling of powerful attraction to the Hebrew literary tradition itself. This feeling, of course, also included our attachment to the War of Independence generation immediately preceding us, but in contrast to this generation, which only latterly (if at all) arrived at academic studies (Matti Megged, Bartov, Yizhar, and Guri), with us it was not only the case that most of the novelists and poets passed through their regular university studies at the usual age but that most of us studied Hebrew literature. We became acquainted with the tradition of Hebrew writing in a systematic and organized way. And we were tested on it.

This feeling on the part of our generation of attraction to, and responsibility for, Hebrew literature made possible a more integrated relation to the Jewish past simultaneous with, and without contradiction to, the celebration of an uncompromised Israeli identity. I emphasize this point because I feel that with the generation of the 1990s in particular, it is as if this dialogue with the tradition of Hebrew literature has ceased entirely. Possibly, this is connected to a postmodernist sensibility of being cut off and fractured. Or perhaps it is linked to some political revulsion against Judaism and Jewishness on the parts of many "cosmopolitan" Israeli writers. (Recently, a journalist didn't know who Agnon's Yitzhak Komer was, which is equivalent to a British TV host not knowing who Mrs. Ramsay is, or Mrs. Dalloway.) In any event I know that without such dialogue, which exists in all literatures to a greater or lesser degree, it is difficult for the literary work to achieve depth and resonance. In the final analysis, who is a writer like Agnon without Mendele or even Brenner? Who is Yizhar without Gnessin, Amos Oz without Berdyczewski, or Appelfeld or myself without Agnon?

A similar point is our experience of the modern world surrounding us, in particular the experience of contemporary world literature that nourished us during the years of the 1950s and 1960s, including, perhaps for the first time, a Jewish literature that identified itself as Jewish and gained recognition as such within world culture. I speak in particular of the impressive appearance of American Jewish literature on the world stage. Now there was Jewish literature in English or French, the important languages of world culture, and it was not only written by Jews or half-Jews like Kafka or Yosef Roth or Yaacov Wasserman or Marcel Proust, but it was written *about Jews*. Bellow, Malamud, Philip Roth, Henry Roth, Patrick Modiano, and others were important to the international literary world and gave us not just legitimitization but also a respect for our Jewishness as a component of our *Yisraeliuth*.

But my last point is, in my opinion, the most important point, at least for me and for some of my fellow authors. This is the quality that gives to the writings of the *Dor Hamedinah* generation their special vitality, which accounts for the generation's distinctiveness and centrality, among all of the literary generations over the last fifty years. So great is the dominance of this generation of writers that even literary critics, who love to produce changes and exchanges in the literary map, placing it before us as a kind of battleground or at least a raging soccer field, in which this or another writer is dismissed in order to crown someone new—these critics are forced to continue making these conversions and exchanges, these dismissals and enthronements, within the framework of the same generational unit.

What accounts for this generation's domination over the Hebrew literary scene, not only from the purely literary perspective, that is, from the point of view of literary scholarship, but also in relation to its community of readers? I think that from the beginning we displayed a compelling balance between what was openly represented in the text and what was concealed there. I speak of the hidden and double meanings that our works contained, which developed during the years of our productivity and that had made the work of Agnon so significant to us: for Agnon was the consummate artist of multiple and subterranean meanings.

The previous generation was more open in its writing. You could read whole pages of Yizhar or Shamir's *B'mo Yadav* [With His Own Hands] without once feeling the need to search for what was buried there. And their openness carried the full force of their conviction. They transcribed a manifest reality directly and boldly because they believed in that reality. For us, on the other hand, hidden meanings always lurked beneath the surface. It is possible that we were not always conscious of these concealed depths, but, from the beginning, we perceived the world as manifold, first saying one thing, and then another. In general the something that was concealed, even from us, was some sort of hidden autobiographical matter, which was kept out of sight for all sorts of reasons and only slowly exposed itself. For example, the Holocaust and exile for Orpaz, which later exploded most provocatively when he added his former family name to his own name: Orbach-Orpaz. Or, the whole Jewish world before the war for Appelfeld, which dominated the Israeli experience of the survivors of the Holocaust and had been his subject at the beginning of his career. For me it was the issue of Sephardism, which began to take form as a question concerning the liminal spaces between North and South and between East and West. There is also the despondent revisionism of the 1950s novels and stories of Amos Oz, which took place under the shadow of his mother's suicide. Or, the deep opposition to the War of Independence generation that broke out in the writings of Amalia Kahane Carmon, and the detached, half-Gentile Germanic features of Yoel Hoffmann's writing. These were the powerful elements that at first were buried in accordance with a desire to conform more completely to the norms of Israeli culture. This was so different from the princedom of Yizhar and his generation. And in time, the seepage throughout the text of revelation and once-hidden meanings intensified in its complexity to produce richness and uniqueness.

Our generation, *Dor Hamedinah,* the "State Generation," is now moving decisively toward the seventh decade of its existence, and if we aren't threatened, as I saw recently in the newspapers, with a living till the age of 140, we have arrived at the final quarter of our lives. Sometimes I identify with the feeling of the younger generation that we have occupied the stage a bit too long; perhaps, indeed, the hour has arrived to exit or at least to move off center. I do not know, however, if we are capable of fulfilling their unspoken wishes. For even though we are sometimes rendered extremely vexed by this State whose name came to identify us as a literary generation, nonetheless we are not yet sufficiently bored with the enterprise to give over our handiwork to others.

Translated by Emily Miller Budick

CHAPTER THREE

The Complex Fate of the Jewish American Writer

Morris Dickstein

As early as the 1960s, some eminent observers argued that Jewish writing no longer existed as a distinct body of work, that younger Jews were so assimilated, so remote from traditional Jewish life, that only nostalgia kept it going. The American critic and editor Ted Solotaroff wrote exasperated pieces about younger writers whose work already seemed to him derivative—thin, tiresome, voguish, and strained.[1] I once heard the Israeli writer Aharon Appelfeld tell a New York audience that authentic Jewish literature was grounded in Yiddish culture and a way of life that prospered in Eastern Europe, something only dimly remembered today. It died, he said, with S. Y. Agnon in Israel and Isaac Bashevis Singer in New York. Gazing down benignly at an audience that included his good friend Philip Roth and the novelist E. L. Doctorow, he said that while there were certainly writers who happened to be Jews, there were really no more Jewish writers.[2]

Other critics have been equally firm in anchoring Jewish writing in the immigrant experience, a point implied by Irving Howe in a famous attack on Philip Roth in *Commentary* in 1972. In a phrase that Roth harbored for years as a stinging personal insult, Howe described him as a writer with "a thin personal culture," suggesting that his work was disfigured by "unfocused hostility" perhaps derived from "unexamined depression." Howe saw Roth, whose first book he had warmly acclaimed, as the kind of writer who "comes at the end of a tradition which can no longer nourish his imagination," or as one who simply has "chosen to tear himself away from that tradition."[3]

Certainly there was very little sense of history, Jewish or otherwise, in Roth's neatly crafted early fiction. Yet in the light of his humor, his characters, his subjects, and above all his later development, Roth hardly stood outside the Jewish tradition—a tradition that is, in any case, too amorphous to have any distinct boundaries. Instead it's clear that he had a family quarrel with the Jewish world in which he grew up, but later began to look beyond it, to see what forces had shaped it. In the end, this profoundly altered everything he wrote. If there is one Jewish writer who constantly uses fiction as a testing-ground for self-definition, it is Roth. Yet at the time Howe's charge struck home. In some respects Roth's later writing can be seen as a rejoinder to Howe's attack, which so rankled him that more than a decade later he wrote a furious novel, *The Anatomy Lesson,* lampooning Howe as a hypocrite, a pompous moralist, and even, in a remarkable twist, a pornographer. He was never a writer to take his critics lightly.

What was the substance of the Jewish literary tradition that Howe and Roth, two of its most conspicuous figures, could come to such angry blows over it? My subject is how Jewish writing has changed, how it has survived even the best-informed predictions of its demise. The conflict between Roth and Howe was partly temperamental, but some of it was also generational. Howe was the child of the Yiddish-speaking ghetto, of socialism, and the Depression; Roth came of age in postwar America, a world he would alternately satirize and idealize. There is a streak of the moralist, the puritan, in Howe's criticism, while Roth took pride, especially when he wrote *Portnoy's Complaint,* in playing the immoralist, or at least in treating Jewish moral inhibitions as an ordeal, a source of conflict. For Howe, as for a contemporary like Bernard Malamud, this moral burden was the essence of our humanity; for Roth it led to neurosis, anger, and dark, painful comedy.

It comes as a surprise to realize that the Jewish literary tradition in America, at its strongest, dates only from the Second World War. Irving Howe once compared the Jewish and the Southern literary schools with a provocative comment: "In both instances," he said, "a subculture finds its voice and its passion at exactly the moment it approaches disintegration."[4] But in what sense was Jewish life in America approaching disintegration in the first two decades after the war, when the best Jewish writers emerged? What was dying, quite simply, was the once-flourishing immigrant culture evoked by Howe in *World of Our Fathers.* After the war Jews became far freer, richer, and more influential. As they moved up the economic ladder, professions like academic life opened to them that had always been off limits. Thanks largely to the sense of shame induced by the Holocaust, social anti-Semitism in America became virtually a thing of the past. Surely the great literary flowering owed much to the way Jews in America had finally arrived, although the writers were often critical of what their middle-class brethren did with their new freedom.

In any ethnic subculture, it's almost never the immigrant generation that writes the books. The immigrants don't have the language; their lives are focused on survival, on gaining a foothold in the new world and ensuring an education for their children. Education not only makes literature possible but ignites a conflict of values that makes it urgent and inevitable. The scattering of excellent novels by individual writers before the war belongs less to a major literary current than to the process by which the children of immigrants tried to assert their own identity. In powerful works of the 1920s and 1930s like Anzia Yezierska's *Bread Givers*, Mike Gold's *Jews Without Money*, and Henry Roth's *Call It Sleep*, the writers pay tribute to the struggles of their parents yet declare independence from what they see as their narrow and limited world. These works could be classed with Sherwood Anderson's *Winesburg, Ohio* and Sinclair Lewis's *Main Street* as part of what Carl Van Doren called the "revolt from the village," the rebellion against local mores and patriarchal authority in the name of a freer, more universal humanity.

Ironically, the parochial world these writers rejected was the only authentic material they had. Their painful memories of small-mindedness and poverty, intolerance and religious coercion fueled their imagination as nothing else could. In all these works, the driving impulse of the sensitive, autobiographical protagonist—Sara Smolinsky in *Bread Givers,* little Mike Gold in *Jews Without Money*, the impetuous Ralph Berger in Clifford Odets's play *Awake and Sing!,* even young David Schearl in *Call It Sleep*—is to get away from the ghetto, with its physical deprivation, its materialism and lack of privacy, its desperately limited horizons, but also to get away from the suffocating embrace of the Jewish family—the loving but overly emotional mother; the domineering but ineffectual father; and the inescapable crowd of siblings, aunts, uncles, cousins, and neighbors, all completely entwined in each others' lives. These works were a blow for freedom, a highly ambivalent chronicle of emancipation, and often, sadly, they were the only books these writers could write. Their autonomy was hard-won but incomplete; their new identity liberated them personally, but it did little to fire their imagination.

Henry Roth once told me that only when he began to depart from the facts of his life did his first novel take on a life of its own;

the book then proceeded almost to write itself.[5] In *Beyond Despair,* Aharon Appelfeld made the same point to explain why he prefers fiction over autobiography, for it gave him the freedom he needed to reshape his own recollections, especially the wartime experiences that bordered on the incredible: "To write things as they happened means to enslave oneself to memory, which is only a minor element in the creative process."[6] The early American Jewish novelists were not so lucky. They were stuck not only with what they remembered but with a naturalistic technique that could not do full justice to the complexity of their lives. Their escape from their origins, never fully achieved, became a mixed blessing. They found themselves caught between memory and imagination, ghetto sociology and personal need. Mere rebellion and recollection, it seemed, could not nurture a full career. Their literary development was thwarted, stymied. It was only the postwar writers who managed to break through this sterile pattern.

Saul Bellow, Bernard Malamud, Delmore Schwartz, Paul Goodman, and their Yiddish cousin, I.B. Singer, were the first Jewish writers in America to sustain major careers, not as immigrant writers but in the mainstream of American letters. As modernism replaced naturalism as the dominant literary mode, as new influences like psychoanalysis and existentialism exploded the sociological approach of most prewar writers, a new generation found powerful vehicles for dealing with their experience. Straightforward realism was never an option for Jewish writers in America; it belonged to those writers who knew their society from within, who had a bird's-eye view and an easy grasp of its manners and values. As newcomers dealing with complex questions of identity, Jews instead became specialists in alienation: they gravitated toward outrageous or poetic forms of humor, metaphor, and parable— styles they helped establish in American writing after the war.

The key to the new writers was not only their exposure to the great modernists—Franz Kafka, Thomas Mann, Henry James— but their purchase on Jews not simply as autobiographical figures in a social drama of rebellion and acculturation but as parables of the human condition. Though Saul Bellow admired the power of authentic naturalists like Theodore Dreiser, his first two novels, *Dangling Man* and *The Victim,* were more influenced by Dostoevsky and Kafka than by any writers in the realist tradition. The new writers were as much the children of the Holocaust as of the ghetto. They did not write about the recent events in Europe—they hadn't directly experienced them—but those horrors cast their shadow on every page of their work, including many pages of desperate comedy.

The atrocities of the Holocaust, the psychology of Freud, and the dark vision of certain modern masters encouraged Jewish writers to find universal significance in their own experience. Kafka was the prophet, not of totalitarianism—that was too facile—but of a world cut loose from will and meaning, the world as they experienced it in the 1940s. Saul Bellow's engagement with the themes of modernist culture can be documented from novel to novel, but even a writer as private as Malamud was able to combine the stylized speech rhythms of the ghetto with a form adapted from Hawthorne and Kafka to turn parochial Jewish tales into chilling fables of modern life. This was the brief period when the Jew became the modern Everyman, everyone's favorite victim, schlemiel, and secular saint. Yet there was also an innovation in language, a nervous mixture of the literary and the colloquial, of art talk and street talk that was almost poetic in its effects. As Saul Bellow put it in his eulogy after Malamud's death in 1986:

> Well, we were here, first-generation Americans, our language was English and a language is a spiritual mansion from which no one can evict us. Malamud in his novels and stories discovered a sort of communicative genius in the impoverished, harsh jargon of immigrant New York. He was a myth maker, a fabulist, a writer of exquisite parables.[7]

We can find these effects almost anywhere we turn in Malamud's stories, from animal fables like "The Jewbird" and "Talking Horse" to wrenching tales like "Take Pity," which he put at the head of his last collection of stories. "Take Pity" includes the following bit of dialogue, supposedly between a census taker, Davidov, and a recalcitrant citizen named Rosen:

"How did he die?"

"On this I am not an expert," Rosen replied. "You know better than me."

"How did he die?" Davidov spoke impatiently. "Say in one word."

"From what he died?—he died, that's all."

"Answer, please, this question."

"Broke in him something. That's how."

"Broke what?"

"Broke what breaks."[8]

This Kafkaesque exchange shows the eternally baffled, fatalistic quality of the Jewish Everyman, trying to evade official scrutiny, too beleaguered and evasive to worry about the meaning of things. Eventually we discover that the man answering the questions so abruptly is himself dead, and his reckoning with the "census taker" is set in some bare, shabby room of heaven or hell, though it feels like a forgotten pocket of the ghetto. Rosen, a former coffee sales-man, has killed himself in a last-ditch effort to impose his charity, pity, or love on the fiercely independent widow of the man who died. Rosen takes pity on her, but she will not *take* his pity. Even after he turns on the gas and leaves her everything, she appears at the window, adrift in space, alive or dead, imploring or berating him in a final gesture of defiance.

Like all of Malamud's best work, this is a story of few words but resonant meanings.[9] Anticipating Samuel Beckett, Malamud strips down the sociology of the ghetto into a spare, postapocalyptic landscape of violently essential, primitive emotions, finding eerie comedy on the far side of horror. After her husband's death, as the business disintegrates, the woman and her children come close to starving, but the story is less about poverty than about the per-verseness of the human will. Again and again, Rosen tries to help the widow out, but she adamantly refuses his help. Both are stub-born unto death, and the story explores the fine line between good-ness and aggression, generosity and control, independence and self-immolation. Rosen will get the proud woman to accept his help, whether she wants to or not, but neither one can truly pity the other; their unshakable self-will isolates and destroys them. And the interrogator, standing in for both author and reader, makes no effort to judge between them. The story leaves us with a sense of the sheer human mystery.

The raw power of Malamud's stories is based on a simple prin-ciple—that every moral impulse has its Nietzschean dark side, its streak of lust or the will to power, just as every self has its antiself, a shadow that exposes its vulnerabilities and limitations. Classic works like Poe's "William Wilson," Dostoevsky's *The Double*, and Conrad's *The Secret Sharer* had developed the figure of the "double," which would prove irresistible to post-Freudian writers exploring the dark side of the mind. This dialectic of self and other is at the heart of Malamud's stories and even his longer novels. The "self" in his stories is often a stand-in for the writer, the artist as assimilated Jew—fairly young but never youthful, well educated but not especially successful, Jewish but nervously assimilated, full of choked-up feeling. Repeatedly, this figure is brought up short by his encounter with some ghetto trickster, a wonder-working rabbi, an ethnic con man who represents the suppressed, tribal part of his own tightly controlled personality.

Malamud's work is full of examples of such admonitory figures, half real, half legendary, including the ghetto rat, Susskind, a refugee in Rome in "The Last Mohican," who steals the hero's manuscript on Giotto, and Salzman, the marriage broker in "The Magic Barrel," whose ultimate gift to a young rabbinical student is his own fallen daughter. These old world characters convey the ambiguous, even disreputable qualities that the young hero has bleached out of his own arid identity. At different times they stand for ethnic Jewishness, carnality, wild emotion, even a sense of magic and the irrational. Like Davidov, the census taker in "Take Pity," Susskind and Salzman are slightly magical figures who come and go with almost supernatural ease. Or else they are figures from another culture—the Italian helper in *The Assistant*, the black writer in *The Tenants*—who test the limits of the protagonist's humanity.

There's a later treatment of this theme in a story called "The Silver Crown." The main character here is a high school teacher named Gans (or "goose"), and the man who puts him to the test is a rather dubious wonder rabbi named Lifschitz. For an odd sum of money, this Lifshitz promises to cure Gans's ailing father by fashioning a silver crown. We never learn whether Rabbi Lifschitz is a holy man, a con man, or both, but when the skeptical Gans loses faith, curses his father, and demands his money back, the old man quickly expires. This could be a coincidence—Malamud loves ambiguity—but he leads us to suspect that the son, who seemed so desperate to save his father, actually does him in. His suspicions about the rabbi and the money signified an unconscious ambivalence, even a hostility toward the father, that he couldn't directly express. Seemingly sensible and cautious, he's only the stunted husk of a man, going from filial piety to symbolic parricide in just a few lines. Malamud took this story from one of the newspapers but shaped it into something entirely his own, a probe of the moral shortcomings of our assimilated selves, our rational and secular humanity, which has killed off some essential part of who we are.

Malamud's own piety toward the past is not something we can readily find in the next generation. Coming of age in the late fifties and early sixties, writers like Philip Roth belonged to a new group of rebellious sons and daughters, even parricidal sons like Malamud's Albert Gans. This was the black humor generation, rebelling not against the constraints of the ghetto—they were too young to have known any real ghetto—but against the mental ghetto of Jewish morality and the Jewish family. If Anzia Yezierska or Clifford Odets inveighed against the actual power of the Jewish father or mother, Roth and his contemporaries, who grew up with every apparent freedom, were doing battle with the internal censor, the mother or father in the head.

The work of these writers proved to be deliberately provocative, hugely entertaining, always flirting with bad taste, and often very funny, but with an edge of pain and giddiness that borders on hysteria. As Portnoy gradually discovers that he's living inside a Jewish joke, the novel's comic spirits turn self-lacerating. Writers like Stanley Elkin, Bruce Jay Friedman, Joseph Heller, Jerome Charyn, and Mark Mirsky practiced an art of incongruity, deploying a wild mockery in the place of moral gravity. Howe's charge against Roth—that he writes out of a "thin personal culture"—could be leveled against them as well, but it would be more accurate to say they looked to a different culture, satirical, performative, intensely oral. They identified less with modernists like Kafka and Dostoevsky than with provocateurs like Céline, Nathanael West, and Lenny Bruce. They looked less to literature than to stand-up comedy, the oral tradition of the Jewish jokes that Freud collected, and the vaudeville *shtick* that brought Jews to the forefront of American entertainment.

The usual targets of their derision, besides Jewish mothers and Jewish husbands, were the new suburban Jews who had made it after the war, the vulgar, wealthy Patimkins in *Goodbye, Columbus*, who live in a posh Newark suburb, play tennis and send their daughter to Radcliffe, and—this got me when I first read it—have a separate refrigerator for fruit in their finished basement. (Actually, it was their *old* fridge they were thrifty enough to save, the way they've preserved remnants of their old Newark personality.) As a foil to the Patimkins of Short Hills, Roth gives us the inner-city blacks of Newark, where the Jews used to live. We get glimpses of the black workmen ordered around by the Patimkins' callow son, and especially of a young boy who runs into trouble simply because he wants to read a book on Gauguin in the local public library. At the heart of Roth's story, then, for all its irreverence, is a sentimental idea of the virtue of poverty and the simple life, something the Jews (except for Neil, the author's surrogate) have left behind but the black boy still seeks in Gauguin's noble vision of Tahiti.

Goodbye, Columbus was published in 1959, just at the outset of a decade in which outrage and irreverence would become the accepted cultural norms. Even Saul Bellow would take a spin with black humor in *Herzog* (1964), as Bernard Malamud would do, unconvincingly, in *Pictures of Fidelman* in 1969. In these books they dipped into sexual comedy as never before, the comedy of adultery in Bellow, of sexual hunger and humiliation in Malamud. But they were soon outflanked by their literary son, Philip Roth, who would make epic comedy out of Jewish dietary laws, rabbinical pomposity, furtive masturbation, plaintive longing for *shikses*, and above all the family romance, centered on the histrionically overbearing mother, the long-suffering father, and the apple of their eye, the young Jewish prince. *Portnoy's Complaint*, with its deliberate vulgarity and broad comic exaggeration, was the work that elicited Irving Howe's sweeping attack. This was the book that famously tried to put the Id back in Yid, and turned the vulgar spritz of stand-up comedy into literature.

The Oedipal pattern in *Portnoy's Complaint* belongs to a larger history. Roth and his contemporaries were rebelling not only against their parents but against their literary parents, the often solemn moralists of the previous generations, who were still around and did not take so kindly to it. Bellow responded to the carnival aspect of the sixties by taking on the voice of the censorious Jewish sage in *Mr. Sammler's Planet*, arraigning middle-aged adulterers along with women, blacks, and young people in one sweeping vision of moral decay—"sexual niggerhood," he called it, in one memorably horrible phrase.[10] The date was 1970, the bitter end of a tumultuous decade; Bellow's and Howe's responses were extreme but typical of the overheated rhetoric of the generation gap and the culture wars. Bellow's outrage perhaps was tinged with the envy many middle-aged Americans, not simply Jews, felt toward the new sexual freedoms of the young.

Bernard Malamud responded just as pointedly in a 1968 story called "An Exorcism," but it is hardly known because he never reprinted it in his lifetime. Unlike Bellow, he wasn't a writer who used fiction as a vehicle for cultural polemics. But more than any other text, this story brings to a head the Oedipal tensions among Jewish writers, to shedding light on their key differences. The central figure is an austere older writer—like Malamud himself, but far less successful—a lonely man rigorously devoted to his craft, a kind of saint and hero of art. An aspiring writer, a young sixties type, attaches himself to the older man at writers' conferences—virtually the only places he ever ventures out. The older man, named Fogel, is grudging and taciturn, but eventually his defenses drop, for he feels "grateful to the youth for lifting him, almost against his will, out of his solitude."[11] Having won his confidence, the boy betrays him; he publishes a story based on an embarrassing sexual episode in the life of the older man, who first confronts, then forgives him. But when the student, as a provocative stunt, seduces three women in a single night, Fogel feels a wave of nausea and exorcises him from his life. (In the incendiary spirit of the young, Fogel sets fire to his camper, the scene of his sexual conquests.)

Malamud clearly felt uneasy with the naked anger of this story, which indicts not simply one unscrupulous young writer but a whole generation for its freewheeling life and confessional style. In the eyes of an exacting literary craftsman, who fears that *his* kind of art is no longer valued, these facile new writers simply don't invent enough. (Fogel accuses the young man of doing outrageous things simply to write about them, of being little more than "a walking tape recorder" of his "personal experiences.") I wondered whether Malamud could be referring directly to Roth in this story, which appeared before *Portnoy's Complaint* was published but after it began appearing in magazines. Certainly when the writer tells his surrogate son that "Imagination is not necessarily Id" (203), Malamud could be referring to Roth's famous line about "putting the Id back in Yid." Roth would give his own version of his spiritual apprenticeship to Malamud and Bellow ten years later in *The Ghost Writer*. In any case, "An Exorcism" remained unknown while *Portnoy's Complaint* became the ultimate piece of second-generation black humor, a hilarious whine against the neurotic effects of prolonged exposure to Jewish morality and the Jewish family.

Portnoy's complaint was an Oedipal complaint, but even at the time, long before he published *Patrimony,* his 1991 memoir of the death of his father, it was clear how deeply attached Roth was to the parents he satirized and mythologized—the eternally constipated father, the operatically self-dramatizing mother, who loved and forgave him as no other woman could, loved him even for his transgressions. (Claire Bloom, Roth's second wife, tells us in her own memoir that Mrs. Roth was nothing like Mrs. Portnoy; when a reporter asked her what she thought of the novel, Mrs. Roth is reported to have said: "We're very happy about Philip's success.") All through the 1970s, Roth kept rewriting the novel in increasingly strident works like *The Breast,* a misconceived fantasy; *My Life as a Man,* a misogynistic account of his first marriage; and *The Professor of Desire.* Roth seemed unable to escape the facts of his life but he also seemed desperate to offend. He attacked critics for taking his work as autobiographical, yet repeatedly fell back on exaggerated versions of the known facts. In *My Life as a Man* he even played on the relationship between fact and invention by giving us what claimed to be the "real" story behind some fictional versions. But of course he felt free to make up the "real" story as well. Years later, trying to work his way out of a nervous breakdown, Roth would tell the *real* real story in *The Facts,* a memoir that itself played on its relation to his fiction.

None of these almost military maneuvers against critics and readers, which Roth also carried on in essays and interviews, quite prepared us for his next book, *The Ghost Writer,* which launched the next stage of Jewish American writing, the one we are still in today. If the second stage was mocking and satiric, even parricidal, the third stage begins with a work of filial homage addressed to the two writers with whom his name had always been linked. Malamud appears in the book as E. I. Lonoff, very much the ascetic devotee of craft as he appears in Malamud's own late work, including "An Exorcism," *The Tenants, Dubin's Lives,* and the earnest essays and speeches collected in *Talking Horse.* Bellow (with a touch of Norman Mailer) figures as the prolific, much-married, world-shaking Felix Abravanel, a man who, as it turns out; "was clearly not in the market for a twenty-three-year-old son."[12] Roth himself appears as the young Nathan Zuckerman, a dead ringer for the author at that age. Zuckerman has just published his first, controversial stories, as Roth had done, and his own father is angry at him for washing the family linen in public. ("Well, Nathan, you certainly didn't leave anything out, did you?" [85]) His father has gotten the elders of the Jewish community on his case, in the person of one Judge Leopold Wapter, who sends him a questionnaire, no less, that concludes: "Can you honestly say there is anything in your short story that would not warm the heart of a Julius Streicher or a Joseph Goebbels?" (103–104)

This Judge Wapter stands for all the professional Jews and rabbinical critics who had been upset by Roth's early stories—stories which, after all, had surely been written to ruffle people's feathers, even to offend them. Under the guise of broad satire, the older Roth is now caricaturing his enemies, nursing old grievances, and parading his own victimization as wounded virtue. Roth demands from his readers what only his parents had given him: unconditional love. He wants to transgress and wants to be forgiven, wants to be outrageous yet also to be accepted, to be wickedly clever and to be adored for it. When his lovers or his critics fail to give this to him, he lashes out at them. This rehearsal of old grievances is the tired and familiar part of *The Ghost Writer,* but the book included much that, in retrospect, was quite new.

First, there is a surprising and insistent literariness that goes well with the book's evocative tone and warm filial theme. Roth's angry iconoclasm has been set aside. *The Ghost Writer* deals with Nathan Zuckerman's literary beginnings, and Roth's virtuoso portraits of the older writers are perfectly in tune with the literary allusions that form the backdrop of the story—references to Isaac Babel, the great Soviet Jewish writer murdered by Stalin; to Henry James's story "The Middle Years," which also deals with a young acolyte's relation to an older writer; and most importantly, to the diary of Anne Frank. She is the figure behind Amy Bellette, the young woman in Roth's story who may actually *be* Anne Frank, and who may be having an affair with Lonoff.

Second, for all the *shtick* and satire in Roth's earlier fiction, this is his most Jewish book so far, not only for Roth's tribute to earlier Jewish writers but in his warm retelling of Anne Frank's story. Both the literariness and the Jewishness had always been latent in Roth's work, just barely masked by its satiric edge, its willed vulgarity. Roth's literary bent had been evident in his essays on contemporary fiction, his brilliant story about Kafka, the interviews he had published about each of his novels, and especially the invaluable series he was editing for Penguin, "Writers From the Other Europe," which launched the Western careers of a number of great (but then unknown) Polish and Czech writers including Milan Kundera. No critic, to my knowledge, has yet tried to gauge the effect of this large editorial enterprise on Roth's later fiction. As his own work bogged down in Portnoy imitations and paranoia, this project took Roth frequently to Eastern Europe where he made a wealth of literary contacts. Thus Roth found himself editing morally serious and formally innovative work which, despite its congenial absurdism, cut sharply against the grain of what he himself was then writing. This material exposed Roth to both the Holocaust and Soviet totalitarianism, and ultimately helped give his work a historical dimension—and a quite different Jewish dimension—it had previously lacked. It brought him back to his European roots. The angry young man, the prodigal son, was gradually coming home.

In *The Ghost Writer* Roth still nurses his old quarrel with the Jewish community, just as he would pursue his vendetta against Irving Howe in *The Anatomy Lesson*. He eulogizes Lonoff as "the Jew who got away" (50), the Jew of the heart, or art—the non-institutional Jew—and portrays Anne Frank as a secular detached Jew like himself. In a bizarre moment, Zuckerman even imagines himself *marrying* Anne Frank, perhaps the ultimate rejoinder to his Jewish critics, to all the Judge Wapters of the world. But apart from this defensiveness, there's a strain of reverence toward art in the book, toward the Jewish historical experience, even toward the Jewish family, which creates something really new in Roth's work.

As Zuckerman realizes "how much I was still my family's Jewish offspring," he pays tribute to the "dour wit and poignancy" with which Lonoff, the Malamud figure, has been able to connect with ordinary Jewish lives (11-12). The "thwarted, secretive, imprisoned souls" in Lonoff's work reunite Zuckerman with his own family. This empathy, some common touch and fellow feeling even in the most refined artist, is something that has clearly eluded Roth himself, which he now desperately wants. Instead of rebelling against the father, he wants to be anointed by him: he's come "to submit myself for candidacy as nothing less than E. I. Lonoff's spiritual son" (9). Adopted by Lonoff, married to Anne Frank, he will be armored against the Howes and Wapters who criticize his writing for not being Jewish or tasteful enough.

In retrospect we can see how so much of value in Roth's later work—the wider political horizons in *The Counterlife* and *Operation Shylock*, the unexpected play with metafiction and textuality in both of those books, with their ingenious variations on what is made up and what is "real," and finally, his loving tribute to his late father in *Patrimony* and to two fictional fathers in *American Pastoral*—can be said to have originated in *The Ghost Writer*. Moreover, they are strikingly typical of what I call the third phase of American Jewish writing, when the Jewishness that once seemed to be disappearing returned with a vengeance. In this phase the inevitability of assimilation gives way to the work of memory.

There's nothing so surprising about this pattern of departure and return. The great historian of immigration, Marcus Lee Hansen, long ago suggested what came to be known as Hansen's Law: "What the son wishes to forget the grandson wishes to remember."[13] For Roth as a novelist this was a more complicated matter. In *Patrimony* he presents his aged father as in some ways a pain in the neck—Claire Bloom's memoir confirms this—but also as the keeper of the past, the storyteller, the Great Rememberer. Driving around Newark with his son, the former insurance agent, like a real census taker, easily recalls every occupant of every building: "You mustn't forget anything—that's the inscription on his coat of arms," his son writes. "To be alive, to him, is to be made of memory."[14]

The father's motto is also part of the artistic credo of the son. Roth's protagonists are always astonished to meet old friends who cannot recall every single minute of their mutual childhood. This is why the narcissistic side of Roth, obsessed with self-scrutiny, cannot let go of any of his old grievances. When Roth in *The Facts* tells us how his first wife pawned his old typewriter, he thinks of it still as the one he got for his bar mitzvah. How could she do this; how could anyone do this, *to his mother's favorite son*? Every object in his life carries this baggage of personal history. It leads him to idealize his youth in *Portnoy's Complaint,* to see the postwar years as a Golden Age in *American Pastoral*. It enables him to remember his past with a hallucinatory intensity. Yet by the mid 1980s Roth also developed a wider historical purview, a sense of all that life that was lived before him, or far away from him—in Eastern Europe, where he sets "The Prague Orgy," in England or Israel, where some of the best parts of *The Counterlife, Deception,* and *Operation Shylock* take place. This is a more cosmopolitan Roth, reaching outside himself for almost the first time, in dialogue with Zionism, acutely sensitive to anti-Semitism, grounding himself in the Jewish identity he had once mocked and scorned.

Much of *The Counterlife* still belongs to the old self-involved Roth of the Zuckerman saga—the fears of impotence, the scabrous comedy, the Wagnerian family uproar—but the sections set in England and Israel are something new. Until the early 1980s there was as little trace of the Jewish state in American fiction as there was of the old European diaspora in Israeli literature. American writers by and large were not Zionists, and Israeli writers were certainly not nostalgic for the shtetl or the Russian Pale. With its insistence on nationhood as the solution to the Jewish problem, Israel was perhaps too insular to capture the imagination of assimilated writers, however much it preoccupied ordinary American Jews. Israel was the place where Portnoy couldn't get an erection—surely the least memorable part of that vivid novel.

But more than a decade later, when Zuckerman's brother Henry becomes a *baal t'shuva,* a penitent, and Zuckerman looks him up among the zealots of the West Bank, Roth's work crosses that of Amos Oz and David Grossman, novelists who had written well about the cultural and religious tensions dividing Israeli society. Like them, Roth brings on great talkers who can articulate sharp ideological differences, which also reflect his own inner conflicts. For Roth this is a new fiction of ideas, much closer to Bellow than to early Roth. *The Counterlife* inaugurates a dialogic phase of Roth's writing that gets played out in *Deception,* an experimental novel that is all dialogue; *The Facts,* where Nathan Zuckerman appears at the end to offer a rebuttal to Roth's memoir; and *Operation Shylock,* which returns to the Israeli setting of *The Counterlife.* In the process, Roth's work acquires a marked historical dimension, which would also lead to an acclaimed but uneven trilogy about postwar America beginning with *American Pastoral.*

Like these later stories, Zuckerman in Israel gives us Roth escaping from the narcissistic limitations of his earlier work. In England, cast among the not-so-genteel anti-Semites, Zuckerman develops an extraordinary pride, aggressiveness, and sensitivity about being Jewish. With their layers within layers, *The Counterlife* and *Operation Shylock* are Roth's most Jewish books, even as Zuckerman defends himself (and Jewish life in the Diaspora) against the demands of both orthodoxy and Zionism. They mark his return to the fold, as well as his most formally complex fiction, pointing not only to the confusions between art and life but to the multiple layers of Roth's identity.

By giving so much attention to Roth, I run the risk of making it seem that it's only *his* development that is at stake, not larger changes in American Jewish writing. But every feature of Roth's later work has its parallel in other writers who emerged in the last twenty years: the more explicit and informed Jewishness, the wider historical framework, the play with metafiction or magic realism, and the more intense literariness. In line with the wave of identity politics in America, there has been a persistent search for roots among younger Jewish writers. The poet and translator David Rosenberg edited two well-received anthologies, *Congregation* and

Testimony, in which secular writers contributed personal essays on
the Hebrew Bible or on the Holocaust. Novelists with little traditional background, such as Anne Roiphe and Leslie Epstein—one
grew up rich on Park Avenue, the other in Hollywood, son of a
leading screenwriter—both mined Jewish material for their fiction,
and so did younger writers like Steve Stern, Allegra Goodman, Lev
Raphael, Thane Rosenbaum, Melvin Jules Bukiet, Pearl Abraham,
Rebecca Goldstein, Aryeh Lev Stollman, Nathan Englander, and
Ehud Havazelet. They have written about subjects as varied as the
old Jewish ghetto of Memphis, the lives of young Jews in Oxford
and Hawaii, the orthodox communities of New York and Israel, the
problems of gay Jewish identity, the surreal experiences of the walking wounded—Holocaust survivors and their children—and the old
world of the shtetl and of Europe after the war. This is a rapidly
expanding group, which reflects a passionate new ethnicity. Some of
their work smells of the library or reads like latecomers' writing,
arduously researched. The large fictional statement, the creation of
a comprehensive world, so far eludes them. They work best in haunt-
ing short novels like Stollman's *The Far Euphrates* or in collections
of overlapping stories like Rosenbaum's *Elijah Visible* or Goodman's
The Family Markowitz, composed of scenes and vignettes that allude
nostalgically to the old-style family chronicle.[15]

The interests of these emerging writers were foreshadowed not
only by the later turn of Philip Roth but by the direction taken by
another older writer, Cynthia Ozick, who, like Roth, spent many
years indentured to the 1950s gospel of art according to Henry
James, and only later discovered a more original vein of Jewish
storytelling typical of the writers of this third stage. To put it
bluntly, Ozick's work too is much more Jewish than her predecessors, richer with cultural information, even sentimentally Orthodox. The title stories of two of her collections, "Bloodshed" and
"Levitation," are stinging attacks on secular Jews, as are some of
her best-known essays, including an assault on Harold Bloom for
worshiping the idols of art and a blistering critique of the editing
and staging of Anne Frank's diary.[16] Yet Ozick began as a feminist
and remains the most articulate woman in a largely patriarchal
line that rarely produced strong writing by women, apart from
such isolated figures as Emma Lazarus, Mary Antin, Anzia
Yezierska, Grace Paley, or Tillie Olsen. This is something else that
has changed dramatically since 1970.[17]

Bellow and Malamud had Jewishness in their bones, but what
they actually knew about Judaism could have been written on one

page. They knew the ghetto neighborhoods, the character types, the speech patterns, and whatever else they took in with their mother's milk. They were born into Yiddish-speaking homes. Their Judaism was all instinctive, domestic, introspective. But their determination to navigate the literary mainstream prevented them from getting too caught up with specifically Jewish subjects. Ozick, on the other hand, like Isaac Bashevis Singer or Steve Stern, is fascinated by the whole magical, esoteric side of Judaism—the popular lore and legend, the Dybbuks and Golems of Jewish mystical tradition. For Singer this was part of his own experience growing up in Poland, but for Ozick or Stern it is a vicarious Judaism based on reading and research. But this very bookishness—a certain remoteness from life—becomes a key theme in their work.

Until quite recently a great fear haunted Jewish-American writing: that the subject was exhausted, that we live in inferior times, that giants once walked the earth and said everything that could be said. From her first important story, "Envy, or Yiddish in America" in 1969, to her keynote story, "Usurpation: Other People's Stories" in the mid-1970s, to *The Messiah of Stockholm* and *The Puttermesser Papers,* Ozick repeatedly wrote stories about writers, or stories about other people's stories. This was a latecomer's literature, almost a textbook example of the postmodern profusion of texts upon texts or of Harold Bloom's famous theory of the anxiety of influence, which emphasizes the Oedipal relations between writers and their precursors. We risk becoming footnotes to our forebears.

Like *The Ghost Writer,* Ozick's "Envy"—the very title is revealing—is most memorable for its portraits of two older writers, one a lethal caricature of Isaac Bashevis Singer—widely translated, fabulously successful, yet cruel, egotistical, and rejected by most other Yiddish writers—the other loosely based on the great poet Jacob Glatstein, widely celebrated among fellow Yiddishists yet never properly translated into English. (Ozick herself later did some translations of his work.) But the key figure is a young woman, perhaps based on Ozick herself, whom the poet grasps as his lifeline into English, the potential savior of all Yiddish culture.

The desperate poet is envious of Singer's success but especially contemptuous of American Jewish writers for their ignorance: "*Jewish* novelists! Savages!" he says bitterly. "Their Yiddish! One word here, one word there. *Shikseh* on one page, *putz* on the other, and that's the whole vocabulary!"[18] Like Roth's novella, this is a kind of ghost story; the characters represent a dead culture trying to come alive. But it's also a vampire tale, since the young woman eventually rejects them as bloodsuckers trying to live at her expense. Fascinated by the high drama of an expiring Yiddish culture, she decides she cannot allow it to take over her own life. Cynthia Ozick is thought of as some kind of pious traditionalist but this, her best story, written with ferocious energy and style, is a work that radiates hostility from first to last, reminding the reader of the polemical turn she often takes in her essays.

In "Usurpation" the spirit of envy takes over the protagonist herself. It begins with a young writer sitting at the 92nd Street Y and listening to a reading by a famous older writer. After two or three sentences, her ears begin to burn for she feels he's telling a story that truly belongs to her, that she was born to write. As it happens, the writer and the story can easily be identified, since Ozick retells it. It's "The Silver Crown," Malamud's story about the wonder rabbi, which is precisely about the conflict of generations that is virtually the signature of this third, or latecomers' generation. It's also a story of the kind of Jewish mystery and magic so dear to Ozick that she burns with resentment at not having written it herself. Like Steve Stern, she makes that literary belatedness the theme of her own story.

It's no accident that Ozick's stories overlap with her fine literary essays, or that metafiction and postmodernism here make a belated and surprising entry into Jewish writing. Postmodernism, as I understand it, conveys the sense that all texts are provisional, that we live in a world already crowded with texts, that originality is a romantic illusion, and that techniques like collage, pastiche, and pseudocommentary are better than realism for conveying our sense of belatedness and repletion.

This feeling of vicariousness is the theme of my last example, Ozick's 1990 story "Puttermesser Paired," the centerpiece of *The Puttermesser Papers*, in which the author's fictional alter ego tries to imagine herself as George Eliot—a writer who was such a severe moralist that she might as well have been Jewish, even apart from the Zionist theme of her last novel. Ozick wonderfully retells the story of Eliot's relationship to two men in her life, her first husband, George Henry Lewes, and her brief second marriage to a much younger man, later her biographer, Johnny Cross, who apparently tried to drown himself in a Venice canal during their honeymoon. Ozick has her protagonist reenact this relationship with a younger man in *her* life—as disastrously as George Eliot. Like other third-generation stories, it's a text about texts, a piece of historical and essayistic fiction about earlier writers' lives, infused with the sense that we are doomed either to repeat them or to fall far short of them.

It's not often that literary history so closely mirrors social history, but the conflict of literary generations described here is part of a larger pattern. It's no news that America has experienced a revival of ethnicity, or that the world has been rocked by waves of resurgent nationalism. With their long-standing commitment to the universalism of the Enlightenment, to which they owed their emancipation, secular Jews have been ambivalent about participating in this process. Thanks to the near-disappearance of anti-Semitism, Jewish life in America has become far more assimilated, but younger Jewish writers have both taken advantage of this and sharply criticized it. They have turned to Israel, to feminism, to the Holocaust, to earlier Jewish history, and to their own varied spiritual itineraries, ranging from neo-Orthodoxy to Eastern religion, as a way of redefining their relation to both Jewish tradition and contemporary culture. If they have lost the old connection to Europe, to Yiddish, or to immigrant life, they have begun to substitute their own distinctive Jewish and American experiences. They are not simply living on the inherited capital of past literary generations. The new writing so far may lack the power of a Malamud, a Bellow, a Grace Paley, the wild intensity and intelligence of a Roth or an Ozick, but it is certainly not hemmed in by the bland, assimilated aspects of Jewish life. Jewish writers have quarreled with each other, but these have been family quarrels, not holy wars. Whatever tension this creates in their work, it certainly gives us no sign that they are about to give up the ghost, especially now that the ghost, the past, has taken on new flesh and blood.

Notes

1. See, for example, his 1964 review of first novels by Jerome Charyn and L. S. Simckes, "Jewish Camp," reprinted in Solotaroff, *The Red Hot Vacuum and Other Pieces on the Writing of the Sixties* (New York: Atheneum, 1970), pp. 87–93.

2. A version of Appelfeld's talk was later published in English, "The Rise and Fall of the Jewish Author," trans. Jeffrey Green, in *The Pakn-Treger* 25 (summer 1997): 27–30. Appelfeld, who grew up in an assimilated family speaking German at home, writes that "with the death of Yiddish, part of the Jewish soul passed away. . . . The Jewish author was the embodiment of Jewishness. Jewishness was body and soul for him. . . . Now we no longer have Jewish authors. Now we only have authors of Jewish descent who also

write about Jewish subjects. . . . The Jewish author lived for about a century, from the mid-19th century to the '50s and '60s of our century. He left behind no descendants" (30).

3. Irving Howe, "Philip Roth Reconsidered," in *The Critical Moment* (New York: Horizon Press, 1973), p. 147. Howe develops his argument about the relation of Jewish writing to the immigrant experience in several places, including his introduction to *Jewish-American Stories* (New York: New American Library, 1977), p. 16.

4. Howe, ed., *Jewish-American Stories,* p. 3. Elsewhere he writes: "The work of American Jewish writers represented an end, not a beginning. . . . By now it is clear that the world of our fathers, in its brief flare of secular passion, gave the American Jewish writers just enough material to see them through a handful of novels and stories." He describes the younger writers as "exhausting the credit of their grandfathers' imaginations." See "Strangers" (1977), in *Celebrations and Attacks* (New York: Horizon Press, 1979), p. 19.

5. See my profile of Roth, "Call It an Awakening," *New York Times Book Review* (November 29, 1987).

6. "The things that happened to me in my life have already happened, they are already formed, and time has kneaded them and given them shape," he says. "Reality can permit itself to be unbelievable, inexplicable, all out of proportion. The created work, to my regret, cannot permit itself all that." Aharon Appelfeld, "A Conversation with Philip Roth," in *Beyond Despair,* trans. Jeffrey M. Green (New York: Fromm International, 1994), p. 68.

7. Quoted by Robert Giroux in his introduction to Bernard Malamud, *The People and Uncollected Stories,* ed. Giroux (New York: Farrar, Straus and Giroux, 1989), p. xv. Malamud's Yiddish-inflected literary language was anticipated in the 1930s by Henry Roth in *Call It Sleep* and by Clifford Odets in the stylized dialogue of his best plays.

8. Malamud, "Take Pity," in *The Stories of Bernard Malamud* (New York: Farrar, Straus and Giroux, 1983), pp. 5–6.

9. See Malamud's own arresting comments on the story in a posthumously published talk, "Why Fantasy?" in *Talking Horse: Bernard Malamud on Life and Work,* eds. Alan Cheuse and Nicholas Delbanco (New York: Columbia University Press, 1996), pp. 59–61. There he describes the setting as "an institutional place in limbo" and the interrogator as a kind of "recording angel" and "symbolic figure . . . who could be anybody listening to a tale."

10. Saul Bellow, *Mr. Sammler's Planet* (New York: Viking, 1970), p. 162.

11. Malamud, "An Exorcism," in *The People and Uncollected Stories,* p. 212. "An Exorcism" has also been reprinted in Malamud, *The Complete Stories,* ed. Giroux (New York: Farrar, Straus and Giroux, 1997), pp. 471–488.

12. Philip Roth, *The Ghost Writer* (New York: Farrar, Straus and Giroux, 1979), p. 66.

13. Hansen's thesis has become a highly contested issue in the historiography of immigration. For Hansen's original essays and some recent critiques see *American Immigrants and Their Generations: Studies and Commentaries on the Hansen Thesis after Fifty Years,* eds. Peter Kivisto and Dag Blanck (Urbana: University of Illinois Press, 1990). First published in 1938, the year of his death, Hansen's lecture on "The Problem of the Third Generation Immigrant" had wide impact only after it was reprinted in *Commentary* in 1952, where its application to the children and grandchildren of Jewish immigrants was underlined. For a review of the debate and a critique of the whole generational paradigm, see Donald Weber, "Reconsidering the Hansen Thesis: Generational Metaphors and American Ethnic Studies," *American Quarterly* 43 (1991): 320–332; and Werner Sollors, *Beyond Ethnicity: Consent and Descent in American Culture* (New York: Oxford University Press, 1986), pp. 208–236.

Since the boundaries of any generation are fluid and inexact, the point of the generational metaphor is that it *is* a metaphor, a suggestive way of shaping what we have observed. "Though it defies measurability," says Sollors, "the generation is first and foremost a mental concept which has been experienced as well as used to interpret experience throughout American history. Generations are no less real because their duration cannot be precisely determined" (210). Sollors quotes F. Scott Fitzgerald: "by generation I mean that reaction against the fathers which seems to occur about three times in a century."

Literary "generations" can succeed each other much more rapidly, as Malcolm Cowley showed in his many studies of the Lost Generation, including *Exile's Return,* rev. ed. (New York: Viking, 1951). This may be due to the cataclysmic changes in twentieth-century history, which constantly alter the influences on writers as well as the cultural demands placed upon them, and make them more likely to react against their immediate predecessors. This speed-up is also fostered by the exigencies of the market, which puts a premium on novelty.

14. Philip Roth, *Patrimony: A True Story* (New York: Simon & Schuster, 1991), p. 124.

15. For more detailed comment on the younger Jewish writers, see Morris Dickstein, "Ghost Stories: The New Wave of Jewish Writing," *Tikkun* 12 (November–December 1997): 33–36; as well as my review of Steve Stern, *Lazar Malkin Enters Heaven, New York Times Book Review* (March 1, 1987). For a more skeptical view of some of the same writers, see Mark Shechner, "Is This Picasso, or Is it the Jews?" *Tikkun* 12 (November–December 1997), pp. 39–41.

16. See Ozick, "Literature as Idol: Harold Bloom, in *Art & Ardor: Essays* (New York: Knopf, 1983), pp. 178–199, which accuses Bloom of erecting

"an artistic anti-Judaism," and "Who Owns Anne Frank?" *The New Yorker* (October 6, 1997), reprinted in *Quarrel & Quandary* (New York; Knopf, 2000). For a rejoinder to Ozick on Anne Frank and a defense of Jewish universalism against cultural chauvinism, see Ian Buruma, "The Afterlife of Anne Frank," *New York Review of Books* 45 (February 19, 1998): 4–8.

17. The best anthologies of the new Jewish American writers give special emphasis to the emergence of women. See especially *Writing Our Way Home: Contemporary Stories by American Jewish Writers,* eds. Ted Solotaroff and Nessa Rappoport (New York: Shocken, 1992).

18. Ozick, "Envy; or, Yiddish in America," in *The Pagan Rabbi and Other Stories* (New York: Shocken, 1976, first published 1971), p. 79.

CHAPTER FOUR

Philip Roth's To Jerusalem and Back

H. M. Daleski

Portnoy's Complaint is a delight, one of those rare books—like David Lodge's *Changing Places*—that repeatedly makes one laugh out loud in the reading, a rare blessing that we should be properly thankful for. It is so deliciously funny that it is hard to credit the outrage it elicited among many American Jews. An extreme instance of this was the response of Marie Syrkin, usually a sensible person. Not only did she regard Portnoy as an anti-Semitic stereotype; apropos of his attempt to persuade a fastidious Gentile woman to engage in fellatio with him, she said this was "a classic description of what the Nazis called *rassenschande* (racial defilement)," and for good measure added that "the anti-Semitic indictment straight through Hitler is that the Jew is the defiler and destroyer of the Gentile world."[1]

This is patently absurd, and also ignores the fact that Portnoy is as scathingly offensive about Christians and blacks, not to mention Poles, as he is about Jews. He is in the business of ridiculing anything and everything, as in the following representative passage:

> Tacked above the Girardi sink is a picture of Jesus Christ floating up to heaven in a pink nightgown. How disgusting can human beings be! The Jews I despise for their narrow-mindedness, their self-righteousness, the incredibly bizarre sense that these cave men who are my parents and relatives have somehow gotten of their superiority—but when it comes to tawdriness and cheapness, to beliefs that would shame even a gorilla, you simply cannot top the *goyim*. What kind of base and brainless schmucks are these people to worship somebody who, number one, never existed, and number two, if he did, looking as he does in that picture, was without a doubt The Pansy of Palestine.[2]

Allegations of Philip Roth's anti-Semitism in his portrayal of Portnoy, moreover, are beside the point. One way of trying to get at the heart of a narrative is to pay attention to recurrent or pronounced elements in it. In Charles Dickens's *Our Mutual Friend*, for example, there are three cases of near-drownings. In one instance a villain, against the odds, is brought back to life, but despite hopes to the contrary he remains the villain he was. His recovery indicates that, whereas life may be physically restored by others, a spiritual transformation can come only from within. Such a transformation is demonstrated in the near-drownings of the two main male protagonists, and the nature of their reentry into life is at the thematic center of the novel. Similarly, in all three of Roth's novels that I propose to discuss, *The Counterlife* and *Operation Shylock* as well as *Portnoy's Complaint*, comparably revealing narrative elements may be discerned.

In *Portnoy's Complaint* what strikes the reader in the eye as well as in that of Portnoy himself on a memorable occasion is his masturbation, his obsessive, prodigious, masturbating capacity. The Victorians had a homely term for masturbation—*self-abuse;* and indeed to this day the only definition of the word *masturbate* proffered by the *Shorter Oxford English Dictionary* is "to practise self-abuse." This is preeminently what Portnoy practices. He traces his feeling about himself to the upbringing he receives at the hands (in more than one sense) of his adoring, guilt-inducing, overpowering, impossible Jewish mother, the woman whom Roth in another context calls "the Cleopatra of the kitchen,"[3] and his beaten-down, Philistine, constipated father, with the masturbation serving as an escape from them and an assertion of his independence. Primarily, however, Portnoy is intent on considering his own weaknesses in continuous self-abuse. In this respect the novel, outrageous though it may seem, conforms to a central American—not American Jewish—pattern, at least as Saul Bellow describes this. "No people," says Bellow, referring to Americans, "has ever had such a passion for self-criticism. We accuse ourselves of everything, are forever under horrible indictments, on trial, and raving out the most improbable confessions."[4]

The nature of Portnoy's self-criticism is epitomized in a vivid passage early on in the novel:

> Doctor Spielvogel, this is my life, my only life, and I'm living it in the middle of a Jewish joke! I am the son in the Jewish joke—*only it ain't no joke!* Please, who crippled us like this? Who made us so morbid and hysterical and weak? Why, why are they screaming

still, "Watch out! Don't do it! Alex—*no!*" and why, alone on my bed in New York, why am I still hopelessly beating my meat? Doctor, what do you call this sickness I have? Is this the Jewish suffering I used to hear so much about? Is this what has come down to me from the pogroms and the persecution? from the mockery and abuse bestowed by the *goyim* over these two thousand lovely years? Oh my secrets, my shame, my palpitations, my flushes, my sweats! The way I respond to the simple vicissitudes of human life! Doctor, I can't stand any more being frightened like this over nothing! Bless me with manhood! Make me brave! Make me strong! Make me *whole!* Enough being a nice Jewish boy, publicly pleasing my parents while privately pulling my putz! Enough! (25)

In this passage it is notable that Portnoy moves beyond the sense of his own neurotic state in an attempt to define a more general malady—that of the American Jew per se. What he invokes is the commonality of the first person plural, asking who made "us" like this, and wondering, at least half-seriously, whether his condition is attributable to his being heir to two thousand years of "Jewish suffering." Later, in querying what is wrong with Jewish parents in general, he insists that he is "not in this boat alone, oh no," but "on the biggest troop ship afloat," one "stacked to the bulkheads" with "the sad and watery-eyed sons of Jewish parents, sick to the gills from rolling through these heavy seas of guilt" (83). Guilt is something Portnoy's parents "render" from him "like fat from a chicken" (25). The paramount desire of this thirty-three-year-old "Jewish Momma's boy" (104) is to be made "whole," to break out of what he perceives as his "crippling" self-division, which he ascribes on another occasion to his being "torn by desires that are repugnant to [his] conscience, and a conscience repugnant to [his] desires" (93). His self-division leaves him with a debilitating sense of being "weak" and "frightened." His plea to Doctor Spielvogel is thus to make him "brave" and "strong," to "bless [him] with manhood."

The only means of breaking out of his "shackled and fettered" existence (111) that Portnoy can perceive is to give himself to sexual adventure or, as he has it, to "put the id back in Yid" (88). Inevitably he is driven to measure himself against the Other that matters, non-Jewish American women. He has no time for Gentile American men, not wanting to do a "pathetic little Jewish imitation of one of those half-dead, ice-cold *shaygets* pricks, Jimmy or Johnny or Tod, who look, who think, who feel, who talk like fighter-bomber pilots" (108). But to American *shiksas* he is insatiably drawn. He has three major lasting affairs: with Mary Jane Reed, the uneducated, sexy ex-model, whom he calls "The Monkey"; with Kay

Campbell, refined and poetic, whom he calls "The Pumpkin"; and
with Sarah Abbott Maulsby, the aristocratic Vassar girl, whom he
calls "The Pilgrim." He tells the doctor that this is how he is able
to "*conquer* America," noting that he does not seem "to stick [his]
dick up these girls, as much as . . . up their backgrounds," as though
his "manifest destiny is to seduce a girl from each of the forty-eight
states"—he doesn't count Alaska and Hawaii (167). It is notable,
however, that he is incapable of forming an enduring relationship
with any woman. There are no flies on Portnoy, and he knows
exactly why this is the case, citing Freud's discussion of "The Most
Prevalent Form of Degradation in Erotic Life," and—the son of *his*
mother—quoting "where such men love they have no desire, and
where they desire they cannot love" (131).

And that is where the novel might have been expected to end—
with Portnoy in Doctor Spielvogel's office, having abandoned The
Monkey in their hotel room in Athens, leaving her threatening to
jump out of the window because he won't agree to marry her. He
does not leave for New York, however, but flies to Israel. The short
Israeli section of about fifteen pages is glaringly tacked on to the
novel, but the novelist would seem to have been driven to append
it. It has been said that "in Israel [Portnoy] rediscovers his Jewish
identity,"[5] but that is something that to his continuous harassment
he has never lost. What is enacted in this section is Portnoy's
confrontation with what the novelist apparently regards as the
really Significant Other—the Israeli Jew. As we might anticipate,
the encounter is essentially confined to Portnoy's chosen field of
battle; but in his engagement with two Israeli women, this sexual
athlete, this virtuoso of the bedroom, proves to be impotent. There
could be no more damning concretization (though that perhaps is
not an altogether apt description) of this American Jew's habitual
inner sense of weakness, of general powerlessness. Clearly, if Israel
could wreak such havoc, could inflict the kind of defeat never experienced in America, it would need at some point to be studied at
greater length and in greater depth. Nearly twenty years later in
The Counterlife, and six years after that in *Operation Shylock,*
Roth finally undertook an extensive depiction of Israel.

The Counterlife is a novel that lives on surprise. In "Basel," the
first named section of the novel, some fifty pages are devoted to an
account of the death and funeral of Henry Zuckerman, the dentist
brother of Nathan Zuckerman, the novelist. In "Judea," the second
section, there is first an abrupt change of narrative method, the
external narrator of the first part giving way to Nathan as a first-

person or protagonist-narrator, and an equally abrupt change of scene, Newark giving way to Tel Aviv. But these jolts are as nothing compared to the fact that in "Judea" Henry, decently dead and buried in "Basel," is now—and with no explanation proffered—very much alive and kicking, studying Hebrew at a settlement near Hebron named Agor. As we read the novel for the first time, all we can do is as abruptly change our generic expectations, putting realistic narrative behind us and settling—though "Judea," apart from Henry's magical reincarnation, is puzzlingly in the same realistic mode—for the genre of the fantastic, as Tzvetan Todorov has distinguished this from the marvelous and the uncanny.[6] In fact, some one hundred and fifty pages later, a simple explanation is provided for the phenomenon by means of two further surprises that the novel has up its sleeve. It apparently has succeeded in keeping the surprises there for some critics, one of whom, for instance, posits a view of "subjectivity" that "makes it plausible that Henry and Nathan Zuckerman should go on with their lives after each of them has died. . . ."[7]

The first of the new surprises, and it is again marked by a change of narrative method as we move back to an external narrator, is the offhand announcement that Nathan has died. The second surprise is the information that Henry has never been in Israel. After Nathan's funeral, Henry, suspecting that a novelist such as Nathan, who makes extensive use of real life in his fictions, may well have drawn on events in his life that he would rather keep secret, invades Nathan's apartment. There he discovers that Nathan has in fact put him into a novel on which he was still working when he died, and we discover that both "Basel" and "Judea" are sections of the work in progress. The mystery of Henry's fantastic reappearance in "Judea," we may now assume, is due to nothing more remarkable than a novelist's false start, the change of narrative method in the second section pointing to Nathan's intention to scrap the first part in the finished work. This assumption is reinforced by what appears to be the projected scrapping of another section, "Aloft," a rather strained account of a planned hijacking of the El Al plane on which Nathan returns from Israel to London, for the fifth section, "Christendom," which comes nearly one hundred pages later, opens with a casual reference to Nathan's "quiet flight up from Tel Aviv."[8] We furthermore discover, when Nathan's mistress Maria visits his apartment for the same reason as Henry and finds that she too is part of a novel, that Nathan has never left New York for London (or Tel Aviv for that matter), that he and Maria have not married, and that she is not pregnant with his child. We discover, in other words, that, apart from the narrative of Nathan's death and funeral and the two surreptitious visits paid to his apartment, the novel we are reading is the novel that Nathan was working on and leaves unfinished at his death.

How we should approach this complex and elaborately confusing narrative is perhaps suggested by Roth's general account of his methods:

> [I]n my [work] virtues and values are "proposed" as they generally are in fiction . . . largely through the manner of presentation: through what might be called the *sensuous* aspects of fiction— tone, mood, voice, and among other things, the juxtaposition of the narrative events themselves.[9]

The juxtaposition of events in *The Counterlife* points, first of all, to the way in which a novelist such as Nathan projects his fears and wishes, not through Freudian dreams, but in his fiction. It is Nathan who suffers from an impaired heart and who is rendered impotent by the drug he has to take to counteract his condition. It is Nathan who decides to risk bypass surgery in order to rid himself of his impotence and dies during the operation. But in "Basel" it is Henry who lives through this, and who dies, for him. Similarly, Nathan's account of his marriage to Maria and of their life together in England is what he conjures up in his New York apartment. The relation between what Roth strikingly calls "the unwritten world"[10] and the written, however, is more significant than that. What it allows for is a Yeatsean play of masks, the "construction of a counterlife that is one's own antimyth" (167). Thus Nathan projects in Henry not only a counterlife to his own but a life in Israel that is set against Henry's life in Newark; similarly, Maria's life in New York as the wife of the man upstairs and Nathan's mistress is set against her life in England as Nathan's wife. The major dimension of the counterlife constructions, however, is not so much the opposition of one individual life to another as of ways of life: this is the mechanism by means of which Roth is able to set life in America against that in Israel and England. And the most telling effect of the juxtaposition of events in this novel is to indicate that for Nathan the novelist—and, we may guess, for the novelist behind him—neither life in Israel nor life in England is real. The only real events in the novel, the only events that belong to the unwritten world, are Nathan's death and funeral and the visits paid to his apartment after the funeral. All the rest has no more reality than the fiction in which it is embodied. Or to put it another way, neither life in Israel nor life in England is a real option for Nathan, as is in fact directly dramatized.

The narrative element, like masturbation in *Portnoy' Complaint,* which draws attention to itself in *The Counterlife* is impotence, this indeed forming an immediate point of contact with the earlier novel. The travails of both Henry and Nathan in their impotent condition are vividly portrayed. Nathan thinks that Henry's impotence is "like an artist's artistic life drying up for good" (38); and Maria in turn reflects that it is Nathan's "unconsumed potency as a man" (279) that goes into his writing. But their suffering takes on a larger significance when Nathan makes it representative of a widespread American malady, if not of the American condition itself: "If that is indeed how these drugs incapacitate most of the men who must take them to live," he muses, "then there's a bizarre epidemic of impotence in this country..." (47). Roth's American abroad is not Henry James's innocent young woman but an impotent middle-aged novelist. He is also an American Jew, but unlike Portnoy, he is not measured against unmanning Israeli women; his antimyth is the potent Israeli man.

Impotent in the section "Basel," Henry is transformed in "Judea." Looking through the window of a "broken-down old cheder" in Mea She'arim at the young children studying within the room, he has a visionary experience of complete identification with the children (66). He tells Nathan that he realized he had never previously "been *anything*" to the same degree as he then felt his Jewishness: "I am not *just* a Jew," he says, "I'm not *also* a Jew— *I'm a Jew as deep as those Jews*" (68). Abandoned in Newark, Henry's wife Carol is immune to mystical transformations; for her, having "a suburban husband who [has] turned himself into a born-again Jew," is "like having a child become a Moonie" (89). But Henry, it turns out, is beyond such denigration. Having moved from Mea She'arim to the settlement Agor, he is now ready to sink his newfound self in a larger communal identity: where he now is, he tells Nathan, "there isn't time for *me*, there isn't need of *me*— here Judea counts, not *me!*" (118). And he who was impotent has now become an unabashed apostle of power: "[The Arabs] don't respect niceness," he says, "and they don't respect weakness. What the Arab respects is power" (119). Henry's transformation is nicely figured (and in more than one respect) by the pistol he carries when he drives with Nathan into Hebron, as is later underlined for us by Nathan:

> I wasn't sure whether the pistol was strictly necessary or whether he was simply displaying, as drastically as he could,

the distance he'd traveled from the powerless nice Jew that
he'd been in America, this pistol his astounding symbol of the
whole complex of choices with which he was ridding himself of
that shame. (121)

Henry in Judea is not only a counterself to what he was in
Newark but also to his brother Nathan, and Nathan is not enam-
ored of what he sees, as the ironic undertone in the quoted passage
indicates. Nathan serves as the unregenerate debunker of the new
Henry. His newfound ideas seem to Nathan "mostly platitudes
gleaned from a turn-of-the-century handbook of Zionist ideology
and having nothing whatever to do with him." Nathan for the most
part keeps his reservations to himself, but they function to undermine Henry's position, particularly when he takes to psychoanalyz-
ing his younger brother and so eliminating ideology altogether.
What Henry has described as "a revolt against the grotesque con-
tortions of the spirit suffered by the galut, or exiled Jew," Nathan
reduces to "an extremely belated rebellion against the idea of
manhood imposed upon a dutiful and acquiescent child by a dog-
matic superconventional father." He then goes even one better when
he imagines himself saying to his brother, "What's Jewish isn't
coming here and becoming a Jew, Henry. What's Jewish is thinking
that, in order to leave Carol, your only justification can be coming
here" (125–126). Nathan even maintains that, following his successful bypass operation, Henry is seeking to escape his "resuscitated potency," being "in crazy flight" from "the folly of sex, from
the intolerable disorder of virile pursuits . . ." (148). There's nothing
much left of Henry's Zionist ardor after all that.

Mordecai Lippman, the settlement leader, is Henry writ large,
but whereas Henry is a convert not yet rooted in his positions,
Lippman is the thing itself. Nathan's left-wing journalist friend
Shuki insists that far from being "the very embodiment of Israel,"
Lippman is no more than "a very peripheral paranoid" (179), but
the fact remains that in this novel he is the representative Israeli.
A paratroop commander, he is one of the heroes of the Six Day War,
having been seriously wounded in the battle for Ammunition Hill
in Jerusalem. Nathan thinks Henry must regard him as "the embodiment of potency" (154), and indeed Lippman is filled with a
sense of illimitable strength: *Nothing is impossible,*" he says. "All
the Jew must decide is what he wants—then he can act and achieve
it" (130). He is also defiantly proud of the new Jew that Israel has
produced:

"Tell me," Lippman said, "can the Jew do *anything* that doesn't stink to high heaven of his Jewishness? . . . First it was Jewish passivity that was disgusting, the meek Jew, the accommodating Jew, the Jew who walked like a sheep to his own slaughter—now what is worse than disgusting, outright *wicked,* is Jewish strength and militancy. First it was the Jewish sickliness that was abhorrent to all the robust Aryans, frail Jewish men with weak Jewish bodies lending money and studying books—now what is disgusting are strong Jewish men who know how to use force and are not afraid of power." (144–145)

Nathan the novelist is more than fair in the space he gives to Lippman's tirades, uncannily suggesting the very inflections of his voice; but Nathan the American Jew is appalled by his crudity. It is not only a question of unacceptable ideas but of taste, and Lippman has a habit, as he himself puts it, of saying what he thinks "as unpalatably as possible" (143). Nathan thinks of him as someone "for whom centuries of distrust and antipathy and oppression and misery have become a Stradivarius on which he savagely plays like a virtuoso Jewish violinist" (163). But he resents the "word-whipping" to which he is subjected in what he sarcastically calls "Lippman's seminar," which leaves him feeling that language, his territory, is no longer his "domain." Lippman effectively reduces Nathan, the word-master, to speechlessness, his way of handling the settler being to remain "practically mute" (147). How remote Agor is to Nathan is conveyed when he and Henry leave Lippmann's house that night and walk along "the unpaved settlement street, as alone together as Neil Armstrong and Buzz Aldrin up there planting their toy flag in the lunar dust" (147). Out in the open, Nathan also feels Agor to be threateningly dark, being thrown back to a childhood memory for anything "as black as Agor . . . at eleven o'clock at night" (149). The blackness supports Maria's later description of Nathan's trip to Israel as his "journey to the Jewish heart of darkness." Nathan grants her the image, but thinks rather of his "plunge into the heart, if not of darkness, of demonic Jewish ardor." With Israel safely behind him, he is inclined not to think of Conrad and "the Kurtz of Judea," but of Melville and of Lippman as "the Zionist Ahab": "My brother, without realizing, could well have signed onto a ship destined for destruction, and there was nothing to be done about it, certainly not by me" (301). So much for the Israeli antimyth for this American Jew.

Nathan is no more comfortable, in the fiction, in England when he goes to live there with his pregnant non-Jewish wife Maria. He finds, to his surprise, that he is assailed by his Jewishness. On the evening of his return from Israel, he accompanies his wife to a carol service in a West End church, and when the congregants are directed to kneel, he finds that he "[remains] obstinately upright" (298). After the service his sister-in-law Sarah sweetly informs him that his mother-in-law is "terribly anti-Semitic" (318); and she adds that Maria should have told him she is from "the sort of people who, if you knew anything about English society, you would have *expected* to be anti-Semitic" (320). Sarah also says that her mother will expect to have their child christened, and Nathan registers that just as strongly he will insist on circumcision: "England's made a Jew of me in only about eight weeks," he states (370). Nathan also experiences an anti-Semitic attack by a stranger in a wonderful scene in a plush restaurant that he goes to with Maria. Looking directly at Maria and him, a woman loudly remarks that it is "simply disgusting," and calls to the headwaiter to open a window—"there's a terrible smell in here." Nathan confronts and confounds the woman, but this too leaves its mark on him: "[U]sually it was the Semites," he reflects, "and not the anti-Semites, who assaulted me for being the Jew I was. Here in England I was all at once experiencing first-hand something I had never personally been bruised by in America" (350–351).

In the final pages of the novel, which present an exchange of letters between Maria and Nathan, the novelist apparently sets out utterly to confound fact and fiction but succeeds only in undermining his own narrative. We are forced to regard the letters as existing outside the novel, belonging neither to its severely restricted unwritten world nor to its fictions, for Maria writes to Nathan as if he were still alive and queries aspects of his fiction of their life together in England that she was only able to read because he was dead; while he, very much alive, relates to their fictional marriage as if it were real. In this never-never land, however, there perhaps sounds the voice of the novelist himself, the novelist behind Nathan the novelist, as the kind of Jew England has made of Nathan is defined for us: "A Jew without Jews, without Judaism, without Zionism, without Jewishness, without a temple or an army or even a pistol, a Jew clearly without a home, just the object itself, like a glass or an apple" (370).

Operation Shylock, unlike *The Counterlife,* is soaked in the real, the unwritten world. First and foremost, the main protagonist and narrator is Philip Roth himself, who appears under his own name. With his alter ego, the novelist Nathan Zuckerman killed off in *The Counterlife,* Roth's stand-in in *Deception* (the novel published between *The Counterlife* and *Operation Shylock*) is once or twice called "Philip," but is not graced with a surname. In *Operation Shylock* Roth not only appears in full person but comes complete with his wife Claire, and with numerous references to facts from his personal history and to his published works and their reception. Nor is he the only real-life novelist in the fiction. Aharon Appelfeld is given the distinction of appearing as a character under his own name in Roth's novel, and he too comes together with his wife Judith and his own works of fiction. His physical presence is strongly evoked: the narrator says he is "a small, bespectacled compact man with a perfectly round face and a perfectly bald head, [who] looked to me very much like a benign wizard, as adept in the mysteries of legerdemain as his namesake, the brother of Moses."[11] Roth has come to Israel at a time that is specified, January 1988, to interview Appelfeld. He published their exchange in *The New York Times* on March 11, 1988; excerpts from this article are quoted extensively in the novel, and the article is also reprinted in Appelfeld's volume entitled *Beyond Despair: Three Lectures and a Conversation with Philip Roth.* A third writer who figures under his own name is Roth's New York friend, Ted Solotaroff, who appears with his son Ivan.

There are also numerous well-known, real-life personages in the narrative, some playing a part in the plot, though off-stage, as it were, such as Lech Walesa, then still the leader of Solidarity in Poland, President Ceausescu, President Kennedy, and Meir Kahane; and others who are incidentally brought into the tale, such as Meyer Lansky, Vanunu, Jonathan Pollard, Leon Klinghoffer, and U.S. Ambassador Pickering. The action takes place in Jerusalem amid familiar landmarks such as the King David Hotel and the YMCA, the American Colony Hotel, Mishkenot Sha'ananim, the Ticho House, and the Mahane Yehuda Market.

The plot is set amid real-life events that occurred in January 1988. Most notably, reference is made to the trial of John Demjanjuk in the Jerusalem District Court. Roth attends several sessions of the trial, records his personal responses to what he sees and hears, and provides extensive excerpts from verbatim court minutes. Real-life people who figure in these episodes are Demjanjuk and the witness, Eliahu Rosenberg, the judges Levin and Tal, and the lawyers Chumak, Sheftel, and Shaked. Roth also attends a session of the Military Court sitting in Ramallah, and observes from the window of his room at the American Colony Hotel Palestinians gathering rocks in the early morning hours for use in the Intifada that has recently erupted.

The narrative technique in *Operation Shylock* is thus the reverse of that in *The Counterlife:* with so large a part of what takes place immersed in the real, the effect is to make real what is clearly fabulous. First, this gives life and credence to a character who would otherwise remain wholly in the realm of the fantastic, a man who goes by the name of Philip Roth, and who is the novelist's exact double—hereinafter (as the lawyers say) referred to as Roth II. The same applies to Roth II's mistress, the oncology nurse named Wanda Jane "Jinx" Possesski. In his preface to the novel, Roth states that a few names have been changed in the ostensibly real-life account that follows, such names being "marked with a small circle" the first time they appear. Jinx's name is so marked. Jinx is of Polish and Irish Catholic extraction, and presents herself as "a recovering anti-Semite," who has been "saved" by the "recovery group" founded by Roth II called A.S.A.—Anti-Semites Anonymous (90). Roth II has formulated "The Ten Tenets of Anti-Semites Anonymous," which Roth edits and reduces to five (101–102 and 108). Then there is the intelligence operation, related to the PLO's activities in Europe, which Roth undertakes for the Mossad, which he refers to as a fact in his preface to the novel, and which he recounts in what was to have been the final chapter of the book, though in the end he agrees to suppress it at the behest of the Mossad. Finally, and most significantly, there is the doctrine of Diasporism promulgated by Roth II, a notably incredible doctrine but one that thus takes on form and substance. It is certainly central to the novel.

The narrative element in *Operation Shylock* that is parallel to that of masturbation in *Portnoy's Complaint* and impotence in *The Counterlife* is uncertain identity. The sequence is launched with Roth's drug-induced breakdown prior to the opening of the action. Regularly taking the sleeping pill Halcion after minor surgery, he finds himself "enveloped" in "the disaster of self-abandonment": "'Where is Philip Roth?' I asked aloud. 'Where did he go?' I was not speaking histrionically. I asked because I wanted to know" (22). His uncertainty about his identity is passed on to the reader, who begins to wonder whether the Philip Roth in the narrative is the same as the Philip Roth who exists outside it. When he employs "the disguise of [his] own face and name" (129) and pretends to be Philip Roth, that is Roth II, who is Philip Roth? George Ziad tells him that he mistook him for himself, but he answers, "I assure you that I am no more myself than anyone else around here" (148).

When George indicates that he can arrange a meeting between him and Arafat, he states categorically that he is ready for this, but thinks that he, Philip Roth, "[doesn't] even exist" (155). George at one point calls him "the Dostoyevsky of disinformation" (283), but he is no mean hand at the game himself. Who indeed among his multiple selves is George? Is the bitter, anti-Israeli Palestinian, whom Roth thinks of as an "overwrought cyclone of distress," the same as the student he knew at the University of Chicago, "the cultivated young gentleman . . . admired for his suavity and his slick composure" (123)? Is he not the nationalist he presents himself as but "a collaborator," an "Israeli spy," whom Roth thinks is spying on him (149)? Or is he really Roth's PLO handler who, Smilesburger suggests, is behind Roth II?: "Perhaps you have been even more misused by your Palestinian friends than by me," he says to Roth (348). But then who is Smilesburger? Is he merely the "very slight, elderly cripple who [seesaws] toward [Roth and Appelfeld] on two aluminum forearm crutches" (108) while they are having lunch at the Ticho House and gives Roth a check for a million dollars in support of the Diasporism movement? But then is he not the man who runs the snack bar off the lobby at the Demjanjuk trial? He certainly is the man who has Roth kidnapped, and turns out to be a Mossad operative, Smilesburger being merely his "code name" (345). Similarly, David Saposnik, who presents himself as "an antiquarian" (269) and prevails on Roth to consider writing an introduction to the diaries of Leon Klinghoffer (which turn out to be fake) is said by George to be "Shin Bet" but is actually working for Smilesburger. As are the two young men in Mahane Yehuda whom Roth takes to be "market workers," and George to be Shin Bet (124).

One of the two major cases of unclear identity is Philip Roth's double, Roth II. He is dressed "identically" to Roth, with even "a nub of tiny threadlets where the middle front button [has] come off his jacket" as it has off Roth's (76). He is "nearly [Roth's] duplicate in every way" (77), even his handwriting resembling that of the novelist (101). The heels of his shoes are "sharply worn away exactly as the heels" of Roth's shoes (206). Roth II is "a usurping self," a "Jerusalem counterself" to Roth (29), but he accuses the novelist of going around "pretending to be *him*" (72). The Mossad identifies him as an impostor hours after he enters Israel on a phony passport (346), but who he really is is never disclosed. In the letter Roth imagines Jinx writing to him, she says Roth II finally revealed "where he really came from and who he really was, a story irreconcilable with everything he had told her before. She refused to

believe him and, in her letter to [Roth], would not repeat even one
detail of the things to which he pleaded guilty" (369). And that is
the last we hear of Roth II, who dies in the United States "on
Thursday, January 17, 1991, just hours after the first Iraqi Scud
missiles [explode] in residential Tel Aviv" (365).

The second case, one that is literally a case in which "the
identity issue" is at its heart (52), is of course that of John
Demjanjuk. Is he merely "a hardworking, churchgoing family
man . . . a father of three grown American children, a skilled
autoworker with Ford, a decent, law-abiding American citizen" (50)
or is he Ivan the Terrible, the perpetrator of unspeakable horrors
at Treblinka? The identity issue, indeed, relates not only to
Demjanjuk but, as Smilesburger insists to Roth, to all Jews because "inside every Jew there is a *mob* of Jews," the Jew being "a
three-thousand year amassment of mirrored fragments" (334). The
central question that the novel insistently poses is who or what is
a Jew? Who is the real Jew?

Diasporism, founded and created by Roth II, has three main
tenets. First, Israel, far from being the solution of the Jewish problem, constitutes "the greatest threat to Jewish survival since the
end of World War Two" (41). Diasporism aims "to avert the catastrophe of a second Holocaust brought about by the exhaustion of
Zionism as a political and ideological force" (44). Israel, says Roth
II, "endangers us all"; and Israel, with "its all-embracing Jewish
totalism," has "replaced the goyim as the greatest intimidator of
Jews in the world" (81). Second, he maintains the time has come for
Jews to return to their "ancestral Jewish Europe" since "virtually
everything we identify culturally as Jewish has its origins in the
life we led for centuries among European Christians" (42). To that
end, he claims he has been negotiating with Lech Walesa for the
return of Polish Jewry. Third, Diasporism opens the way to a settlement of the Arab-Israeli conflict. Israeli Jews whose "origins are in
Islamic countries" will continue to live in Israel after European
Jews have been resettled in Europe. As a result the population of
Israel will be halved, the state can then be "reduced to its 1948
borders," the army "can be demobilized," and "peace and harmony"
will be restored between Israel and its Arab neighbors (42).

Diasporism, not unexpectedly, appeals to the Palestinian George
Ziad, but in talking to Roth he adds a dimension to it that is not
specified by Roth II. What, George asks, have Israelis created "like
you Jews out in the world? Absolutely nothing." If you compare
Israeli to American Jewish culture, he says, "it is pitiable, it is

laughable." For good measure he adds that there is "more Jewish heart at the knish counter at Zabar's than in the whole of the Knesset!" (122). A little later he makes a statement that bears directly on the question of who is a real Jew:

> I lived with *real* Jews, at Harvard, at Chicago, with *truly* superior people, whom I admired, whom I loved, to whom I did *indeed* feel inferior and *rightly* so—the vitality in them, the irony in them, the human sympathy, the human *tolerance,* the goodness of heart that was simply *instinctive* in them, people with the Jewish sense of survival that was all human, elastic, adaptable, humorous, creative . . . (126)

We may think the man protests too much, spattering his speech with italics, but the question is how his interlocutor, Philip Roth, and behind him the Philip Roth who has created both of them, views what he says. The short answer is that in the fiction Roth does not respond, there being a significant gap in the narrative at this point, a break in time marked by a short line, that leaves George with the last word. A longer answer is that, following George's tirade in the market, Roth suddenly changes his plans and goes back with him to his home in Ramallah, where on an impulse he "[usurps] the identity of the usurper" (156) and proceeds at length to advocate Diasporism, playing at being Roth II. In a climactic statement, he defines a Diasporist as "a Jew for whom *authenticity* as a Jew means living in the Diaspora, for whom the Diaspora is the normal condition and Zionism the abnormality" (170). The real Jew, that is, is the Diasporist. Roth describes his behavior at George's home as a "mild exercise in malicious cynicism," but grants that he was "hidden no more than an inch or two behind [it]" (163). The cap still fits, that is to say, even though Roth, acting as Philip Roth in the open, later declares the idea of Diasporism to be "spurious," a scheme that is "antihistorically harebrained" (287). The proof of the pudding is in the eating, at any rate. Roth returns to his home in New York, for, as he reflects when he sees the Palestinians gathering rocks outside the American Colony Hotel, the rocks may be intended "to split open the heads of Jews," but he "[belongs] elsewhere," the struggle being over "territory that is not [his]" (216). *His* territory has produced Jews who "[have] it in their heads to be Jews in a way no one [has] ever dared to be a Jew in our three-thousand-year history: speaking and thinking American English, *only* American English, with all the apostasy that [is] bound to beget" (312). These, we are to take it, are the real Jews. We last see Roth, if not at Zabar's, then at "a Jewish food store on Amsterdam Avenue" (378), where he meets Smilesburger, who has come to persuade him not to publish the last chapter of his book. It is a place that Roth regularly patronizes, coming there to satisfy his "inextinguishable appetite for the chopped-herring salad [that is] unceremoniously served up" at its tables (379). It is of course a place in which he truly feels at home.

Notes

1. Letter published in *Commentary* (March 1973). Quoted in Philip Roth, *Reading Myself and Others* (London: Cape, 1975), p. 244.

2. *Portnoy's Complaint* (New York: Bantam, 1970), p. 119. Further references are incorporated in the text.

3. "On *The Breast,*" *Reading Myself,* p. 66.

4. Saul Bellow, *To Jerusalem and Back: A Personal Account* (New York: Viking, 1976), p. 77.

5. Jay L. Halio, *Philip Roth Revisited* (New York: Twayne, 1992), p. 76.

6. Tzvetan Todorov says that when an unnaturally strange event can be explained only in terms of the supernatural, we are in the realm of the marvelous; when such an event is susceptible of a natural explanation, we are in the realm of the uncanny; and when we can opt neither for a natural nor a supernatural explanation but are left hesitating between the two, we are in the realm of the fantastic. See *The Fantastic: A Structural Approach to a Literary Genre,* trans. Richard Howard (Cleveland, London: Press of Case Western Reserve University, 1973, first published in French, 1970), pp. 25 and 33.

7. Joseph Cohen, "Paradise Lost, Paradise Regained: Reflections on Philip Roth's Recent Fiction," *Studies in American Jewish Literature* 8 (Spring 1989): 202.

8. *The Counterlife* (Harmondsworth: Penguin, 1988), p. 291. Further references are incorporated in the text.

9. "Document Dated July 27, 1969," *Reading Myself,* p. 27.

10. "After Eight Books," in ibid., p. 106.

11. *Operation Shylock* (New York: Simon & Schuster, 1993), p. 53. Further references are incorporated in the text.

CHAPTER FIVE

Contemporary Israeli Literature and the Subject of Fiction: From Nationhood to the Self

Gershon Shaked

As I have argued at length elsewhere, the tradition of Hebrew fiction during the years immediately preceding the declaration of the State in 1948 was primarily a realist tradition, serving the ideological and cultural needs of a newly established nation in the process of consolidating its identity. For the most part, the writers of the second generation of native authors, the *Dor Hamedinah* writers born in the 1930s and 1940s such as A. B. Yehoshua, Amos Oz, Aharon Appelfeld, and Yehoshua Kenaz, challenged and resisted such realism, introducing into the literary canon alternative, antirealist modes of representation (often inspired by the example of Agnon). These strategies came to be adopted by some of the previous generation of writers as well (e.g., Benjamin Tammuz, Yitzhak Orpaz, Yehuda Amichai, Nissim Aloni, Amalia Kahana-Carmon, David Shahar, Amos Kenan, and Yoram Kaniuk). Already in the late 1950s the attitude of Hebrew fiction to the large ideological metaplot of Zionist history and realization began to change. There was a general sense of disillusion in the literary community as what used to be a community of voluntary idealism turned into a bureaucratic state swamped by waves of immigration. The writers reflected the feelings of the cultural, intellectual, and political elite, which felt it was losing the identity that the Hebrew community had forged for itself since the 1920s. The Sinai War, the Eichmann trial, the Lavon Affair, the revolt against Ben Gurion, the Six Day and Yom Kippur wars, and the political upheaval of the late 1970s—all of these events left their marks on creative people of all ages, but especially on the younger ones, for whom the Holocaust and the War of Independence had not been formative experiences. In the early 1950s Amos Kenan responded to the "outbreak of the State" in his satiric column "Uzi & Co" in the newspaper *Haaretz*. And in 1963 he returned to the subject in a modernist-absurd novel *Batahanah* [At the Station]. But it was in the 1960s that the new, postrealist Hebrew fiction of disillusion took hold, with the first short story collections of A. B. Yehoshua *(Mot Hazaken)* [The Death of an Old Man] and Aharon Appelfeld *(Ashan)* in 1962, followed by Yoram Kaniuk's *Hayored Lemalah* [*The Acrophyle*] 1963, Yehoshua Kenaz's first novel *Aharai Hahagim* [After the Holidays] 1964, and Amos Oz's first short story collection *Artzot Hatan* [Where the Jackals Howl] 1965.

Struggling against imaginary external censors and genuine internal ones, the major writers of this New Wave of Israeli authors (as they were dubbed) produced anti-establishment allegories that to some degree veiled their intentions. This accounts for works like *Mikreh Hakesil* [Fortunes of a Fool] 1959 and *Haberihah* [The Escape] 1962 by Aharon Megged (a member of the older generation), as well as the early allegories of A. B. Yehoshua, which began to appear in the late 1950s in the newspaper *Lamerhav* and in the periodical *Keshet*. Yehoshua's story "Hamefaked Ha'aharon" [The Last Commander], for example, which appeared in the collection *Mot Hazaken* in 1962, is about a group of soldiers who prefer sleeping to fighting. It evokes the weary distaste for war felt by the post-Sinai Campaign generation. A more direct response to the transformations in attitude effected by the Sinai Campaign and by the Lavon Affair, in which Israelis plotted, and failed, to blow up Americans and incriminate the Egyptians, was mounted in Yariv Ben-Aharon's book *Hakerav* [The Battle], which was published in 1967—the year of the Six Day War. In *Or Be'ad Or* [Skin for Skin] 1962, Orpaz protested the war and the values that led up to it. So did Amos Oz in one of his major works of fiction, *Mikha'el Sheli* [My Michael]. Though the book appeared only in 1968, nonetheless its inner climax corresponds, not to the Six Day War, but to the Sinai Campaign. It discharged tensions that had built up during the years of living on the edge.

Various aspects of the Holocaust, which the Israelis had been unable to contend with directly, remained suppressed until the 1960s. Secular Zionism had rested on the negation of the diaspora and diaspora Judaism. The Eichmann trial revalidated the old Jew in Israeli eyes. The Jews who had been slaughtered were not guilty of anything, not even of having failed to heed the Zionist message in time. They were innocent victims of a hostile world. Therefore, the Jewish metaplot, of which the Zionist metaplot was one part, had to acknowledge these Jews as equally legitimate protagonists in the unfolding of the national narrative.

This realization concerning European Jewry took an even more radical turn following the Six Day War, in which the corollary of diaspora weakness as opposed to Israeli strength and invulnerability, came to be tested. On the one hand, the impending conflict revitalized and revivified national myths, as the nation envisioned a second Auschwitz. Accordingly, one euphoric response to the victory of 1967 was a reconfirmation of divine promise and Zionist vision finally realized. But such triumphalism angered many leftist intellectuals, whose outcry determined the dominant post-1967 note, especially as Israel, in the wake of its self-confidence, nearly lost the Yom Kippur War. In the autumn of 1974, the periodical *Akhshav* published a "we told you so" editorial, as if Israel's near-defeat at the hands of the Arabs was a sort of moral victory, not only for the political left, but for avant-garde literature: "Are we, as writers and intellectuals, supposed to keep silent in the face of this foolish refusal, which harms Israel, to recognize the right of the other nation in this country, namely the Palestinian people, to self-determination at our side?"

Repelled by the exultant society around her, writers such as Ruth Almog, for example, in her novel *Mavet Bageshem* [Death in the Rain] 1982, presented post-1967 Israel as a land of contractors, snobs, and the newly affluent. Or take the following passage from Oz's *Laga'at Bamayim, Laga'at Baruah* [Touch the Water, Touch the Wind] 1973, which was published a little before the Yom Kippur War and is set in the moment of 1967:

> Yotan and Audrey... had decided that words were not enough. They resolved that it was their duty to set out that very night on foot for the mountains over the border. There they would try with all their might and main to meet, to talk, to explain, to persuade, to extinguish with the right words the flame of blind hatred. Not that they had any confidence in the success of their experiment, but they both shared a feeling that there was nothing else in the world to compare to it, even if it failed, and that the almost certain defeat they faced would be far more glorious than all the magnificent victories of which the history books are full.[1]

Amos Kenan went still further in his grotesque-satiric novella, *Shoah II* (1975), in which he suggested that occupation, not the '67 threat, would be what produced a second Holocaust.

Following the change of government in 1977, when the Likud took over from the Labor Party, such propeace responses by the intellectual left grew even stronger. An increasing number of didactic writings warned against the right-wing government, Gush Emunim, and the Orthodox community. Benjamin Tammuz's *Pundako shel Yirmiyahu* [Jeremiah's Inn] 1984 and Yitzhak Ben-Ner's *Mal'akhi Baim* [Angels Are Coming] 1987 satirized Orthodox Jewry. Amos Kenan's *Baderekh Le'ain Harod* [The Road to Ein Harod] 1984 was an antiestablishment dystopia, and Kaniuk, Orpaz, and Oz likewise confronted the new political situation in their fiction. All of them issued warnings against an extreme right-wing and Orthodox-Jewish takeover of the State. A novel that attempted to deal with the social as well as the political problems of the late 1970s was Ben-Ner's *Eretz Rehokah* [A Far Land] 1981, which ranged over such topics as the decline of the Labor movement, the rise of the right-wing Likud, Sadat's visit, and relations between Ashkenazi and Sepharadi Jews. A political novel with an element of nostalgia, it assessed the years since the change of government in light of the Zionist metaplot.

Thematic changes brought with them formal changes. Beginning in the late 1950s, the fiction was characterized by a certain deflation of style and rhetoric. Attention was paid to marginal and unrepresentative aspects of reality. As the narrative shook off the constraints of realist conventions and social realist intentions, it began to open up to the modern world, and its plots became more fluid. Hebrew fiction began to construct its own literary history, returning to earlier, largely abandoned writers such as Mendele, Brenner, Agnon, Gnessin, and Jacob Steinberg, and discovering neglected authors such as Aharon Reuveni, David Vogel, Dov Kimchi, and Yaakov Hurgin. In the spring of 1959 the editor of the literary periodical *Akhshav*, Gabriel Moked, expressed the case as follows:

> We must tackle not only the pseudo-metaphysical view of our reality, but also the attempt to memorialize it as a metaphysical process. Our literature must not be compelled to depict the armed forces, the underground movements, kibbutzim, the desert, immigrant villages, old settlements and new. Altogether, literature must not be obliged to do anything, either in accordance with pseudo-messianic prescriptions, or with mini-Bolshevik, leftist, super-responsible social-democrat prescriptions. There is a whole generation of native writers who produce chiefly folkloristic sketches, rarely literature. The dramatists of that generation are incapable of writing anything higher than commonplace skits, and the prose

writers cannot go beyond stories for secondary-school and youth-movement textbooks, or readable childhood memoirs. You can count on the fingers of one hand the genuine poets among the group which arose in the mid-'40s. Most of these people became involved in literature by accident, either because they were the first native-born generation, or because of the social-national themes they dealt with – principally the themes of the War of Independence. By and large, they were meant to be youth-movement leaders, senior functionaries of the Broadcasting Corporation, spokesmen for the Ministry of Education, skit-writers for TELEM, public-relations people at the military high command, editors of kibbutzim leaflets. But perhaps now, when the freshness of the newly-depicted social phenomena has worn off, our literary world can shake them off, discard their primitive babbling and anachronistic spiritual and cultural affiliations, and return to a healthy, personal, intellectual and literary tension. Only this kind of mental tension, in which every problem is experienced without being first refracted in the metaphysical-ideological prism of the "redemption of Israel," or the social-national prism of "constructive enterprise" and "rebirth of the Homeland"—only such a tension can help us to confront our reality as it is, in literature and philosophy alike. [TELEM was an establishment organization marketing to villages of new immigrants.][2]

The influence of Agnon on the major writings of Yehoshua, Oz, and Appelfeld is marked, as it is as well on the surrealism of Yitzhak Orpaz, in, for example, "Mot Lysanda" [The Death of Lysanda] 1964; "Tzeid Hatzeviyah" [The Death of the Doe] 1966; "Nemalim" [Ants] 1969, and "Madregah Tzarah" [A Narrow Step] 1972. The pull of the Western literatures also becomes manifest at this time. The surrealism of Kafka served well writers like Yehoshua and Orpaz, who sought to break out of the realist mode of Hebrew writing. In many ways, he fulfilled the same functions as Agnon. He provided a kind of mythical foundation for the depiction of the human condition in general, and the Jewish condition in particular. As Appelfeld put it:

> Help came from an unexpected source, from a man who had not been in the Holocaust, but had envisioned the nightmare during the serene days of the declining Hapsburg empire, namely, the Jew Franz Kafka. No sooner did we touch the pages of *The Trial*, than we felt that he had been with us in all our wanderings. Every line expressed us. In Kafka's language we found the suspicion and doubt as well as the unhealthy yearnings for meaning.[3]

Appelfeld spoke for Kaniuk, Orpaz, and Yehoshua, as much as for himself.

The most direct heir of the 1960s generation was David Grossman, who revolutionized the heritage from within. Though his early stories and novels showed the same social involvement as the novels of Oz and Yehoshua, in *Ayen Erekh: Ahavah* [See Under: Love] 1986, he declared his independence as a writer. A highly allusive and intertextual work, the book wove together different narratives and different literary styles. It disrupted familiar literary boundaries and produced a wholly original work of art. The first part of the novel is a neorealist rendering of a child's experience of the survivor community in Israel, focalized through the child's own consciousness. The second and third sections, moving back into the period of the Second World War, are fantastic and parodic grotesque. And the work culminates in a decidedly postmodernist move. Instead of narrative, it provides an encyclopedia of names, terms, events, and concepts, many of them connected to the Holocaust and to events that appear elsewhere in the novel itself. Invoking the real-life figure of the Polish Jewish author and painter Bruno Schultz, who does not belong in the lineage of Hebrew writers and who was killed by the Nazis during the Second World War, the book is particularly influenced by the writings of Günter Grass. Thus, even though the book also carries traces of internal Hebraic influences, such as the Holocaust fiction of Yoram Kaniuk (*Adam Ben Kelev* [Adam Resurrected]) and Oz's metahistorical grotesques *Laga'at Bamayim, Laga'at Baruah* and *Har Haetzah Haraah* [The Hill of Evil Counsel], it also places itself within an unmistakably European context.

At the same time, it forges new territory in Holocaust fiction. It insists that nothing less than phantasmagoric representation can get at the reality of the death camps. And it proclaims the efficacy of art in attempting to come to terms with the horror. By dealing with the Holocaust, Grossman violated sacred taboos, which held the Holocaust as an inappropriate subject for fiction of any sort, most especially fiction of the wildly imaginative but also redemptive variety Grossman himself produced. Nonetheless, despite its apparent rebellion against the literary tradition of the 1960s, *Ayen Erekh: Ahavah* also reaffirms an aspect of that tradition, namely the importance of the collective experience as the locus of Hebrew fiction.

The writings of Oz, Yehoshua, Kaniuk, Orpaz, and most of their contemporaries were all susceptible of socio-allegorical interpretation, as the authors observed and commented on the national scene. In the 1980s writers permitted themselves to turn inward toward more idiosyncratic and sui generis experiences. Thus, for example, in Amos Oz's novella concerning a child during the War of Independence *(Har Haetza Harah)* the focus is, despite the child character, on a confrontation among a British officer, an underground leader, and a terminally ill man, who is expending his last energies trying to invent weapons to defend against the Arabs. By contrast, in Grossman's *Sefer Hadikduk Hapnimi* [The Book of Internal Grammar] 1991, the Six Day War serves only as background for an apolitical narrative. Tracing the maturation of a sensitive, introverted young boy growing up in Jerusalem in the 1960s, the novel does not attempt to confront the main issues of the times, such as the Jewish-Arab conflict (as in Grossman's earlier *Hiyukh Hagdi* [The Smile of the Lamb] 1983), or the Holocaust and its survivors. Rather, despite its being thoroughly anchored in time and place, it does not presume to define this time and place. Nor is the novel overtly ideological. The protagonists are socially and politically marginalized individuals, going through the ordinary, prosaic course of their lives (as in Albert Suissa's novel *Ak* [Bound] 1990). The children are all familiar with the ins and outs of the buildings in their working-class neighborhood, with the gossip that spreads like wildfire through the flats, and with the life that flourishes within its confines. Far more important than major national events is the life of the neighborhood.

In this the novel resembles Henry Roth's classic *Call It Sleep*. Whether or not Grossman was familiar with Roth's novel, both *Call It Sleep* and *Sefer Hadikduk Hapnimi* recall their original source of influence, namely, James Joyce's *Portrait of the Artist as a Young Man* and *Ulysses*. In books of this genre, ordinary family life moves to the center, and what appears to be merely bourgeois and banal is made to reveal hidden depths of mental and emotional experience. Grossman's Kleinfelds are both typical and atypical of Israeli families. In the background are the father, once imprisoned in a Soviet labor camp in the steppes, and the mother, an orphaned refugee who had brought up her own sisters. Even though these historical backgrounds are important, nonetheless, the novel, unlike *Ayen Erekh: Ahavah,* is less concerned with the sweep of history and its consequences for the collective consciousness than with the very specific effects of family biography on the family itself. Of primary importance is the distance between the communal and the private. Thus, when a siren suddenly goes off, what is more important to fourteen-year-old Aaron than the possibility that the war has begun—maybe *their* war has begun, he says—is his own, very different, personal liberation.

In focusing on private, interpersonal relationships rather than on the group, *Sefer Hadikduk Hapnimi* recalls the early novels of Yehoshua Kenaz, *Aharei Hahagim* [After the Holidays] and *Haishah Hagdolah Min Hahalomot* [The Big Woman of Dreams] and Yeshayahu Koren, *Levayah Batzohorayim* [Funeral at Noon] 1974. Grossman draws from the neorealism of the bildungsroman (Kenaz's *Moment Musicali* [Musical Moment] and *Hitganvut Yehidim* [Heart Murmer]), but also introduces grotesque elements, as in the long episode concerning one of the neighbors, whose relationship to the boy's father verges on the absurd. In this the book recalls the example of A. B. Yehoshua. It produces a neorealism committed to flitting on the margins of history.

Two other writers who built on the innovations of the 1960s generation are Meir Shalev and Dan Benaya Seri. Adapting Yehoshua's grotesques to explore as yet uncharted territories, Shalev produced sociohistorical pageants, with nostalgic overtones: *Roman Russi* [The Blue Mountain] 1988, *Esav* [Esau] 1991, and *Keyamim Ahadim* [As a Few Days] 1994. The fictions are carnivalesque, almost in the manner of English and French Renaissance writing. They proceed through secondary tales and anecdotes, producing an amazing conjunction of laughter and tears, an uninhibited use of strange and contrasting materials, and tribal rather than personal perspectives on sexual relations. In some ways the obverse of the decadent novels of 1970s Hebrew fiction, Shalev's fiction incorporates myths, legends, rituals, and visions in a danse macabre mingled with a dance of life. Thus, the author plays endless games with the primary elements—fire, water, and sun—while mixing and leaving unreconciled bizarre and tragic events, such as (in *Esav*) a son (the narrator-protagonist) who does not return for his mother's funeral; a woman who refuses to return to life after her son's death (Leah); a woman who saw her family massacred by an Arab mob (the aunt); a young girl abandoned by her father and married to a man she was not meant for (Leah); two ridiculous, short-sighted brothers; and the failed marriages of the two principal couples.

Of the three novels, *Esav* is in all ways the most important. On the face of it, it is about a family of bakers. One of the brothers (Esau) leaves the country, gives up the trade, and writes cookery and baking books. The other brother remains in the country, loses his son in a military incident, and continues his father's trade. But the novel is intertextual and allusive, such that the relationships also signify biblical and historical archetypes. This is history as myth, the names of the characters—Abraham and Sarah, Jacob and Esau, Leah and Benjamin—and their various activities making their biblical overtones unmistakable. It is also parody. In the fraternal struggles of the novel, it is Jacob who is the earthy man, not Esau, Leah who is loved by the brothers, not Rachel, and the United States that is the Egypt to which the protagonist emigrates. Parody does not cancel the text's symbolic force. Thus, for example, the author insists that fraternal conflict is one of the basic elements of the human condition, especially in the direct descendants of Cain and Abel, Isaac and Ishmael, Jacob and Esau, and Joseph and his brothers. In the biblical tradition, the older brother served the younger, because the younger was more spiritual. In *Esav* the picture is reversed and reversed again. The narrator, Esau, seems to be spiritual, but his spirituality is barren. He can write about bread but he cannot bake it. He sleeps with many women, but he fathers no children. Jacob is the material brother: an absurd lover and a bereaved father. A baker of bread, it is he who conveys the positive vision of the text.

Another writer who, like Shalev, adapted the grotesquery of Yehoshua's fiction to new purposes, is Dan Benaya Seri. Even before Yehoshua had expanded his own techniques in *Molcho* and *Mar Mani* [Mr. Mani], Seri had turned the grotesque inward to examine the mythical and psychological depths of the communal psyche. "Elef Neshotav al Naftali Siman-Tov" [The Thousand Wives of Naftali Siman-Tov], which opens the collection *Tzipporei Tzel* [Birds of the Shade] 1987, deals with the impossibility of human sexual relations. Its male and female protagonists are incapable of entering into direct conversation concerning any of the issues that connect them, most especially sexuality itself. Sex, in the world of this text, is outside language. Not only do men and women refrain from conversing either before or after engaging in sexual relations, they do not seem even to understand what is happening to them. Thus, for example, one pregnant woman does not even know that she is pregnant. One of the male characters, who does know, cannot tell her, because he also knows that he is not the one who had impregnated her, preferring, as he does, masturbation to sexual intercourse. By his use of communal materials, the euphemistic avoidance of the subject, and the grotesque depiction of his protagonists, Seri succeeded in painting a picture of a society that avoided conflict by escaping into its unconscious and repressing its psychosexual needs. In this way, it perverted itself and courted disaster. Seri's writing provides insights into a particular Israeli community. Yet it is not ethnic fiction per se. Rather, the stylized, antimimetic quality of the writing produces a universalized portrait of the human condition, cast in Middle Eastern terms.

Quintessentially postmodernist, the fiction of Yoel Hoffmann also has discernible roots within the tradition of Hebrew writing. His stories "Katzchen" (about a young immigrant boy who eventually gets delivered to a kibbutz) and "Sefer Yosef" [The Book of Joseph] (which takes place in Europe before the war), both of which appear in the collection *Sefer Yosef* (1988), have much in common with Appelfeld's inventory of alienated and uprooted immigrants and refugees (as do the figures in David Schütz *Ha'esev Vehahol* [The Grass and the Sand] and *Shoshan Lavan, Shoshan Adom* [White Rose, Red Rose]). But whereas Appelfeld downplays his characters' ethnic origins, Hoffmann highlights them, incorporating German phrases directly into the narrative, with translations provided in the margins of the text. Hoffmann's structure is fragmentary in the extreme, creating the sense that something is being suppressed or left unsaid or otherwise cannot be rendered articulate. Like Appelfeld, Hoffman is grappling with the forces of Jewish identity and assimilation both preceding and following the war. But whereas Hoffmann's dry, alienated style modifies the pathos implicit in both of these situations, his depiction of the characters and their plights evidences a greater sympathy and warmth than, for example, the parallel representations in Appelfeld.

In his later fiction, Hoffmann became even more experimental. From brief poetical sketches he moved into a novel of snapshots, raising questions about the nature of reality and the continuities and discontinuities of its unfolding. The author employs various typographic techniques, for example, short units of text, printed on a single side of the page, in order to stress discontinuity, fragmentariness, and the role of the interpretive imagination in creating order and meaning.

For Hoffmann (as for Appelfeld and others), the immigrant is an alien in his homeland. As marginal outsider, he is also, however, the central protagonist of the national story. As he puts it in *Bernhard* (1988):

In his childhood Bernhard flew over Finland on the back of a wild goose. Many strange things happened to him and Sigmund and

Klara. Sigmund and Klara died and Bernhard came to Palestine on his own and married Paula, and Paula too died, and all through those years Bernhard never once said "Ahalan" . . . [an Arabic greeting used by native-born Sabras (Israelis)]. He detests those double-chinned types who walk about Palestine saying "Ahalan." He wants to ask: "And Bernhard, Sigmund's son, is he not a human being?"

Sometimes even skinny, skeptical types say (unnaturally) "Ahalan." And when Bernhard sees them he feels uncomfortable, as if they'd showed him their private parts.[4]

The hero remains culturally a part of the world he left behind (signified, e.g., by the allusion to Selma Lagerlf's children's classic *The Wonderful Journey of Nils Holgersson with the Wild Geese* [1907]). He loathes immigrants who betray their European origins in their hurry to assimilate. This problematic had been raised earlier by Ben-Zion Tomer in his play *Yaldei Hatzel* [Children of the Shade] 1963, and by Appelfeld. It receives a new clarity and sharpness of definition in Hoffmann's writing.

Hoffmann's *Christus Shel Dagim* [The Christ of Fish] 1991 is an even more innovative and daring book. No longer dependent on the thematic or stylistic conventions of the 1960s, it represents a wholly new departure in Hebrew fiction. As in *Bernhard* the structure consists of small poetic units. They are parts of an ongoing narrative, yet each is self-defined and autonomous. Representation does not exist apart from interpretation. The whole is fragmentary, its pieces either arbitrarily or inevitably associated—it is impossible to decide. In effect, the novel is a discursive poem, with many gaps, recalling Japanese haiku and the miniature art *(Kleinkunst)* of turn-of-the-century Austria, in which the text's caesuras are no less important than the rhythmic units themselves.

As in other of Hoffmann's writings, the text is extremely intellectual and allusive, assuming familiarity with Western and German as well as Hebrew culture. The reader is expected to know, for example, who Anton Wildgans was (an Austrian expressionist poet and dramatist, who lived from 1881 to 1932), and to have knowledge of the myths of Parsifal, Nefertiti, the albatross, the ideas of Spinoza, Moses Mendelssohn, Leibniz, Hume, Ignatius of Loyola and the Bhagavad-Gita, and any number of other mythological, literary, and historical materials. Needless to say, the very title of the book recalls Christian tradition.

As in his earlier fiction, Hoffmann mounts a critique of the nation in relation to its unassimilatable European immigrants:

After the war (in winter seventy-four) / the godhead sent chill winds over the world. / The waking-up mechanisms (cuckoos and the like) / in the wall-clocks froze. Aunt Magda ignited / a blue flame in her kerosene heaters and sat down / she and Frau Steir on the old sofa / in tandem. . . . At five Frau Steir said "Ignatius." Did she mean the bishop of Antioch (Antiochos/Theophoros) who in his epistles called for / bishops to be reverenced like god? Did she mean / Ignatius of Loyola who founded in the church of / St Mary in Montmartre / the Society of Jesus?"[5]

Two temporal continuities, one historical, the other natural, and two image fields (wars juxtaposed with cuckoo clocks and kerosene heaters or the two Ignatiuses) reflect the divergence between the external world in which these women live and the inner contours of their lives. For them Christianity is as much a part of their experience as Judaism is to their immediate environment. This contrast between cultures is often conveyed in comic-grotesque images: "In fact, the life-story of Aunt Magda / is the life-story of Aunt Magda in a slip. / Guns shelled the 'Altalena'. Begin cried. / But Aunt Magda stood / (such decisiveness has no equal!) like a lump of earth, beside the harpsichord, in a slip" (passage 98). "Perhaps the English had a mandate on Palestine," the text writes elsewhere, "but my Uncle / Herbert had a mandate on all the worlds" (passage 102). This is an elegiac saga about the decline of a culture, and of alienated immigrants in a strange nonhomeland.

Hoffman is not the only writer of the 1980s to write postmodernist fiction, employing documentary and pseudo-epistolary texts and self-consciously exposing the fictional devices of fiction making. Among the prominent examples are Avraham Heffner (*Kolel Hakol* [All Inclusive] 1987) and Itamar Levy (*Agadat Ha'agamim Ha'atzuvim* [The Legend of the Sad Lakes] 1988). The most interesting of these is Yuval Shimoni. The grandson of the Zionist poet David Shimoni, Yuval Shimoni turned his back on his genealogy, and just as Vogel wrote German novels in Hebrew, so he wrote an American French novel in Hebrew. Like Hoffmann, Shimoni also sought resources outside Hebrew fiction. He also experimented with typographic devices. His novel *Maof Hayonah* [The Flight of the Dove] 1991 is written in two facing columns, each of which narrates a different story. In the right-hand column the protagonists are an American couple in Paris, though this is of little significance, since they emerge as universal rather than national figures. The left-hand column concerns a lonely Frenchwoman contemplating suicide, who is equally universalized. Though the novel does not offer any obvious links between the two stories, despite its hints toward some interconnection, the novel's patterning ipso facto presupposes the human mind as a synthetic entity, capable of creatively collating and organizing otherwise disparate materials. Symmetries of composition—the room, the metro, and the pigeons—emphasize asymmetries. Yet they also construct parallels that go to the shared humanity of the characters. The tourist couple on the right have both been defeated in the battle of the sexes. Their relations to each other share nothing more than common space and habit. Yet this fate it not particular to them. It is the destiny of monogamy itself.

Time emerges as the destroyer, which marriage attempts, vainly, to defy but that cannot be held back. Speaking about their children, the husband says: "They are our fucking hour-glass. . . . What rises for them goes down for us."⁶ Aging is only an external manifestation of an inner process of change that causes people to draw apart, even to feel repelled by one another: "She turns her face to him, compels him to see the flesh which has thickened and grown flabby. The empty bags under her eyes and the loose skin of the neck" (65).

In the opposing column a different story goes forward, told in a different style as well. External observation is abandoned and stream of consciousness takes over. We know nothing about the past of the lonely woman protagonist, only her immediate and pitifully mundane present, which is depicted with intensely poetic imagery: "So it should be closed. The lid. The lid of the salt-cellar should be closed. There, now it's closed. It's closed. It has turned and reached the big hole, so it has to go on a bit, to this point. To here. The salt-cellar lid is receding from view, and with it the table under it. The tablecloth has red and white checks" (71a). Objective description and subjective feeling continuously displace each other, until one can hardly tell if there is, indeed, an outside world. If, in column a, we have the depiction of waning libido, the physical world coming to substitute for the world of emotions, and loneliness encroaching on the shared life of the couple, in column b we have heightened sexuality and emotionality, driven by a death wish more vital and potent than the couple's commitment to enjoying life and having a good time. For the American couple the compelling existential problem is whether to visit the Centre Pompidou or the Eiffel Tower: "In the end everything falls apart," the wife says. "They don't put it together properly, they give no warranty, so what can you do. Your shoelace" (79). The banality of the words expresses the insignificance and meaninglessness of their lives.

In Shimoni's novel we experience not only the end of the plot, but the end of psychological characterization as such. The assumption is that fiction must find a new position among the media, because its plots cannot compete with the cinema, nor its psychological characterization with psychoanalytic research. What it can do better than any other medium is to depict human behavior more meticulously than even a close-up photograph. Therefore, instead of speeding up the plot, Shimoni slows it down, and instead of building up tension, he depicts the minutiae of everyday life as a drama—or antidrama—of a couple's life, and of the monodrama of a solitary woman.

The isolated, lonely woman, however, even though she is not in dialogue with anyone else, still maintains within herself a kind of internal dialogue, and in this, the book suggests, there is meaning. To be sure, the ending is ambiguous. The flight of the dove may represent the woman's death. It may also, however, signify only her disappearance or escape from the world. The right-hand column had charted the dying of communication; the left—the intensity, madness, and self-destructiveness of internal human monologue. But a paragraph in the left-hand column on the penultimate page suggests a more optimistic possibility:

> And in lighted rooms, in a bright light gentled by a lampshade; there, subdued even as they approached, were the touches which longed to touch, man touching woman, human to human; hopeful and hesitant, fearful, approaching and clutching each other, there was nothing else but they. Somewhere beyond the crowded mass of buildings, a woman stood at a counter and sprinkled white grains of sugar. Water spouted from a little fountain beside her. A dove, like this one here, strutted towards some breadcrumbs. (96a)

"The ends of the roads are only longings," the text tells us; beyond death-in-life, there may be, like a twinkling light, a touch, not merely between people but between the human and the nonhuman (the dove). In his flight from the Israeli scene and from the collective experience, Shimoni finds, in the intensity of solitude, a certain measure of hope.

A subject that has occupied many scholars of Hebrew literature as of late, including Esther Fuchs, Naomi Sokoloff, Anne Hoffman, Yael Feldman, and Hanna Naveh, is women's fiction, which is another area of radical revision in the tradition.[7] Though in poetry, women have always assumed a prominent place, in fiction the situation was somewhat different. The novels and stories of Dvora Baron, Elisheva Bikhovski and Esther Raab, and Leah Goldberg never received sufficient reception, even though Goldberg's *Vehu Haor* [And He is the Light] is probably the originating text in Hebrew literature's women's tradition.

In the 1940s and 1950s many women writers appeared on the scene. Naomi Frenkel wrote the trilogy *Shaul Veyohanna* [Shaul and Yohanna] and Yonat Sened cowrote (with her husband Alexander) many works of fiction. Yehudit Hendel, who started out as a writer of impressionist-realist fiction, moved on to produce impressionist fiction in *Hakoah Ha'aher* [The Other Power], *Leyad K'farim Shketim* [Near Quiet Places], and *Kesef Katan* [Small Change]. Rachel Eytan promised great things in her *Haraki'a Hahamishi* [The Fifth Realm] 1962, while Shulamith Hareven contributed short stories, a novel (*Ir, Yamim Rabbim* [A City of Many Days] 1973), and several historical fictions (*Sone Hanissim* [Miracle Hater] 1983 and *Navi* [Prophet] 1988).

If there is a single woman writer who set standards, produced a style, and created feminist consciousness, it was Amalia Kahana-Carmon who, though a contemporary of Hendel and Yonat Sened, made her debut only in the late 1950s. One of the most stylized authors since Yizhar, Kahana-Carmon is perhaps the major woman author of the 1960s. Thematically, she deals with relations between men and women and family experiences, set in various periods, regions, and classes in Israel. Stylistically, her writing is characterized by an intricate lyrical manner, with minute observations of her heroine's emotions and longings. Also important is Ruth Almog, who appeared on the literary scene somewhat later and who produced unmistakably feminist fiction in her short story collection *Nashim* [Women] 1986 and in her novels *Be'eretz Gezairah* [The Exile] 1970, *Mavet Bagashem* [Death in the Rain], and *Shorashei Avir* [Roots in the Air].

Indeed, in the 1980s a large number of women appeared on the literary scene: Savyon Liebrecht, Leah Aini, Yehudit Katzir, Hannah Bat-Shahar, Dorit Peleg, Nava Semel, Noga Treves, Lilly Perry, Tzipporah Dolan, Orly Castel-Bloom, and many others. The very appearance of so many women writers in a short space of time is noteworthy in itself, and may have something to do with the tendency, within the literature generally but more pronounced among the women writers, to withdraw from the large dimensions of political scene, or to observe it through miniature synecdochic portraits. Ruth Almog's *Shorashei Avir*, for example, begins as a family tale about a girl growing up in a small town in *Eretz Yisrael*, and concludes as a feminist depiction of the young woman's rebellion against her Israeli background: her father and the men who tried to dominate her.

Some of the 1980s women writers (e.g., Yehudit Katzir and Savyon Liebrecht) adapted rather than overturned the dominant tradition. Katzir evokes the example of Yaakov Shabtai, while Liebrecht, in *Tapuhim Min Hamidbar* [Apples from the Desert] 1986, reexamines old subjects from new, female, perspectives. Thus, in "Heder Al Hagag" [A Room on the Roof], she describes Arab Jewish relations from the viewpoint of a Jewish woman, who is alone with Arab workers while they build her new room (recalling Amos Oz's "Navadim Vatzefa" [Nomad and Viper]); while "Yonim" [Doves] concerns a Communist Holocaust-survivor mother struggling to dissuade her son from turning Orthodox.

Hannah Bat-Shahar's *Likro La'atalefim* [Calling the Bats] 1990 presents a different collection of bizarre and depressed characters, extremely lonely, complexly related to their parents, and suffused with unfulfilled erotic desire. As she writes of one of her characters: "her condition is a subject which always causes her gravity and awe. It sets her apart from other people and justifies her strange way-of-life. It makes her suffer, but she is also attached to it, as to a secret which gives her a different outlook on reality, a different yardstick."[8] Dushka lives in a boardinghouse, where Paul (whom she secretly loves) is employed. She wants to leave the boardinghouse and move to the apartment where her mother had lived and committed suicide and of which property her uncle is the executor.

Such peculiar and intricate situations recur in most of Bat-Shahar's fiction. Her characters are crippled by love, which cannot be realized because of their personal defects or because of their subjugation by ailing or tyrannical parents, as in "Behadarayikh Tzel" [Thy Shaded Apartments]). Most of the characters have non-Hebrew names (Lotti, Edith, Dushka, Teta, Paul, Larry, Laibe, Mensel, Polina, Amalia, and Gerda), strengthing the impression that the setting is essentially non-Israeli, a different world from that of the average sabra (native-born Israeli). Bat-Shahar focuses on erotic frustration. All of the stories are thickly sensuous, the landscape serving as images of the protagonist's despair and dysfunction.

Women's fiction has also produced more experimental forays into women as the literary subject. Rejecting traditional modes of representation altogether, Lilly Perry and Orly Castel-Bloom have done nothing less than change the face of Hebrew fiction. Castel-Bloom's *Haikhan Ani Nimtzet?* [Where Am I?] 1990 is certainly one of the strangest books to appear in recent years. Whereas a writer like Kahana-Carmon produced a dense poetic prose, Castel-Bloom stripped her text of all cultural allusion and poetical metaphor, producing a comic absurdity out of disrelation and the unexpected: "When you dive, all people are equal. You dream you're flirting with a tall Negro as you flirt with your first husband. The minister of police looked into my computer and spoke to me in a friendly way."[9] Such unlikely juxtapositions as the Negro, the husband, and the minister of police recur on the level of the macrotext. The story revolves around divorce, marriage, a typist's job, visiting cousins from France, an attempt to enter drama school, university studies, an attempted rape, seduction by a pimp trying to get the heroine to act as a "companion" for an unnamed figure, a meeting with the prime minister—for whom she is also intended—and similar developments that do not add up to a logical and coherent story. The materials all reflect the genuine realities of Tel Aviv, gleaned from the press, the campus, the underworld, or—which is much the same—the secret services. But this reality lacks coherence. There is nothing here about longing for true love, and there are no erotic descriptions. Insofar as there is any sexuality, it is as mechanical as the girl's work at her computer.

This is the antiromantic antithesis of Kahana-Carmon's writing. Castel-Bloom's character is swept along by her own narrative, which is as prosaic as possible, leading to a postmodernist dead-end in word and plot. The author seems to be saying, in so many words, that the world she lives in, the world of computers, journalists, politicians, imaginary husbands, and imaginary lovers is devoid of emotions and dead: "It was probably at the beginning of winter. A thunderstorm raged outside. But it had nothing to do with my state of mind, which was as indifferent as a dried-up well in the desert" (22). The heroine's unemotional floundering is the social meaning of the text. It is difficult to identify Castel-Bloom's literary point of departure: perhaps the endings of Shabtai's two novels, *Zikhron Devarim* [*Past Continuous*] and *Sof Davar* [*Past Perfect*]. It is not impossible to imagine her heroine the daughter of Caesar, Ervin's son. But if Shabtai's Caesar is a child of pioneers, whose dream is being lost, for Castel-Bloom the dream is so long gone, it can only be recalled in its absence:

> A relative of mine, he's sixty years old. He has silver hair. I like
> him. He wrote a book about his life in his native country. His
> decision to go to *Eretz Israel*. His activity in Zionist organizations.
> His wonderful years in a kibbutz in the north. How he joined the
> banking system. The opening sentence in the book says every-
> thing: "I was not always a banker," this relative wrote. I've adopted
> this opening sentence and write: "I was not always a typist. I did
> not always know how to touch-type." (21)

The equation between the banker's prebanking existence (Zionism,
pioneering, and kibbutz) and the narrator's pretyping life annuls
both nostalgia and the satire of disillusion.

If thematically Castel-Bloom picks up where Shabtai left off,
formally she recalls the modernist collages of Yitzhak Oren and
Menashe Levin (though she may never have read them) and the
bitter satires of Hanoch Levin. A not dissimilar 1960s writer was
Yitzhak Orpaz, whose urban trilogy (*Bayit Le'adam* [A House for
One], *Hagevirah* [The Mistress], and *Ha'elem* [A Charming Trai-
tor]) was also written in an absurdist prose and contained the
kernel of Tel Avivian desperation, though in Orpaz there still remained an aching nostalgia for a lost experience. Like Hoffman
and Shimoni, Castel-Bloom communicates the despair of a generation that no longer even dreams the dreams of Zionist history. It is
not so much that she writes either for or against the Zionist
metaplot. Rather, like others of her generation of Israeli authors,
she simply writes outside it.

There is, of course, no saying, where Israeli literature will go
from here. Postmodernist and feminist tendencies share space
with other more traditional forms of literary representation. The
major authors of a generation ago—Appelfeld, Yehoshua, and Oz—
continue to hold sway, and writers of different national backgrounds (in particular, Sephardic) command greater and greater
attention. What is clear is that the historical circumstances that
founded a nation, a language, and a literature will continue to
influence cultural production, and that this cultural expression
will itself be the product of, and simultaneously construct, Israeli
Jewish identity.

Notes

1. *Touch the Water, Touch the Wind,* trans. Nicholas de Lange (San Diego: Harcourt, 1974), pp. 173–74.

2. "Comments on a Possible Argument," *Achshav* 3-4 (spring 1959), 24–36. [Hebrew]

3. *Essays in the First Person* (Jerusalem: Zionist Library Press, 1979), p. 15. [Hebrew]

4. (Jerusalem, Keter Publishing, 1989), p. 37. [Hebrew]

5. (Jerusalem, Keter Publishing, 1991, passages 179–180 [Hebrew]

6. (Tel Aviv: Am Oved, 1991), p. 69. [Hebrew]

7. See, for example, the chapters in *Gender and Text in Modern Hebrew and Yiddish Literature,* eds. Naomi B. Sokoloff, Ann Lapidus Lerner, and Anita Norwich (New York: Jewish Theological Seminary, 1992) and in *The Boom in Contemporary Israeli Fiction,* ed. Alan Mintz (Hanover: University Press of New England, 1997, the articles; "Bodies and Borders: The Politics of Gender in Contemporary Israeli Fiction," pp. 35–70 and Yael S. Feldman, "From Feminist Romance to an Anatomy of Freedom: Israeli Women Novelists," pp. 71–113.

8. (Jerusalem: Keter, 1990), p. 166. [Hebrew]

9. (Tel Aviv: Zmora, Bitan, 1990), p. 12. [Hebrew]

This chapter has been adapted from Gershon Shaked, *Modern Hebrew Fiction,* trans. Yael Lotan, ed. Emily Miller Budick (Bloomington, Indiana: Indiana University Press, 2000).

CHAPTER SIX

Magnified and Sanctified:
Liturgy in Contemporary Jewish American Literature

Hana Wirth-Nesher

In Leon Wieseltier's scholarly elegy for his father, *Kaddish,* he weaves personal and philosophical reflections concerning the recitation of the Kaddish during his eleven months of mourning with accounts of rabbinic debates and social commentaries on what emerges in his book as the ritual of rituals in Judaism. Several of his statements serve as touchstones for introducing the subject of collective memory in contemporary Jewish American culture. A child of Holocaust survivors, Wieseltier recalls that after delivering a speech at the Holocaust Museum in Washington, his friends arrange a minyan for him in the vestibule where "I say the kaddish for my father, who cherished this place. . . . Now the words of his kaddish float high into the concentrationary ether of the atrium, and fly past the glass on which the name of his burned birthplace in Poland is carved."[1] Although the Kaddish Yatom, literally the Orphan's Kaddish, is a prayer in memory of a particular parent or other close relative, when recited in this setting it necessarily also becomes collective. In post-Holocaust Jewish American literature, whenever the Kaddish is invoked—and it is with uncanny regularity—it bears this symbolic weight as well. Maybe that is one of the reasons why it is ubiquitous.

On another occasion his rabbi asks him to help two guests in his congregation who have come to recite the Kaddish but are not knowledgeable about Jewish practice: "As I watched the brothers struggle with the transliterated prayer, I admired them. The sounds they uttered made no sense to them. But there was so much fidelity, so much humility, in their gibberish" (18). Fidelity to gibberish is an odd way to characterize Kaddish observance, and Wieseltier's sentence draws attention both to the way the Kaddish must sound

to their own ears as the brothers recite what they cannot understand and can pronounce only haltingly, and to the way their stum-
bling recitation of it sounds to Wieseltier's more practiced and
knowledgeable ear. Why, Wieseltier's text seems to be asking, this
stubborn and somehow admirable insistence on mouthing what is
incomprehensible and unutterable?

One possible answer is the notion that the Kaddish is endowed
with the power to save the souls of the dead from hell. Although
this idea can be traced back to the seventh or eighth century, it has
been contested and railed against for centuries by rabbis who see
in this claim the encroachment of medieval Christianity on Judaism. American rabbis have openly lamented what they believed to
be a superstitious turn in Kaddish performance: "The influence of
Catholicism has doubtless colored these prayers," complained one
rabbi at the end of the nineteenth century, pointing out that many
Jews, ignorant of its history, equated the Kaddish with a mass for
the dead (JS, 283).[2] That the Kaddish was written and recited in
Aramaic, a language not understood by most American Jews, may
have contributed to what one Omaha rabbi called "the blind spirit
of superstition."[3] He urged its translation into English, in order to
dispel its mystique, but American Jews preferred to stumble through
the "authentic" text, so much so that as early as the 1890s transliterated cards began to appear with the Kaddish in Latin print.

Popular imagination continues to invest the prayer with legendary powers, and Wieseltier is himself aware that the mystical
belief in helping the souls of the departed alone cannot account for
the widespread devotion to this practice. Therefore he makes sure
to provide testimony from a free thinker as well. In Zeev Jabotinsky's
novel about an Odessa family written in the 1930s in Paris, a
mourner objects to the obsequiousness of the Kaddish and to its
lack of any mention of the loss suffered. Nevertheless, he decides
to recite it anyway because it defeats evil by not giving into despair
and bitterness: "So the man with a kaddish has a mission," writes
Wieseltier. "He speaks up against darkness, against nothingness.
This, too, is humanism, with or without God" (165).

As early as 1928, the monopoly of the Kaddish in America with
regard to minimal religious affiliation was noted by Rabbi Joseph
Schick of the West Side Jewish Center in New York: "The Kaddish,
perhaps more than any other prayer, has become a soul-searching
agency which brings back to the Jewish fold numerous erstwhile
indifferent sons and daughters. Its mysterious charm cannot be
rationalized. It perplexes the mind of the Theologian and fasci-

nates the mind of the laymen. Practical business men, who otherwise remain unmoved by sentiment, melt wax-like when called upon, at the demise of a near or dear one, to 'say' the Kaddish."[4] In 1948 Rabbi Israel Goldstein in his book on mourners' devotions claimed that "If one were called upon to designate the prayer which has come to be regarded as the irreducible minimum of Jewish religious allegiance, one would probably say, 'It is the Kaddish.' "[5] So deeply engrained is the practice in America that it is now marketed online by the Kaddish Foundation—"Is it difficult for you or a friend to go to shul to say kaddish? Call Toll-Free to see if we can help you," followed by a fax number and a website.[6]

What is this ritual, that it should have acquired such an aura? "Kaddish" means "sanctification" in Aramaic, and the prayer originally had nothing to do with bereavement. It was a synagogue formula with which all religious discourses concluded, a doxology hallowing God's name and heralding his kingdom of peace on earth. The Kaddish is a prayer expressing faith in Israel's messianic redemption. It came to be associated with death as during the one week period of mourning the bereaved family remained at home and it was customary for a portion of the day to be devoted to Jewish study. The scholar who delivered the address would conclude in the usual way, with the Kaddish formula, adding one or two words to comfort the bereaved. Gradually, this text became associated with the house of mourning and later it came to be recited by the mourners themselves in memory of the deceased.

Since the language of the Kaddish is almost entirely Aramaic, scholars have concluded that it must have originated in Babylon and at a time when Aramaic was the Jewish vernacular (about eighteen hundred years ago). Some scholars date the practice of Ashkenazi mourners reciting the Kaddish back to the thirteenth century. In traditional Orthodox practice, a son is obligated to say Kaddish for a parent daily during the eleven months of mourning commencing with the beginning of the shivah period. Because it is a part of the religious service, it can be recited only in the presence of a minyan (ten males) and facing in the direction of Jerusalem. Daughters are prohibited from reciting it. As Jewish culture in modernity invests the Kaddish with ever increasing significance, the traditional gender restrictions in Orthodox practice also serve to call attention to the prayer as a symbol of exclusion.

When the mother of Henrietta Szold died in 1916 (Szold was a philanthropist and Zionist, the first president of Hadassah), a male friend volunteered to recite Kaddish, and her reply addressed

the issue of woman as public person, as mourner, as American Jew
dedicated to tradition:

> The Kaddish means to me that the survivor publicly . . . manifests
> his wish and intention to assume the relation to the Jewish
> community which his parent had, and that the chain of tradition
> remains unbroken from generation to generation. . . . You can do
> that for the generations of your family. I must do that for the
> generations in my family. I believe that the elimination of women
> from such duties was never intended by our law and custom. . . .
> When my father died, my mother would not permit others to take
> her daughters' place in saying the Kaddish, and so I am sure I am
> acting in her spirit when I am moved to decline your offer.[7]

In 1994 E. M. Broner published *Mornings and Mourning: A Kaddish
Journal* in which she recorded the day-by-day experience of reciting the Kaddish for her father in an Orthodox minyan in New York:
"I am sitting like a fool on the opposite side of the room. It does not
matter that I stood near the curtain, kept to the bench, that I was
pleasant, friendly, trusted the rabbi, or took the group into my
heart. I am the Other."[8]

Wieseltier sums up commonly held beliefs about the Kaddish
this way: "That the dead are in need of spiritual rescue; and that
the agent of spiritual rescue is the son; and that the instrument of
spiritual rescue is prayer, notably the kaddish" (126). Yet as Edward Alexander has observed in his essay on Wieseltier, "considerable weight of rabbinic opinion says no—the son's kaddish does not
request a good fate for his father, but demonstrates why the father
deserves a good fate: namely, because he taught his son to sanctify
God before the congregation. The son is said to 'acquit the father'
because the father, whatever his sins may have been, arranged for
his son to study Torah and to do good deeds" (421).[9]

Before examining specific cases of the Kaddish in Jewish
American literature, where it is prevalent, let me put it into the
context of Jewish ritual and identity by comparing it to another
Jewish ritual that I would identify as its antithesis, the Passover
seder. The role of Passover in Jewish American literature requires
a full length study of its own, but beginning with Mary Antin's *The
Promised Land,* it figures as a trope that is entangled with the
Christian world and with American Puritan rhetoric, just as Passover and Easter are entangled theologically and historically. Mutual suspicion has always characterized the Passover-Easter nexus

as the Easter holiday is the only sacred time on the Gregorian calendar that is not fixed. This is because the church fathers' main motive for the dating of Easter as the Sunday following the first full moon that coincides with the vernal equinox was to separate it irrevocably from Passover, always celebrated at the full moon. To prevent backsliding into Jewish practice, the church decreed at the meeting of the First Council in Nicaea in 325 C.E. that celebrating Easter with Passover constituted an act of heresy. In the Protestant New World, emphasis on the Old Testament may have mitigated some of this tension, but Puritan rhetoric situated the Jew in a peculiar cultural space: the Promised Land is not only overlain with the deterritorialized Christian appropriation of it, but even further overlain with America as site of both new sacred territory and of personal salvation born of faith. Insofar as the Puritan vision of the New Jerusalem required that the American Promised Land supercede the Land of Israel, Americanization for Jews required renunciation of basic tenets of Jewish culture. Since Passover consists of the retelling of the founding of the Hebrew nation in its journey from enslavement in Egypt toward return to their Promised Land, it serves as an annual reminder of the Jews' difference and their prior claim to the story of Exodus. In Henry Roth's *Call It Sleep,* for example, Passover serves as the dominant trope for the highly charged process of the Americanization of the Eastern European Jewish immigrant.

Passover observance is marked by its communal dimension. It invokes a collective history that is retold in a community, as Jews gather around a table to read, chant, and sing from the Haggadah. Because it is a festival of freedom celebrated in the spring, it has lent itself to a variety of interpretations to accommodate the needs and ideologies of different Jewish communities throughout history. Because it is celebrated in the home and embraces multigenerational participants, it has emerged as the most family-oriented holiday in the Jewish calendar. In fact the cover design for two recent reprintings of prominent Jewish American novels feature families at a seder: Jo Sinclair's *Wasteland* (1946) and Isaac Rosenfeld's *Passage from Home: The Erotic Awakening of a Young Intellectual.* In *Wasteland,* Jake's break with his family and his psychological journey to redefine himself is triggered by his sudden feeling of estrangement at the seder: "It was at Passover, at the Seder, and I was just sitting there and asking the questions, and all of a sudden I looked up and saw them. My God, it was just like I'd never seen them before—the way they really were."[10] For Jake, demystifying the seder is a painful enterprise; he keeps returning to the seder as the site of wholeness that is irretrievable: "He followed his father's chanting voice that always seemed to cry when it prayed. Oh, it was so beautiful, it was so strange and so much the-whole-world-is-doing-this. He pretended he could understand the Hebrew as he read the English. *Blessed are thou, Eternal our God, King of the Universe, Creator of the fruit of the vine.* He didn't understand it, no, but it was so beautiful." After years of inner struggle and after accepting the inadequacies, in turn, of each member of his family, Jake's maturation is signaled by his return to the very ritual that alienated him. The book ends with his resuming his former role, the son who asks the questions: "He stood up, began reading to them with all his heart: 'Wherefore is this night distinguished from all other nights?' " (348).

Published that same year, Isaac Rosenfeld's *Passage from Home: The Erotic Awakening of a Young Intellectual* begins with the Passover seder seen through the eyes of the adolescent bohemian in the making, for whom the ritual is a sensuous occasion

> on which I was permitted to drink wine—and it was to wine, rather than the history of my people, that I owed my sense of reverence. The wine would stand throughout the long ceremony in its special Passover decanter, surrounded by the Passover goblets which were of a single pattern, fashioned of a brownish-rose glass and blown with clusters of grape, vine, stem, leaves and all. In the center of each grape stood a point of light, reflected from the chandelier overhead, stained with the color of the glass and the color of the wine within, and shooting off rays of beaded green and red and purple in all directions. . . . They were the original Egypt, colored and revived, the parting of the waters, the Red Sea agape, the journey through the desert.[11]

The aspect of the Seder celebration highlighted in Rosenfeld's work that is also prevalent in Jewish American fiction and nonfiction is its adaptability, its openness to its immediate cultural environment. In *Passage from Home,* the seder rises to an ecstatic ending as the Gentile guest Willy, inspired by the singing of Elijah the Prophet, strikes up a Bible Belt song of his own: "It's that old time religion / and it's good enough for me." "It was Passover in the hill country," writes the narrator, "celebrated by the lost tribes," and the grandfather leading the seder chimes in with "Amen!"(20). In fact, it is the malleability of the seder that becomes the target of

Allegra Goodman's recent satiric novel, *The Family Markowitz*. On this occasion, the four sons—the wise, wicked, simple, and the lacking in knowledge to ask—are transformed into the committed, uncommitted, unaffiliated, and assimilated. Reading from the New Revised Haggadah, the father can adapt the ceremony to current events: "We eat this matzoh so will never forget what slavery is, and so that we continue to empathize with afflicted peoples throughout the world. . . . In particular we meditate on the people in our own country who have not yet achieved full freedom; those discriminated against because of their race, gender, or sexual preference."[12] By the time he extends the story of the Exodus from Mitzrayim ("to differentiate it from modern Egypt") to "sexual harassment, verbal abuse," his daughter Miriam has had enough. Digging in with her Orthodox Birnbaum Haggadah, she accosts him: "Why do we have to spend the whole time talking about minorities? Why are you always talking about civil rights?" "Because that's what Passover is about" (197).

Like the Passover seder, the Kaddish is an act of remembering. But that is where the resemblance ends. Instead of referring to a formative moment in history for the nation, it remembers the soul of one person. Instead of telling a story, it praises God; instead of placing the reciter on a historical continuum, it removes him from the temporal. Instead of including all of the assembled in a collective action, it enlists the congregation to enable the single mourner to fulfill his duties. It is not linked to a specific holy day, but rather to the calendar of the bereaved, to the timetable of his grief. Nor is it associated with any natural or seasonal cycle. It is one individual marking one personal loss by praising one God in public. Moreover, and this may be its most compelling feature: it is a fixed liturgy that has not lent itself to interpretation, accommodation, or revision. It is pristine, unwavering and therefore familiar even in its alien tongue. Unlike a seder, or other rituals in Jewish life, it is either performed or not; there are no variations. Art Spiegelman makes this abundantly clear in *Maus* after his mother's suicide. His father is seen reciting the Kaddish and Art recites from the Tibetan Book of the Dead. He is not negotiating with his heritage at this point; he is rejecting it.[13]

In his essay "The Dialectics of Assimilation," Amos Funkenstein observed that Jewish historians have usually operated within a dichotomy that designates past phenomena, cultural or social, as testimony of assimilation or its opposite:

Attempts to separate a stable "essence" which accounts for the
continuity of the Jewish past as against a margin of changing
"appearances," or attempts to separate that which is original and
therefore homegrown, authochthonous, from that which has been
absorbed—these characterize not only the traditional self-perception
of Jews but, in a transformed and more nuanced language, also
the perception of many, if not all, Jewish historians today.[14]

Funkenstein exposes these as false dichotomies and false questions. I would like to suggest that Jewish American fiction has tended
to treat the Kaddish as a signifier of the "essence" of Judaism or
Jewishness, as a ritual untouched by the processes of assimilation
or accommodation. The eruption of the Kaddish into so many Jewish American works of literature is usually not a sign of the theological, of the transcendent or the divine, but rather an affirmation
of the continuity of Israel based on immanence, within history. It is
an appeal to the essential, the "national spirit" or *volksgeist.*

The Kaddish has left, and continues to leave, an indelible mark
on literature written by Jews in America. In a volume of poems by
Alter Abelson published in 1931, a narrative poem entitled "The
Lost Kaddish," tells the mournful tale of the ghost of two parents
who perished in a tenement fire and now peer through the window
of their son's house, a son who has "slurred the law" by not reciting
the Kaddish: "Beneath their breath they mumbled; / "A heathen is
our son; / We have no other Kaddish, / He is our only one. / We
never will have a Kaddish, / Unless we cry our woe / Each mid-
night, by his window, / Until he godlier grow."[15] But the Kaddish
was not to remain in sentimental doggerel, not after Allen Ginsberg
published his poem "Kaddish" in 1960 dedicated to his mother
Naomi. More of the poem is given over to a Whitmanesque catalog
of hers and society's ills and to raging indictments of capitalism as
Moloch than to praise of God. Yet it adopts the meter and sound of
the Kaddish long before the transliterated second line of the prayer
appears on the page, in midchant, the first line taken for granted:
"Magnificent, mourned no more, marred of heart, mind behind,
married dreamed, mortal changed." The Hebrew prayer blends in
with the other sounds in Ginsberg's 1960s America, with the Bud-
dhist Book of Answers, and the Evangelist's God is Love: "I've been
up all night, talking, talking, reading the Kaddish aloud, listening
to Ray Charles blues shout blind on the phonograph/the rhythm,
the rhythm."[16] Ginsberg was not the only one among Jewish American writers to adopt the rhythm of the Kaddish in his works. Two

years later Charles Reznikoff in his poem entitled "Kaddish" set English words to the familiar incantation. Its first lines: "Upon Israel and upon the rabbis / and upon the disciples and upon all the disciples of their disciples / and upon all who study Torah in this place and in every place / to them and to you / peace."[17] Its rhythms pervade the prose of Saul Bellow's writing as well; Mr. Sammler on the last page of *Sammler's Planet,* whispers to his dead nephew in the New York hospital room: Remember, God, the soul of Elya Gruner, who, as willingly as possible and as well as he was able, and even to an intolerable point, and even in suffocation and even as death was coming was eager, even childishly... even with a certain servility, to do what was required of him."[18]

By the 1980s, Johanna Kaplan satirizes the displacement of the traditional Kaddish by the poetry of the Beats, and the displacement of traditional Judaism by American culture. The last chapter of her novel *O My America!* describes the memorial service of Ezra Slavin, son of Russian Jewish immigrants and a leftist writer and intellectual, which takes place in a library in midtown Manhattan. After the eulogies by family and friends, one of his former students reads Pablo Neruda's poem "For Everyone," followed by a song performed by the guitarist who introduced the deceased at an antiwar rally in 1965. Familiar to his audience and to Kaplan's readers as Pete Seeger's "Turn! Turn! Turn!" (To Everything There Is a Season), the words are taken from the book of Ecclesiastes. Just as he repeats the last line without guitar accompaniment: "And a time to every purpose under heaven," presumably the conclusion of the service, Slavin's estranged son Jonathan unexpectedly takes the microphone and "gulps out, 'I'm going to read the Kaddish.'" "Oh! Allen Ginsberg! What a wonderful *idea!*" whispers one of the assembled, "I saw him on the street the other day, and I really didn't think he looked at all well." Jonathan's recitation appears in full in the text, a complete transliterated Kaddish in italics, and it stuns the listeners: "How could you and Dave possibly have allowed something so-so *barbaric!*" charges one of his friends. "It's a *prayer,* dear," assures another.[19]

Recited in part, in full, with errors, or only alluded to, the Kaddish becomes a recurrent sign of collective memory and Jewish identity, a religious text turned marker of ethnic origin. In *Roommates,* Max Apple whispers "Yisgadal, v'yisgadash *[sic],*" unable to go on until he hears his grandfather's Yiddish words. "'Shtark zich!' I told myself, and I did... my voice steadied, and I made no mistakes. By the last stanza everyone could hear."[20] Robin Hirsch's memoir *Last Dance at the Hotel Kempinski* ends at his father's gravesite, the new rabbi admitting: "Ladies and gentlemen, I didn't know Herbert Hirsch . . ." into which the son splices the words: "Yiskadal v'yiskadash."[21] The African American writer James McBride's recent tribute to his white Jewish mother who converted to Christianity in the memoir *The Color of Water* recalls the custom among pious Jews of reciting the Kaddish for a child who left the faith: "I realized then that whoever had said kaddish for Mommy— the Jewish prayer of mourning, the declaration of death, the ritual that absolves them of responsibility for the child's fate—had done the right thing, because Mommy was truly gone from their world."[22] This uncapitalized kaddish whose words are already forgotten along with its alphabet is a stark representation of assimilation into Christian America.

The Kaddish is invoked in American literature for its rhythm and cadence (as in Ginsberg and Bellow where English words are recited with echoes of the familiar incantation), for its content, which has at times been modified as praise for particular human beings rather than for God (Ginsberg, Reznikoff, and Bellow), for its foreign resonances in the original Aramaic (in Kaplan, Apple, etc.), and for its performative aspect as a prayer for the dead, which, in post-Holocaust texts, serves as an overdetermined sign, almost a requiem for Jewish life in Europe (for example, in the work of Elie Wiesel). Perhaps its most universalist expression was Leonard Bernstein's use of the motifs of Ravel's *Deux Melodies Hebraiques* (1914) in his "Kaddish" Symphony (1963), a work for narrator (a female speaker), soprano, chorus, and orchestra. Bernstein conducted it himself for its premiere in Tel Aviv and dedicated it to "the beloved memory of John F. Kennedy" who was assassinated earlier that year.

In almost all cases, the Kaddish appears in transliteration, perhaps because publishers' policies and budgets don't allow for the printing of the Hebrew alphabet, perhaps because the mere introduction of a foreign language into a text already estranges the reader somewhat and authors fear alienating readers altogether with unfamiliar scripts, perhaps because the authors know that even Jewish readers may not be able to recognize the Hebrew whereas the sound of the transliterated prayer still has the power to remind and to stir. In light of the tendency to transliterate, when the Hebrew alphabet does appear on the page in an English text it is all the more dramatic, as in the two following cases, Art Spiegelman's *Maus* and Tony Kushner's play, *Angels in America*.

The child of Holocaust survivors, Spiegelman is haunted by languages other than English, as the German spelling of *maus* in the title testifies along with the heavily accented English of his father, Vladek, narrating his life story to his son. There are only two instances of Hebrew print in the book, neither one translated into English. The first takes place early in the war when Vladek is imprisoned and he recounts: "every day we prayed. . . . I was very religious, and it wasn't *else* to do." Right above the drawing of three mice in prayer-shawls in a prison camp are the Hebrew words from the daily prayer service *Mah Tovo O'holechah, Ya'akov, mishkenotecha Israel.* (How goodly are thy tents, O Jacob, thy dwelling places, O Israel) (54). The painfully ironic juxtaposition of place and language in this frame is available only to the reader literate in Hebrew. The actual words of the Kaddish in the Hebrew alphabet are reproduced in the text in the inserted section entitled "Prisoner on the Hell Planet," an account of Art's mother's suicide when he was twenty. The words of the prayer are divided between two frames, which show Art and his father in front of his mother's coffin; his father recites it in contrast to Art who recites an English translation of an excerpt from the Tibetan Book of the Dead. Recalling that "I was pretty spaced out in those days" (102), he chooses to document the Kaddish even though he is not the one reciting it. In a work in which all of the nations speak a language rendered in the Latin alphabet (even the occasional word in German), it is all the more striking when an untranslated and illegible type infiltrates the page, as if to perversely validate the epigraph to *Maus* by Hitler—"The Jews are undoubtedly a race, but they are not human." What could be comforting because it is familiar rhetoric for Jewish readers could be, and has been, perceived as foreign and menacing to others. What is most striking about Spiegelman's incorporation of the first few lines of the Kaddish is that there is no explanation for the reader who cannot identify this, and there is scrupulous attention to aspiration marks that would not assist the reader in pronouncing the words, because anyone capable of reading this would not need such a nuanced transcription. In other words, the Aramaic words of the Kaddish are treated with reverence and precision while simultaneously remain invisible to the uninitiated.

Tony Kushner's play *Angels in America Part One, Millennium Approaches*, opens with a rabbi in prayer-shawl at the funeral rites of Sarah Ironson, grandmother of Louis Ironson and Russian Jewish immigrant whom the rabbi calls "the last of the Mohicans."

Encompassing a dizzying array of America's problems, including
the ozone layer as one of the last frontiers, religious fundamental-
ism, racism, and government corruption, the play focuses on the
plight of a gay AIDS patient named Prior Walter, descendant of
Mayflower WASPS and Louis Ironson's lover. Louis's New York
Jewish upbringing accounts for the few obligatory Yiddish phrases,
among them a Yiddish translation from King Lear about the in-
gratitude of children and Louis's recalling that his grandmother
once heard Emma Goldman give a speech in Yiddish. All of this
lends weight to Yiddish as a defining feature of Louis's ethnicity,
his claim to significant difference. But midway through the play,
Hebrew displaces Yiddish as Prior's Italian American nurse involuntarily begins to chant excerpts from Hebrew prayers for the dead
that have a cabalistic resonance: "I think that shochen bamromim
hamtzeh menucho nechono al kanfey haschino." "What?" asks Prior,
and she continues with "Bemaalos k'doshim ut'horim kezohar
harokeea mazhirim. . . . "[23] Spoken in an automatic trance, unintel-
ligible to both speaker and listener, and never translated for the
audience, the lines describe Prior's soul departing the earth on the
wings of the Shekhina. When the nurse takes her leave of Prior,
the stage directions magnify the transcendence of this moment by
Hebrew erupting literally on the set: "Suddenly there is an astonishing blaze of light, a huge chord sounded by a gigantic choir, and
a great book with steep pages mounted atop a molten-red pillar
pops up from the stage floor. The book opens; there is a large Aleph
inscribed on its pages, which bursts into flames" (99).

The letter *aleph* maintains a special place in Jewish tradition.
According to one view of the revelation at Mount Sinai, all that the
children of Israel heard of the divine voice was the letter *aleph*
with which in the Hebrew text the first commandment begins,
anokhi, "I." The Kabbalists have always regarded the *aleph* as the
spiritual root of all of the other letters, encompassing in its essence
the whole alphabet.[24] Moreover, the monotheistic credo, the *Shma,*
ends with the affirmation that "the Lord is One," thereby emphasizing the word *ekhod,* which begins with an *aleph* as well. It is the
first letter of the first creature into whom God breathed life, Adam,
and it is the letter whose erasure from the word *emet* saps the
golem of life, renders him *met,* dead.

This mystical letter, prior to all others and source of all articulate sound, is revealed to the American Adam named Prior, shortly
before the ghosts of his ancestors Prior 1 and Prior 2 assemble at his
bedside to await his departure from earth, to await what Prior 1

calls *Ha-adam, Ha-gadol,* the "redemption." At the play's end the Hebrew words uttered by his nurse are literalized on stage; after a blare of triumphant music and light turning several brilliant hues ("God Almighty. . . . " whispers Prior, "*Very* Steven Spielberg"), a terrifying crash precedes an Angel's descent into the room right above his bed. What is this blazing *aleph* doing in a play by a Jewish playwright in which a gay dying WASP is surrounded by a Jew, Mormon, African American, and Italian American, as well as the ghosts of English ancestors? By signifying the anticipated redemption of AIDS victims in what is depicted as a homophobic America, it enlists Jewish sources on the side of transcendence. And by being prior to Prior, it relocates Judaism at the very center of Judeo-Christian America. Prior 1, his thirteenth-century ancestor, is heard chanting words from the Kabbalah such as *Zefirot* and *Olam ha-yichud* in contrast with the contemporary Prior who sings lyrics from *My Fair Lady,* a Lerner and Lowe musical. His observation that the arrival of the Angel is very Steven Spielberg momentarily shifts the tone of the scene from the sublime to the ridiculous, from its contents to its special effects. The *aleph* is indeed just that, a special effect, a foreign letter that both gives the play an ethnic marker while simultaneously recognizing that marker as being at the very core of some fundamental American discourse that subsumes all ethnic difference. It is a theatrical special effect that can be claimed by all.

It is in the sequel to *Millennium Approaches* entitled *Perestroika* that the Kaddish appears. Louis is asked to recite "the Jewish prayer for the dead" for Roy Cohn, lawyer and power broker who has just died of AIDS. "The Kaddish?" he asks the Gentile who made the request. "That's the one. Hit it." Louis insists that "I probably know less of the Kaddish than you do," a point he proves by beginning the Kaddish and quickly swerving into the Kiddish and the *Shma.*[25] But a ghost comes to his rescue, softly coaching him through the entire Kaddish, the ghost of Ethel Rosenberg, presumably another Angel of America, another victim of prejudice. (In an earlier scene, Ethel sings "Tumbalalaike" to Roy Cohn in Yiddish.) In this play, predictable American Jewish ethnic markers such as the Kaddish and the *aleph* are paraded before the viewer in a spirit of self-conscious theatricality.

Which brings me to my final point, the paradox of the Kaddish as marker of Jewish identification, affirming Jewish continuity through a ritual connected with death. This seeming contradiction is partly endemic to the prayer itself that is performed in the context of mourning but whose content does not relate to this fact. Moreover, the proliferation of the Kaddish in Jewish American literature after the Second World War may be a response both to the Holocaust and to assimilation, as the act of mourning becomes an essential aspect of Jewish American identity. In "The Magic Barrel," published in 1954, the matchmaker Salzman reacts to a young rabbinical student courting his daughter Stella, portrayed as a streetwalker, by leaning against a wall and chanting "prayers for the dead."[26] Whereas pious Jews recite prayers for the dead when their child marries out of the faith, this story's strange reversal suggests that the student's marriage to Stella would be tantamount to abandoning Judaism. Although Salzman's daughter would become a rabbi's wife, her father is saying Kaddish for his prospective son-in-law and for the world that he represents. One year later, Malamud published another story in which Jewish identity and mourning are conflated, "The Mourners," a twentieth-century Jewish version of Herman Melville's "Bartleby the Scrivener." Despite repeated eviction notices from his landlord Gruber, Kessler refuses to budge from his flat where he lives alone. He does not answer his summons to appear in court, and when he is deposited on the street by the marshal and by his two brawny assistants, fellow tenants break the padlock to reinstate him. Nearly catatonic, he reviews his past actions: "How, in so short a life, could a man do so much wrong?" Unresponsive to knocks at his door or the ringing of his doorbell, Kessler sits bunched up on the floor "white from fasting, rocking back and forth" when his landlord Gruber forces his way into the apartment. Sizing up the scene, Gruber concludes that Kessler was "engaged in an act of mourning." "Somebody's dead," Gruber muttered. "Then it struck him with a terrible force that the mourner was mourning him: that it was *he* who was dead." Suffering remorse at the way in which he had treated the old man, Gruber cries out in shame. . . ." he pulled the sheet off Kessler's bed and, wrapping it around himself, sank to the floor and became a mourner."[27] In a self-reflexive turn, the mourner recites the Kaddish for himself.

These stories of the 1950s portray acts of mourning for a Jewish past, as if the act of mourning were itself the ultimate Jewish marker. Books of the past two decades that bear traces of the Kaddish, however, blend the mourning and the praise, the looking back with the looking forward. At the end of Aryeh Lev Stollman's tender novel *The Far Euphrates,* Alexander, child of Holocaust survivors, recites the Kaddish at his father's graveside, the prayer referred to as "the language of earliest times." The very letters themselves take on life as they "hovered over me. They assembled themselves not only into my father, but into the Cantor, Hannelore, Marla, even into Berenice," all of his loved ones. As the letters of the prayer dance before him in a mystical and Kabbalistic vision, they are transformed into the souls of the departed; the text takes on magical and human attributes; the mystical and the humanistic merge. Alexander asks "what choice . . . remained for me at that moment and on that sanctified ground, but to bless God's Holy Name forevermore."[28] Leon Wieseltier concludes *Kaddish* on a similar note, at the unveiling of his father's tombstone: "Magnified, I said. Sanctified, I said. I looked above me, I looked below me. I looked around me. With my own eyes, I saw magnificence" (585).

Notes

This research was supported in part by a grant from the Israel Science Foundation and by the Samuel L. and Perry Haber Chair on the Study of the Jewish Experience in the United States.

Parts of this essay appeared in slightly different form in *Insider / Outsider: American Jews and Multiculturalism* edited by David Biale, Michael Galshinsky, and Susannah Heschel, University of California Press, 1998.

1. Leon Wieseltier, *Kaddish* (New York: Knopf, 1998), p. 17.

2. Jenna Weissman Joselit, *The Wonders of America: Reinventing Jewish Culture, 1880–1950* (New York: Hill and Wang, 1994), p. 283.

3. Leo Franklin, "A Few Words about Funeral Reforms," *CCAR Year Book* 7(1898):35. Reprinted in ibid., p. 283.

4. Joseph Schick, *The Kaddish: Its Power for Good* (New York: Memorial Publishing Co., 1928), p. 13. Reprinted in ibid., p. 13.

5. Israel Goldstein, *Mourners' Devotions* (New York: Bloch Publishing Co., 1948), p. 65. Reprinted in ibid., p. 65.

6. Wieseltier, *Kaddish,* p. 48.

7. Letter to Haym Peretz (September 16, 1916), in Marvin Lowenthal, *Henriette Szold: Her Life and Letters* (New York: Viking, 1942). Reprinted in *Four Centuries of Jewish Women's Spirituality: A Sourcebook,* eds. Ellen Umansky and Dianne Ashton (Boston: Beacon, 1992), p. 164.

8. E. M. Broner, *Mornings and Mourning: A Kaddish Journal,* p. 165.

9. Edward Alexander, *Judaism* 48 (fall 1999): 421.

10. Jo Sinclair, *Wasteland* (Philadelphia: Jewish Publication Society, 1987), p. 48.

11. Isaac Rosenfeld, *Passage from Home: The Erotic Awakening of a Young Intellectual* (New York: Markus Wiener, 1988), p. 14.

12. Allegra Goodman, *The Family Markowitz* (New York: Washington Square Press, 1996), p. 193.

13. Art Spiegelman, *Maus: A Survivor's Tale* (New York: Pantheon, 1973).

14. Amos Funkenstein: "The Dialectics of Assimilation," *Jewish Social Studies* 1 (winter 1995): 5.

15. Alter Abelson, *Sambatyon and Other Poems* (New York: Ariel Publications, 1931), pp. 190–191.

16. Allen Ginsberg, *Collected Poems: 1947–1980* (New York: Harper, 1984), p. 212.

17. Charles Reznikoff, "Kaddish," in *Jewish-American Literature: An Anthology of Fiction, Poetry, Autobiography, and Criticism,* ed. Abraham Chapman (New York: New American Library, 1947), p. 319.

18. Saul Bellow, *Mr. Sammler's Planet* (New York: Viking, 1969), p. 313.

19. Johanna Kaplan, *O My America!* (Syracuse: Syracuse University Press, 1995), p. 282.

20. Max Apple, *Roommates: My Grandfather's Story* (New York: Warner Books, 1994), p. 210.

21. Robin Hirsch, *Last Dance at the Hotel Kempinski: Creating a Life in the Shadow of History* (Hanover, Ill.: University Press of New England, 1995), p. 292.

22. James McBride, *The Color of Water: A Black Man's Tribute to His White Mother* (New York: Riverhead Books, 1996), p. 222.

23. Tony Kushner, *Angels in America: Part One: Millennium Approaches* (New York: Theatre Communications Group, 1992), p. 98.

24. Gershom Sholem, *On the Kabbalah and Its Symbolism* (New York: Schocken, 1969), p. 30.

25. Kushner, *Angels in America. Part Two: Perestroika,* p. 125.

26. Bernard Malamud, "The Magic Barrel," in *Bernard Malamud: The Complete Stories* (New York: Farrar, 1997), pp. 134–150.

27. Malamud, "The Mourners," in ibid., p. 156.

28. Aryeh Lev Stollman, *The Far Euphrates* (New York: Riverhead Books, 1997), p. 206.

CHAPTER SEVEN

Jazz and Jewspeech:
The Anatomy of Yiddish in American Jewish Culture

David G. Roskies

The Klezmer Revival

A Jumpin' Night in the Garden of Eden is the title of Michal Goldman's documentary (1988) that traces the birth of two klezmer bands, Kapelye of New York and the Klezmer Conservatory Band of Boston. The movie begins with Henry Sapoznik telling us about his country music band called the Delaware Water Gap, all of whose members—naturally enough—were Jewish. Then one day in 1976 an old-timer named Tommy Jarrell turned to him and said:

"Hank, how come you people don't play your own music?"

Now Hank, or Henry, the son of a cantor, was no ignoramus when it came to Jewish music, but surely the synagogue was not where it was at. His search for the grass roots of Jewish music led Sapoznik to the YIVO Institute on New York City's Fifth Avenue, the central repository of Eastern European Jewish culture. There, in the cellar, he was shown a huge uncataloged collection of old 78s:

"I felt like Howard Carter opening up the tomb of King Tut."

Here was a treasure trove of Yiddish theater hits sung by the original stars, of klezmer orchestras playing Old Country *doinas* and New World Yiddish jazz. An irreverent mishmash of satire and schmaltz. Strange enough to sound ethnic and American enough to be hip, klezmer music had the added advantage of "proletarian" roots. One musical tradition could effectively antagonize the bourgeoisie, the Zionist dreamers, and an Orthodox father.

Meanwhile, in Philadelphia, Hankus Netsky was poking around in his grandmother's basement. He came upon a photo of a klezmer band conducted by none other than *zeydee* himself. Though his grandfather's career had never been mentioned, musical talent clearly ran in the family. Netstky's mother had once hoped that her son would be another big band leader like Elliot Lawrence. Instead, Hankus took up jazz at the New England Conservatory, and now, like Sapoznik, Netsky was prompted to cross over the generations to reclaim his lost Jewish patrimony.

So, too, Netsky's lead singer, Judy Bressler, whose grandfather was a trouper on the Yiddish stage. When she displays his theater memorabilia to the camera, she does so with a gentleness and piety usually reserved for the Torah: "A life in the theater," she quotes him as saying, "it's very hard." To retrace his steps, she must learn the language first. We see her taking Yiddish lessons from a twenty-seven-year-old graduate student at Harvard named David E. Fishman. Yiddish courses are few and far between, so this is a lucky break.

These three biographical sketches have several features in common. Here are second- and third-generation Jews fully at home in the Western world and fully conversant with its artistic idioms. They have "made it" in America and have left the first, immigrant generation, far behind. The grandchildren then experience a sudden loss. It may happen, most directly, when someone from the majority culture pops the innocent question: "How come you people don't? . . ." which then jars them into searching for their roots. What exactly is "our kind of music"? How come no one ever told us about it? Is that what we've been looking for all along? Or it may happen in the family, when the discovery of a lost art suggests a way of suffusing one's modernity with something old and, therefore, authentic. In either event, the discovery of loss is the beginning of the slow return.

How then are the roots uncovered? Where does one find the authentic sources of the lost culture? In an age of mechanical reproduction, one begins with old 78s, photos, and films. For a nonmusician like myself, the most enlightening part of *A Jumpin' Night in the Garden of Eden* was hearing Netsky's painstaking efforts to reconstruct the scratchy records, to transcribe the precise orchestration of every cut so that he could notate it for his own twelve-piece band. Even more fortunate than the discovery of the records, however, is the discovery that some of the old-timers are still alive, though no one's heard much from them for years. We see Leon Schwartz explaining the place of music in Hasidic life to a

Kapelye musician Michael Alpert. The two of them then engage in poignant dialogue through their fiddles.

It emerges that the first immigrant generation of musicians and actors learned their art through personal transmission: Dave Tarras played in *his* father's band; Schwartz heard Hasidic *niggunim* (melodies) in their real-life setting; Bressler's grandparents were part of a family of actors. That living link would seem to make all the difference, because nowadays the reconstructed art has been alienated from its source. No sooner was the rich klezmer repertory packaged into 78s, Sapoznik explains, than each tune was given its own title, and each title was published in a catalog. The music became a marketable ethnic commodity. Whatever didn't fit or didn't sell, just didn't make it. As for the Yiddish theater that once flourished on Second Avenue and elsewhere, what survives in 1988 is the actor Ben Gailing in his rinky-dink radio station. This is your genuine Sunday morning ethnic music radio program, where the DJ does his own commercials with a heavy Yiddish accent. He's been doing it for fifty-seven years. When Ben Gailing goes, so too does the program. Whereas once the arts of storytelling, folk singing, and theatrics enjoyed a generational life span, their mechanical remains became obsolete.

So folklore becomes the art of restoration. Here there are two ways to proceed: the Sapoznik-Alpert way, through archives and interviews, and the Netsky-Bressler way, through the blood. Sapoznik and Alpert, by hooking up with the YIVO, buy into its folkist ideology. According to folkist doctrine, klezmer music is the music of the *people*; ergo, learn as much about the people as about their forms of self-expression. Alpert's interviews with Leon Schwartz are wide-ranging. The music punctuates Schwartz's lessons in ethnography. When it comes to performing on its own, the Kapelye band slants the klezmer repertory toward the "authentic" Eastern European sound and toward songs of social protest, supposedly typical of the toiling, outspoken people. Sapoznik even updates one of his songs with a stanza about nuclear disarmament!

Netsky, unencumbered by all this folkist baggage, states outright that the Eastern European past cannot be resurrected. Besides, the first generation of American klezmer musicians had to learn jazz; for him, it's second nature. Thus the Boston group, in contrast to Kapelye, celebrates the Americanness of the music, with Judy Bressler reviving the schmaltziest hits from the American Yiddish stage. Perhaps because Netsky and Bressler are harnessing a personal past, they feel no need to saddle it with a borrowed ideology as well.

Now for the clincher. Despite the profound generational gaps within Jewish life; despite the need for a catalyst from without (Sapoznik) or a goad from within (Netsky); despite all the problems of gaining access to a culture that only exists within a mechanical setting or in the minds of a few lone survivors; despite the revisionism or ethnic pride that inform the whole enterprise—despite all that, the new art takes on a life and authenticity of its own. In Michal Goldman's documentary, we see the Klezmer Conservatory Band—not all of whose members are even Jewish—performing at a Simhath Torah party at Temple Beth El in Sudbury, Massachusetts, where raucous, irreverent klezmer music transforms the members of this Reform congregation into dancing Hasidim!

Irving Howe's Anthological Imagination

Yiddish, then, has been reclaimed and resuscitated in present-day America, at least among that most eclectic of all guilds—performing artists. Using the klezmer revival as my master metaphor, I therefore ask the following: (1) What constitutes a usable Yiddish past? (2) What are the catalysts or ideological determinants for such a search operation? (3) What forms are most compatible for transmitting a re-created past? (4) Who are the Sapozniks and Netskys of American Jewish letters? (5) Who needs Yiddish anyway?

The story of the klezmer music revival confirms the Roskies axiom: In modern times, the only usable past is an isolated, segregated, obsolete, past.[1] Henry Sapoznik, as we have seen, could not reclaim his father's *hazzanut* (cantorial singing) because it was much too close to home. Only something as esoteric as klezmer music could be betrayed in the name of his American ethnic sensibilities. So too the New York Jewish intellectuals of the forties and fifties.

Located but a few city blocks away from their Greenwich Village cafés was an avowedly secular American Yiddish culture, which once shared with the rebellious sons of Yiddish-speaking immigrants a commitment to the twin ideas of modernism and Marxism: "At the end of the 1930s," writes Ruth Wisse, "these same two principles of Jews without accents and Jews without money... became the twin pillars of the *Partisan Review* and its dominantly Jewish circle of New York intellectuals who were then coming of age." But with the rise of Hitler there came a parting of the ways. The Yiddish modernists, led by the great poet-polemicist-novelist Jacob Glatstein (1896-1971), perceived the approaching destruction of European Jewry. In so doing they discovered a nonelective affinity between their own fate and that of their European, Yiddish-speaking, brethren. Language, for the American Yiddish writers, was fate, and that fate was inexorable.[2] Not until the early 1950s, however, and outside the influence of their Yiddish counterparts, did the New York intellectuals begin to search for their severed Jewish roots.

That search, which even then they saw as secondary, tangential to the real business of cultural criticism, is without doubt their most lasting legacy, at least to their fellow Jews. Unconsciously, their rescue operation turned out to be Jewish in form as well as content. The obvious prooftext is Isaac Rosenfeld's phlegmatic, world-weary, and zanily anachronistic "King Solomon." Of the New York group, Rosenfeld (1918-1956) was the closest to Yiddish and the only one who ever tried his hand at writing creatively in that language.[3] Less obvious are the anthologies of Yiddish literature in translation done by Irving Howe (1920-1993). His *Treasury of Yiddish Stories* (1954), coauthored with the poet and essayist Eliezer Greenberg (1896–1977), became a foundational text of postwar American Jewish culture. As well as wishing to preserve several pieces of the Eastern European Jewish past, Howe was guided by very strong principles of selection. In addition to translating and transmitting the lost legacy of Yiddish to an American-born generation, Howe was intent upon establishing a modern Yiddish literary canon. It is not too much to say that in focusing on a particular aspect of the Jewish experience of the Old World, Howe was also trying to create or re-create a Jewish culture and community in the New. As a Jewish anthologist, then, Howe ranks alongside such members of the Hebrew intelligentsia as Louis Ginzberg, Hayyim Nahman Bialik, Micah Yosef Berdyczewski, Jacob Fichmann, and Israel Halperin.[4]

Howe's coconspirator, his stand-in for the old-timers Leon Schwartz and Dave Tarras, was Eliezer Greenberg. Although Howe depended on Greenberg to lead him through the hidden byways of modern Yiddish prose, it was Howe who selected both the texts and the translators. Through his selection, Howe put Yiddish back where it belonged: in the shtetl. Of the fifty-two modern stories in the anthology, only five have America as their backdrop, and in two of them (by Sholem Asch and Isaac Bashevis Singer), the Old Country looms larger than the New. Howe later justified his choice on the grounds that American Yiddish tales fell flat when rendered into English, so much of their appeal lying in the transcription of American speech or in the novelty of the theme to a Yiddish audience. In a more candid moment, Howe argued that if he wanted the "real thing"—Ernest Hemingway, F. Scott Fitzgerald, Theodore Dreiser, or William Faulkner—he could get it without recourse to Yiddish. Like Hankus Netsky, the American-born cultural impresario did not need klezmer music in order to learn jazz.[5]

Howe's own predilection for social realism, for literature as a critique of observable reality, made him partial to the tougher, leaner prose style of Lamed Shapiro, David Bergelson, and I. M. Weissenberg, and alternatively, made him reject the revival of folklore, myth, and messianism in the writings of S. Ansky, David Ignatoff, Ber Horowitz, Moyshe Kulbak, and especially, the enigmatic Der Nister. The one notable exception was Isaac Bashevis Singer, whom Howe elevated to canonical status in his Modern Library edition of *Selected Short Stories of Isaac Bashevis Singer* (1966). How fortunate that for so many years Singer consciously eschewed an American subject matter, having decided, in 1943, to limit his fiction exclusively to a world in which Yiddish and Yiddishkayt had been the warp and woof of everyday life.[6] Otherwise Irving Howe would never have become his most influential advocate.

The identification of Yiddish culture with storytelling was now complete. Howe and Greenberg rounded out the *Treasury of Yiddish Stories* with some tales of Chelm and Hershele Ostropoler, a famous wag. This left the impression that Yiddish culture was oral and thoroughly ironic, partaking of what Walter Benjamin termed "the world of experience," as opposed to the alienated world of "facts." Henceforth, Yiddish culture was viewed, in Hana Wirth-Nesher's words, as "frozen socially and historically, embedded forever in a milieu of poverty, parochialism, and salty vernacular."[7] At best, its retrieval would be an act of filial loyalty; at worst—of noblesse oblige. Although not a single woman writer was included in the Howe and Greenberg *Treasury of Yiddish Stories*, Yiddish was supposed to signify "a maternal embrace, a home long since outgrown" (Wirth-Nesher). In Delmore Schwartz's fictional kitchen, Mama no longer spoke in Yiddish, even if she did tell stories, about the Great Depression.

Irving Howe's most famous act of retrieval, *World of Our Fathers* (1976), bears out once and for all that the only usable past is an obsolete one. I am persuaded by the argument that what prompted Howe in this instance was not so much filial piety as an aching sense of loss, now that the New Left, historyless and vain, had refused to acknowledge its debt.[8] *World of Our Fathers* was Howe's tribute to the Old Yiddish Left, a monument to an engaged political culture that fused literature with life. Tillie Olsen's feminist tract, "Tell Me a Riddle" (1960), told from the perspective of the sensitive granddaughter, is of a piece with Howe's paeon to the Yiddish socialists of old, and as such was enshrined in Howe's very influential anthology of *Jewish American Stories* (1977).

The Novel between Past and Present

Nothing in the mental curriculum of postwar American Jewish writers inspired them to ask: why aren't you Jews plumbing your own past? Neither the novels of Dreiser, John Roderigo Dos Passos, Hemingway, Fitzgerald, or Faulkner, nor the novels of their beloved Fyodor Dostoevsky. The overwhelming focus of nineteenth- and especially twentieth-century American fiction has been on the lived present, the contemporary social panorama, and the preferred venue for such an exploration has been the novel. Self-reliance, after all, was Ralph Waldo Emerson's credo, and the Horatio Alger story was a favorite fictional trope, in which the hero measured himself against himself. Even David Levinsky, who ultimately found the new self wanting as compared to the old, would never go home again.

So long as the novel, as opposed to the short story, enjoyed cultural preeminence, the search for usable pasthoods, Yiddish or otherwise, was marginalized. It is also easier to vivify the past in story form than it is to sustain that past in a novel, especially if, as we have seen, Yiddish culture was itself considered to be synonymous with the story. The urban, urbane, secular, omnisciently narrated novel was deemed to be incompatible with a Yiddish past. What little room was accorded to Yiddish in postwar American-Jewish fiction was proffered through the back door.

Thus, in the midfifties, Bernard Malamud (1914-1986) introduced his Yiddishized English prose in such short masterpieces as "The Magic Barrel" and "The Jewbird," while his solo attempt at an historical novel, *The Fixer* (1966), set in Kiev, was a totally un-Yiddish work.[9] The situation did not change in the sixties when Cynthia Ozick (b. 1928) made her Jewish debut. Alone in the annals of American Jewish writing, her celebrated story-enclef "Yiddish, or

Envy in America" (1969), describes the Yiddish cultural movement in its death throes. Baumzweig, modeled on Eliezer Greenberg, is a *baum* (or tree) without a *zweig* (branch), as Edelstein (modeled on Jacob Glatstein) is a poet without a translator. Although Ozick places into Edelstein's mouth and letters a passionate critique of the historyless American Jew, and while she ends with a dramatic paraphrase of Glatstein's most famous poem, "A Good Night, World," there is no escape from the story's cul-de-sac. In her later fiction, the only East European Jewish writer worthy of becoming the subject of a novel is Bruno Schulz, who wrote in Polish, a language Ozick does not speak.

Only in the seventies, riding the same highway as the klezmer music revival, do born-again storytellers appear who give free rein to a Yiddish sensibility: Max Apple, who comes by it through the blood, the Netsky-Bressler way; and Steve Stern, who discovers a Yiddish past in Memphis, Tennessee, by retracing the route taken by Sapoznik and Alpert. Yiddish-English storytelling is here the beneficiary of countercultural forces and an ethnic revival at work in America, just as in the eighties, the feminist and gay movements will lead to the discovery of Yiddish women precursors, none of them novelists. In the land of the folkfest and regional storytelling workshops, a male or female storyteller with a Yiddish inflection can finally become king—or drag queen.

The one place where the European Jewish past is not effaced is, of course, in the story of its final destruction. Here one would expect Yiddish, *leshon hakedoshim* (the language of the martyrs), to play a central role. Except that it doesn't. Responding to the Holocaust, the novelist Arthur Cohen revisits the Lower East Side in his novel *In the Days of Simon Stern* (1973). Leslie Epstein, responding to the Holocaust, re-creates Chaim Rumkowski, *King of the Jews* (1979). Saul Bellow gives us *Mr. Sammler's Planet* (1970), Philip Roth resurrects Anne Frank in *The Ghost Writer* (1979), and Susan Fromberg Schaeffer becomes the amanuensis of *Anya* (1974). All five novelists circumvent Yiddish in exchange for domesticating, or Americanizing, the Holocaust. Conveniently, Anne Frank and Artur Sammler do not speak Yiddish to begin with. The playwright Barbara Lebow would have done well to follow their example, or to have taken Yiddish lessons before writing the Yiddish dialogue for *A Shayna Maidel* (1985), her play about a Holocaust survivor who arrives in New York to a long-lost family.

If pre- and postwar American culture was not particularly fertile ground for sowing Yiddish seeds, there might at least have been a figure to bridge the cultural abyss. Isaac Bashevis Singer, for reasons already mentioned, was the ideal candidate to become for postwar American-Jewish writers what S. Y. Agnon was to Israeli writers: the repository of the European Jewish past, its language and lore. Although Agnon may not be read much nowadays among Israelis under thirty, his influence on Israeli literary culture has been enormous. His prose style inspired Aharon Megged (b. 1920) and his young Sabra friends to write ornate and learned Hebrew letters. Amos Oz (b. 1939) took off time from his novels to produce a "strong" revisionary reading of Agnon's oeuvre titled *The Silence of Heaven: Agnon's Fear of God* (1993). Meanwhile, the Israeli novelist Haim Be'er (b. 1945) produced *Their Love and Their Hate* (1992), a biographical essay on Bialik, Brenner, and Agnon.[10] There is nothing comparable for Singer: no stylistic parodies, no revisionist readings, no study of Singer's love-hate relationship with Sholem Asch and I. J. Singer (although we can expect to hear about his love-hate relationship with his private secretaries). Pitifully few American Jewish novelists can read Singer in the original, while Singer himself radically simplified the linguistic and cultural surface of his fiction for the sake of translation and reception. Singer also loved to grant interviews, the thrust of which was to deny any connection whatsoever between himself and the legacy of Yiddish secular culture.[11]

Howe was absolutely right, in my opinion, to have championed Singer qua storyteller, just as Cynthia Ozick was right to have characterized Yankel Ostrover, his fictional stand-in, as a cynical opportunist. More to the point, Singer decried all attempts to make Yiddish into a self-sufficient, secular culture, so that he, least of all, would have led his young admirers through a tour of the landsmanshaftn (hometown associations), the Yiddish theaters, the Workmen's Circle, the offices of the Yiddish daily press, the Sholem Aleichem schools, the YIVO, the Yiddish bookstores, or the Yiddish-speaking Amalgamated housing cooperatives in the Bronx. Singer openly dissociated himself from the Yiddish literary past, and his American critics all took him at his word. Those surviving Yiddishists, in contrast, who might have opened the filing cabinet crammed full of old 78s or have unearthed the old family photos were either too traumatized by the incalculable losses of the Holocaust or too demoralized by the total abandonment of Yiddish on the part of their own children. Yiddish America was peopled with Edelsteins and no City College graduate (as in Ozick's story) was likely to listen to their rantings.

So whom did that leave? The "Other" New York Jewish intellectuals, as Carole Kessner has recently dubbed them, those, like Maurice Samuel, Marie Syrkin, Ludwig Lewisohn, Milton Steinberg, and my own landsman, A. M. Klein, who were, as she puts it "nominatively, not nominally, Jews," were relegated to the parochial sidelines by virtue of their passionate defense of the Jews.[12] It was a stigma they carried with pride, but that cost them dearly. Although Samuel delivered exponentially more public lectures than did Irving Howe, the former was to attract but a single, influential young disciple, Cynthia Ozick, while Howe's popularity has not diminished since his death. *My Glorious Brothers* (1948), a schematic historical novel about the Maccabees by fellow traveler Howard Fast, easily eclipsed Milton Steinberg's philosophically and theologically nuanced portrait of Elisha Ben Avuyah, *As a Driven Leaf* (1939). A. M. Klein went mad, at the peak of his career, after burning his lifetime's work on Joyce's *Ulysses*.

Jewspeech, Yiddish, and the Folk

In the climate of the forties, fifties, and sixties, less was more. Those who were to occupy the forefront of American Jewish letters did so by introducing a Jewish cadence to their narratives of self-definition, a Yiddish inflection. Thus the famous opening line of Bellow's *Adventures of Augie March* (1948–1953) marked a complete change of rhythm from his previous novels, written in clear English diction:

> I am an American, Chicago born—Chicago, that somber city—and go at things as I have taught myself, free-style, and will make the record in my own way: first to knock, first admitted; sometimes an innocent knock, sometimes a not so innocent. But a man's character is his fate, says Heraclitus, and in the end there isn't any way to disguise the nature of the knocks by acoustical work on the door or gloving the knuckles.

If Tevye's son had attended the University of Chicago, this is how he would have spoken. From here on in, Bellow was not only free to address an explicitly Jewish subject matter, whenever he so desired, but also to sustain a narrative voice that was distinctly

American Jewish. As Ruth Wisse demonstrated in her marvelous little book on *The Schlemiel as Modern Hero*, Bellow achieved the perfect marriage of Jewish voice and Yiddish subject matter in *Herzog*.[13]

The first postwar generation invented a kind of "Jewspeech" that would do double duty. In "The Jewbird," Bernard Malamud expanded the linguistic field by creating a triple discourse. First, there is the narrative voice, which speaks a mediated Yiddish: "The window was open so the skinny bird flew in. Flippity-flap with its frazzled black wings. That's how it goes. It's open, you're in. Closed, you're out and that's your fate." This is Tevye talking, as an American Jewish immigrant. Second, the black bird, reeking of herring, speaks "real" Yiddish: "*Gevalt*, a pogrom!" are his opening words. (Not a few of his lines are conscientiously glossed by the editors of the *Norton Anthology of American Literature*. The Jewbird's "If you haven't got *matjes*, I'll take schmaltz" is glossed "If you don't have prime herring, I'll accept the greasy kind.") Finally, there's the implied author's American voice, deliciously parodying Poe's "Raven." The stately raven of the days of yore, who must tap to enter the poet's private domain and perches upon a bust of Pallas is here replaced by a skinny, frazzled, smelly refugee from Eastern Europe who lands atop a lamb chop in a Lower East Side kitchen. The Raven's oracular "Nevermore!" gives way to "*Gevalt*, a pogrom!" followed by a loquacious, argumentative, and stereotypically, Jewish discourse. Unfortunately, the implied author burdens his Jewspeech with a message, an ideology of Judaism, in which suffering ennobles, and the real "anti-Semeets" are the enemy within.[14]

Something of this preciousness and cult of Jewish suffering are still evident in Philip Roth's "Eli, the Fanatic." Here the lost world of East European Jewry is represented by a world-weary but hardnosed Rosh Yeshiva and by a mute and traumatized survivor of the Holocaust. The story's climax, in which Eli, the eponymous hero, exchanges his tailored suit for the survivor's hand-me-down, is a perfect, if unintended, metaphor for Roth himself: Dressed in borrowed clothing, he tries Jewspeech and Judaism on for size. Later, however, when Roth hits his stride with *Portnoy's Complaint* (1969), he reverses Malamud's ideological direction by "putting the id back into Yid."

Because the generation of Bellow, Malamud, and Roth rarely moved beyond its own lived experience, and because for them the actual experience of Yiddish and Yiddishkayt was essentially limited

to the family and to its inner sanctum—the kitchen—any attempt
to build an ideology of Judaism out of this minimal space was
bound to be less than the real thing. The one writer who fully
reimagined a Yiddish-speaking, American Jewish experience in
which less was indeed more was Henry Roth (1906-1995). Remarkably, he did it not once, but twice. Just as Roth's evocation
of spoken Yiddish through the medium of an earthy, expressive,
highly figurative English prose style remains the unique achievement of his first novel, *Call It Sleep* (1934), so his rich employ-
ment of unmediated (and sometimes untranslated) Yiddish words
and phrases makes a different but equally authoritative statement in his semi-autobiographical novel *Mercy of a Rude Stream*
(1994). The six decades that bracket his career not only close the
chapter of Jewish acculturation in America, and not only incorporate the destruction of Yiddish-speaking Jewry in the Holocaust,
but also mark a profound ideological shift from communism to
Zionism. It is the latter ideology, I would argue, that finally allows Yiddish to be what it is—a language of the folk—and perhaps to someday form the basis of a new, postfolkloric exploration
of the Yiddish past.

Henry Roth uses his last novel to examine the self-betrayal of
his autobiographical protagonist *as a Jew*. Young Ira Stigman,
recently moved to goyish Harlem, is thrilled at the imminent
arrival of new relatives from the Old Country. These great expectations, however, are dashed by the recognition that they are
greenhorns:

> Greenhorns with uncouth, lopsided and outlandish gestures, green-
> horns who, once they cried out how big Leah's infant had grown
> since they last saw him, paid no more attention to him, green-
> horns engaged in all manner of talk too incomprehensible for him
> to understand, speaking "thick" Yiddish, without any English to
> leaven it, about the ways of the New World, the kosher shopping
> nearby and the work to be found here, and about relatives and
> friends and affairs in the little hamlet they had left behind: dull,
> colorless, greenhorn affairs. (18-19)

This is immediately followed by a sober, Zionist critique from the
perspective of the adult narrator:

Once again—Ira would reflect later—had their advent into the New World taken place in the ambience of the East Side, their outcry, their foreignness, their Yiddishkeit would not have seemed so garish. But here, already translated from that broader, homogeneous Jewish world, already glimpsing, perceiving on every hand, in every cautious exploration of the surrounding neighborhoods, how vast and predominant was the goyish world that surrounded the little Jewish enclave in which he lived, almost at once, a potential for contrast was instilled, a potential for contrast that waxed with every passing day on 114th Street. From erstwhile unawareness, awareness became insupportable; contrast became too much to bear: The newcomers' crudity and grimace, their green and carious teeth, the sense of oppressive orthodoxy under Zaida's sway—how they rushed to the sink at his behest to rinse their mouths in salt water—their totally alien behavior combined to produce in Ira a sense of unutterable chagrin and disappointment.

Ira Stigman junior pays an enormous moral and psychological price when he abandons the mother tongue, the pain of which is underscored by the ironic, lyrical, self-reflexive voice of Ira Stigman senior. Ira is EveryJew exiled from the promised land.

What Henry Roth calls a "potential for contrast" is an either-or proposition: either you're protected within a moral, Yiddish-speaking universe, or you are damned, and your soul goes up for grabs. There is something very Christian about this fall from grace, this vision of purgatory, the bleakness of damnation that has blighted an entire life. Yet within this medieval morality play, Yiddish remains the touchstone of reality—and memory.

The use of Yiddish both by the characters and by their aged "biographer," moreover, casts a harsh light on the role of Yiddish in American Jewish fiction. Exposed herein is the cosmopolitan ideology of high modernism, which informed the writing of *Call It Sleep*. As Hana Wirth-Nesher pointed out, the polyphonic medium of the earlier novel is its message. At novel's end, David Shearl not only conquers the fear of death; he embodies within his psyche the language of Everyman.[15]

Yiddish for Henry Roth the Elder is the first among many *lieux de memoire* in a gritty, cluttered, and endlessly stimulating past. His Zionist pilgrimage to the Lower East Side and *goyish* Harlem retrieves an urban folklife with deep roots in the Old Country. Whereas Roth's fellow writers reify Yiddish as the Borscht Belt; as beacon of social conscience and as emblem of loss; it is the otherness of Yiddish that turns it for Henry Roth into an object of desire.

Mercy of a Rude Stream does not argue for facile continuities. The past cannot be re-created without breaks, digressions, and persistent computer glitches. By remaining stubbornly true to his lived experience, in the grand tradition of the American novel, Roth demonstrates how terribly difficult it is just to get the "facts" straight. In effect he is telling us that after he goes, there will be no one left to conjure this immigrant experience from within.

Which may be all for the best. For if the logic of my thesis holds true, now that the saga of the Jewish mass immigration is a closed book, it belongs to the dead and therefore resurrectible past.

Perhaps all great literature is fueled by a profound sense of loss. Certainly the loss of faith, or what modern Jewish critics call *hurban beit hamidrash*, the collapse of traditional faith once centered in the House of Study, was the major theme of modern Jewish writing, both in Hebrew and to a lesser degree, in Yiddish: Bialik and Berdyczewski, Greenberg and Agnon, Isaac Bashevis Singer and Grade. Can the loss of a civilization, of a millennial-old culture, stimulate the same degree of creativity? I believe that it can, if the act of retrieval is commensurate with the loss.[16]

Here, klezmer music ultimately falls short of the mark, because it is an easy fix. It makes no serious demands of the audience, and most klezmer bands have only one lead singer who knows (or pretends to know) Yiddish.

The same holds true for the Holocaust, so long as it is rooted in nothing more than personal trauma.

So too the Jewish immigrant experience. Strip away Yiddish and Yiddishkayt, and you are left with Jewspeech, a narrative style and ironic sensibility.

Riding the crest of the immigrant wave, American Jewish fiction has completed its second great phase without significant recourse to a usable past. This route, it seems to me, has reached a dead-end. Even magic realism needs some basis in reality for the magic to work. And so I see but three possible roads that lie ahead: Either to continue on its present course, skirting a vicarious past that leads from Chelm to Chelmno, from folklore to mass martyrdom; to study Hebrew and visit Israel, where the literary exploration of all Jewish—and Zionist—pasthoods is proceeding apace; or to learn Yiddish. If the Yiddish path is the one taken, then this chapter will have been its manifesto.

Notes

1. For a more in-depth discussion, see my book, *The Jewish Search for a Usable Past* (Bloomington and Indianapolis: Indiana University Press, 1999).

2. Ruth R. Wisse, "Jewish Writers on the New Diaspora," in *The Americanization of the Jews*, eds. Robert M. Seltzer and Norman J. Cohen (New York and London: New York University Press, 1995), pp. 60–78; the quote is on p. 73, and ibem, "Language as Fate: Reflections on Jewish Literature in America," in *Literary Strategies: Jewish Texts and Contexts*, ed. Ezra Mendelsohn, vol. 12 of *Studies in Contemporary Jewry* (1996): 129–147.

3. Isaac Rosenfeld, "King Solomon" (1956), in *Preserving the Hunger: An Isaac Rosenfeld Reader*, ed. Mark Schechner (Detroit: Wayne State University Press, 1988), pp. 373–388. Also anthologized in *Jewish-American Stories*, ed. Irving Howe (New York: New American Library, 1977), pp. 67–81. Shechner's Reader also reprints three of Rosenfeld's Yiddish "fables" in English translation.

4. See David Stern, Introduction to *The Jewish Anthological Imagination, Prooftexts* (1997): 1–7; and Israel Bartal, "The Ingathering of Traditions: Zionism's Anthology Projects," pp. 77–93.

5. For a more in-depth discussion of this and other relevant anthologies, see David G. Roskies, "The Treasures of Howe and Greenberg," *Prooftexts* 3 (1983): 109–114.

6. See Isaac Bashevis Singer, "Problems of Yiddish Prose in America" (1943), trans. Robert H. Wolf, *Prooftexts* 9 (1989): 5–12.

7. Hana Wirth-Nesher, "The Languages of Memory: Cynthia Ozick's 'The Shawl'," manuscript.

8. Carole S. Kessner, Introduction to *The "Other" New York Jewish Intellectuals* (New York and London: New York University Press, 1994), pp. 6–9.

9. See Bernard Malamud, "Source of the Fixer," in *Talking Horse: Bernard Malamud on Life and Work*, eds. Alan Cheuse and Nicholas Delbanco (New York: Columbia University Press, 1996), pp. 88–89. In a posthumously published talk, Malamud traces the origins of "The Magic Barrel" back to an invitation from Howe to translate a story for the forthcoming *Treasury of Yiddish Stories*. See "The Magic Barrel," in ibid., p. 80.

10. See Aharon Megged, "Natnu li kah vekah otiyot likhtov bahen, ve'ani kotev bahen," *Ha'aretz, Literary Supplement* (March 1, 1996); Amos Oz, *Shtikat hashamayim: 'Agnon mishtomem 'al elohim* (Jerusalem: Keter, 1993); and Haim Be'er, *Gam ahavatam gam sin'atam: Bialik, Brenner, Agnon ma'arakhot yahasim* (Tel Aviv: Am Oved, 1992).

11. See *Isaac Bashevis Singer: Conversations,* ed. Grace Farrell (Jackson Florida and London: University Press of Mississippi, 1992), especially pp. 8, 34, 71, and 95. For a good laugh, see my review, "The Fibs of I. B. Singer," *Forward* (December 18, 1992).

12. Kessner, ibid., p. 10.

13. Ruth R. Wisse, *The Schlemiel as Modern Hero* (Chicago and London: University of Chicago Press, 1971), chap. 6.

14. Malamud makes no mention of Poe in his various autobiographical talks. Instead, he credits a story by Howard Nemirov titled "Digressions on a Crow." See "Jewishness in American Fiction," in *Talking Horse,* p. 140.

15. See Wirth-Nesher, "Between Mother Tongue and Native Language in *Call It Sleep,*" afterword to *Call It Sleep* (New York: Noonday Press, 1991). See also, Roth's spirited repudiation of Joyce in *A Diving Rock on the Hudson* (New York: St. Martin's, 1995), pp. 115–119.

16. These concluding paragraphs were stimulated by a critique of my chapter by my friend and colleague Abraham Novershtern.

CHAPTER EIGHT

The Yiddish and the Hebrew Writers Head for Home

Ruth Wisse

> But trailing clouds of glory do we come
> From God, who is our home.
> —William Wordsworth

> My grandchildren. . . .
> I haven't fled as far
> from the Baal Shem
> As you flee from your grandfather.
> —Jacob Glatstein

I

At the end of the 1930s, with no apparent knowledge of one another's work in progress, the Yiddish poet Jacob Glatstein in New York and the Hebrew writer S. Y. Agnon in Jerusalem wrote autobiographical novels about the writer who revisits his native city in Poland. It was even less fashionable then than it is sixty years later for a modern writer to identify with the beleaguered Jewish people and to draw attention to their political isolation. In those years, the liberal elites were convinced that socialism was the only moral road to progress, and that the Soviet Union the only bulwark against Fascist and capitalist rule. In the United States, ambitious Jewish intellectuals were making their way into the main-stream culture while many of their counterparts in Palestine were redefining Jewish priorities to secure the new society of *Eretz Yisrael*. The trendy twin movements, modernism and Marxism, were equally contemptuous of Jewish national concerns. The almost simultaneous

departure of Glatstein and Agnon in the same conservative, coun-
terclockwise literary direction is the more unusual because of the
way they rejoined their fate to the Jews of Poland, then cast themselves as survivor witnesses of the Jewish crisis in Europe.

Both S.Y. Agnon and Jacob Glatstein had left their native cities before the First World War, traveling in opposite directions,
Agnon to *Eretz Yisrael,* Glatstein to America. Glatstein felt he had
barely escaped the carnage when he arrived in America just before
the outbreak of hostilities in 1914. Agnon spent the war years in
Germany, having returned to the continent between 1912 and 1923.
While Agnon then moved permanently to Jerusalem and pioneered
a unique modernism in Hebrew, Glatstein slowly settled into New
York and gained coterie recognition as a Yiddish modernist poet.
They raised their families, and while struggling over their work,
experienced personal and material upheavals—Glatstein coping with
a failed marriage and the Great Depression, Agnon as a member of
the embattled yishuv of Palestine.

Yet at one crucial juncture, their lives took a common turn.
Leaving their families, both men took a solitary voyage back to
their native cities, Agnon to Buczacz in August 1930, Glatstein to
Lublin in 1934 when he learned that his mother was dying. Their
cities had become part of the independent republic of Poland at the
end of World War I, Galician Buczacz having been under the aegis
of Austria, and Lublin under czarist Russia when the writers had
lived there in their youth. The works they spun out of these visits
upon their return, Glatstein to New York, and Agnon to Jerusalem,
Glatstein at once and Agnon eight years later, were not investiga-
tive journeys through the newly reconstituted Polish Republic, like
Alfred Doblin's 1925 *Journey to Poland.* They were private and
filial studies of a Jewish space so cramped as to create the sensation of claustrophobia. It would be mischief to suggest that these
writers "foresaw" the catastrophic ends of their communities, because only Hitler had the imagination to launch the all-out war on
Europe's Jews. What seems to us prophetic in hindsight was their
impression of the seeping *aftermath* of catastrophe, the fallout from
World War I among Jews who could not recover their earlier economic, political, or social equilibrium in a country that now re-
sented their very presence.

Working within already saturated genres of the travelogue and
the memoir, both authors contrived to make their stories new. They
placed the autobiographical narrator at the center of their work,
splitting the focus and the narrative tension between the creative,

mobile individual and the stagnant community he has come to review. They invited identification of the fictional narrator with the author by including information about their own life and works, confessional revelations, and discussions of their literary craft. Through disjunctive methods of narration they drew attention to the modernist's anxieties, but also to his ambition to encompass "everything" in a single work. The trip back to their native cities evoked aspects of psychoanalysis, for Glatstein's narrator by locating the source of his adult crisis in the traumas of earliest childhood, and for Agnon's through the investigation of personal and collective myth.

But writing in different languages, the two authors experienced the Jewish condition in different ways. Once twinned in the premodern period, the destinies of Yiddish and Hebrew diverged so sharply by the end of the First World War that competing ideological parties had actually formed along linguistic lines. Yiddish was the adaptive diaspora language, easily turned into an argument for "diasporism," for the perpetuation of Jewish autonomy through a national culture wherever Jews lived in sufficient numbers. Hebrew was the centripetal language, the only tongue that united the Jews through time and space, hence the only potential unifying language of a sovereign Jewish nation; it carried the aura of remembered majesty. Although Glatstein and Agnon were among the least ideological writers of their day, their artistic intuition was guided by the potential of their languages, which was waning in one case, and gaining strength in the other.

It cannot be accidental that of the two writers, Glatstein lost the race with history, although Agnon began his work much later. The creative instinct that prompted Glatstein to organize a major work of fiction around a voyage back to his native city made it impossible for him to complete the project as planned. He published only two volumes of the projected trilogy, *Ven yash iz geforn* [Yash's Outbound Voyage, 1938, published as *Homeward Bound*], and *Ven yash iz gekumen* [Yash's Homecoming, 1940, published as *Homecoming at Twilight*], eventually abandoning the third volume when the mass murder of European Jews began.[1] With the passage of years, that incompletion became an organic part of the work.

II

Glatstein had emerged as a poet out of World War I. In 1920, six years after he arrived in New York from Lublin, he coauthored the manifesto of Yiddish introspectivism, insisting that Yiddish poetry was part of an international literary avant-garde with no special loyalties to Jewish literary traditions or national interests. Introspectivism, or *Inzikh,* falls well within Benjamin Harshav's observation that every modern movement of change, either personal or institutional, was borne by negative and positive impulses alike.[2] As one manifest proof that they were breaking with the past, the poets of *Inzikh* rejected the universal Jewish practice of maintaining the orthography of Hebrew root words in Yiddish, and spelled them phonetically instead, so that the eye could rejoice in what the ear perceived. Over in the Soviet Union, the Yiddish literary establishment was neutering Yiddish orthography for blunt political ends, to deprive the Hebraic component of any pride of place. Ideologues of the Revolution leveled Hebrew as the first step toward eliminating the language that represented the religious and "learned" components of Yiddish. Glatstein and his fellow *Inzikhistn,* Aaron Glanz-Leyeles and N. B. Minkoff, intended no disrespect to the language they knew and loved, but felt they had to "naturalize" the sacral Hebrew component (the phrase is Leyeles's) to free up the sound patterns and rhymes and to gain equal status for all Yiddish words. Their rebellion was cast as an American declaration of independence, much as E. E. Cummings tried to "democratize" English by eliminating its capital letters. They exploited the suppleness of their vernacular by opening it to other languages, paralleling the modernists like Ezra Pound and James Joyce who had reimagined English as the universal tongue. In concert with this aesthetic of freedom, Glatstein published the first of these two novels (but only the first) in the dehebraized spelling the group had adopted.[3]

But other influences were also at work. In 1926, having abandoned his legal studies at New York University, and realizing that he needed a paying profession, Glatstein took a job on the news desk of the *Morgn Zhurnal* [Morning Journal], a Yiddish daily with a traditionalist Zionist orientation that prided itself on the high level of its writing and on the extent and reliability of its news coverage. Glatstein was a very clever man, an intellectual as well as a poet. ("Why should I say, he *may have been* our smartest writer?" one critic blurted, "He *was* our smartest writer.")[4] The daily bombardment of news could not help but challenge some of his aesthetic priorities. While modernism and the rhetoric of class conflict insisted that national boundaries were obsolete, the Jews had actually begun to loom more menacingly than ever in the sights

of Europe, and increasingly of nativist America; anti-Semitism defied
the rational calculations of intellectuals. At the same time, America's
opportunities were proving to be a mixed blessing: the Yiddish
writer might turn cosmopolitan, but acculturation also encouraged
Jews to switch into English, abandoning the Yiddish writers faster
than they had abandoned religion. Glatstein's poetry quickened
with such contradictions and, under assumed names, he also reg-
istered his conflicts in short stories and political commentary.

But he had never undertaken a large-scale literary project until
his mother's illness summoned him home to Lublin and provided
him with the scaffolding for a major narrative. In practical terms,
the mother's fatal illness allowed for his first "furlough" in twenty
years, and the paradox was driven home when the writer found
inspiration from a community in fatal decline. The midlife journey
served the writer as an occasion for both *kheshbon hanafesh,* "spiritual self-scrutiny," and exposure to the widest possible cross section
of people across national frontiers. The strange relation between
the voyaging author and narrator is suggested by the latter's ano-
nymity throughout the book, except for the name Yash in the title.
Yash may be a Polish Jewish version of Jacob, the man Glatstein
would have become had he remained in Poland. He returns like a
demobilized soldier to his devastated home.

Yash realizes upon leaving the country how much of an American he has become. His first encounter as the *Olympic* sets sail is
with a band of college musicians from the University of West Vir-
ginia on their maiden trip to Paris. When he speaks to these boys—
who are the same age he was when he arrived from Europe—he
discovers the English language tripping "acrobatically" from his
tongue. He alone seems to appreciate the sadness of the jazz they
play, the "uncertain" and even "funereal" quality of their leave-
taking from America. The scene between Yash and the musicians
introduces the method of the Yash novels as a whole. It sounds the
musical motif that will weave through the entire narrative (opening the second book on a very different note) and it establishes
Yash as the ideal listener who discovers himself mostly through
conversations with others. One of the passengers later compliments
him on his "golden ears."

Yash exults in the newfound freedom of being able to meet so
many strangers on equal terms. He interacts with a variety of
individuals who, "having existed through all the time that you
didn't see them, want to set out their lives for you on a platter." A
keen observer, Yash sees lovers slipping into trysts and cabins, and

feels no want of opportunity himself, being among the most sought after companions on his (second-class) deck, a magnet for all sorts of outbound and homebound passengers. Yet contrary to the expectations that he and the travel genre arouse in us by throwing strangers together, Yash has only verbal brushes with other people, and none of those intense, transforming interactions that threaten to change the direction of a life.

Quite simply, the novel lacks incident. The missing dramatic action of Glatstein's book takes place within the narrator, between the middle deck where Yash moves by day and the cabin to which he retires by night. The first night out to sea in his narrow bunk, Yash is reminded of the "teacher Fishl Dovid who is going home for the holidays in a rowboat." This is the first Jewish reference in the book, and it appears without commentary, just as it emerges unbidden in Yash's consciousness. Fishl Dovid is the hero of Sholem Aleichem's "Home for Passover," a *melamed,* or teacher, from the shtetl Khatchevate who must earn his living in the distant city of Balta, but who really lives for his twice yearly visits back home with his family. The teacher's journey is threatened, as happens so often in Sholem Aleichem, by a succession of obstacles that evoke the nightmare of Jewish life, ending with a trip in a narrow boat across a thawing river, rowed by a sadistic Gentile ferryman. Yash's literary allusion connects the terrified Fishl Dovid stretched out on the bottom of his potential coffin with the dapper American poet who is suspended between America and Europe. Jewish apprehension overtakes the narrator at the boundary between wakefulness and sleep, anticipating the conclusion of this book that leaves us wondering whether Yash did, indeed, reach his mother before her death. Sholem Aleichem drains us by anxiety before providing a happy end, but Glatstein provides no catharsis at all.

Yash's anxieties are compounded because he is traveling through real historical time. In the early hours of June 30, 1934, Hitler executed his former comrades among the storm troopers, and that slaughter, reported by the ship's bulletin on the third day out at sea, subtly but inevitably separates the Jews from the rest of the passengers. Until that point, Yash enjoys conversations pretty much indiscriminately with Christian and Jew alike, and he admits he is pleased to shuck off, at least temporarily, his concerns for the Jewish people. But now the equanimity of his shipmates oppresses him:

> I realized that Hitler means something different to them and to me. Hitler is to them (with or without rage) the German dictator,

and to me—600,000 German-Jewish brothers—my 17 million brothers and our hysterical fear of fascism. . . . Hitler is a paw forcibly writing chapters of Jewish history and so I have to pay bloody attention to him.[5]

Alas, Yash does not discover any sense of community in his ensuing search for fellow Jews. A pious Jew in slippers: "with the aphoristic wisdom of Lao Tse," assures him that the enemies of Israel vanish whenever he immerses himself in a holy text. A Dutchman is angry to have been recognized as a Jew. A coarse Bessarabian from Bogotá "with the accent on the *a*," spins out a miniature history of Jewish assimilation in South America. Yash betrays a touch of cynicism when he suggests to the Jew from Bogotá that he could solve both his own and the Jewish national problems were he to launch a Yiddish newspaper in New York. Neither Yash nor any of the other Jews he meets has any notion of how to respond to Hitler's threat. Later, toward the end of his trip, when Yash is surrounded by merry Nazi youth on the train through Germany, the protection afforded him by his American passport allows him to experience even more acutely his impotence as a Jew.

Yet if the Hitler news allows no illusions about Jewish national solidarity, that first encounter with the pious Jew in slippers does overtake Yash with his first remembrance of childhood:

> The Jew exuded the atmosphere of Sabbath rest that hung like a secret in our home, when parents closed the door and went to lie down for a while after the *tcholnt* [baked stew]; a calm that was broken only when father removed the iron bars and unbolted the store. The smell of iron-rust, the frozen scrape of cold keys and the first customer of the long week were the signals that the God/of/Abraham had turned on all the lights and Holy Sabbath had departed and the careworn week had returned.
>
> And suddenly the Jew in slippers had connected my first seventeen-eighteen years at home with the present journey home to see my mother. Her ears are yellow as wax, writes my aunt, pack your things immediately and come and may the good Lord help you arrive in time to see her.[6]

This triggered sensation, like the madeleine of Marcel Proust's epic, opens a rush of memory that then intensifies and expands. As a child, he had felt the secrets of Sabbath from behind a closed door, marvelously paired with the secrets of his parents' union. "God/of/Abraham" was not a distant deity, but the homey lamplighter. The boy's exclusion from the sacred may have sharpened his sense of the profane. But why has it taken a sudden jolt—of his aunt's letter, of the slippered Jew—to recall him to what he ought never to have left behind? And what will become of him now that he has been recalled to his past?

In a poem of Glatstein's entitled "At Sea" and possibly written aboard ship, the speaker confesses to being charged by guilt like the ancient mariner's, except that his guilt is strictly within himself. He had carelessly overthrown tradition, and for what?

> *gefresn, gezoyft, gehulyet, getroyert un gelakht,*
> *getrakht, gefresn, gezoyft, gehulyet, geshlofn un gevakht.*

The heavy repetitiveness of sound and sense in this string of past participles, with the first person pronoun only implied, as Yiddish grammar allows, contradicts the hedonism they describe: "[I] gobbled, swilled, caroused, mourned and laughed / pondered, gobbled, swilled, caroused, slept and stayed wakeful."[7] Like the speaker in this poem, Yash realizes that sanctity quickens, and its absence dulls, human experience. Thus, already at the beginning of the voyage that was to take the poet out into the world, news and memory suck him powerfully back into his people and his past. But the elegiac connection between the mother's yellow ears and the poet's golden ears, cited by Dan Miron as the dominant image of the novel, does not result in any action, and neither does the poet's response to the news of Hitler.[8] The tension between politics and poetry has no practical issue in this book. Glatstein and his narrator are obliged to create a novel around an absent society.

On the second day at sea Yash hears news of Hitler, and on the third, of Stalin. And the closer he gets to home, the less patience Yash has for the great wide world. His sojourn in Paris is a cruel parody of the expatriate adventure that the young American musicians were hoping to enjoy. Trying to squeeze in a couple of hours of the city's "magic" before his train leaves for the east, he makes his way in the rain to the famed Café Dome. There, a Jewish artist whom he had briefly met in New York condescends to sit down with an "obscure" Yiddish writer, and gives Yash the unhappy news that Bialik had died the previous day: "The greatest Jewish poet since Judah Halevy! He would surely have won the Nobel Prize!"[9] Yash is shaken by Bialik's death, but also by the memory of having heard Bialik during a visit to New York foretell the demise of the Yiddish language. The sting of Bialik's prediction has entered his bloodstream like venom. In place of the Montmartre literary scene he was hoping briefly to join, Yash receives a compounded death notice for the Jewish poet, and for his Yiddish tongue.

The journey that began so expansively with the appearance of "that famous couple, sky-and-water," tunnels to its conclusion through fascist Germany and the impoverished Polish countryside. By the end of the trip, the original proportion between encounters with other people and private reflection has been inverted, so that Yash has to apologize to his train companion for being lost in his own thoughts. All that "flutter of talk" that he found so interesting gives way to "the sad tonality of home." He enters Warsaw as though it were Zion:

> See, I have never been false to you. My tongue may be cleaving to my gums, but I have never forgotten you, my Jewish Poland, with all your terrors and sorrowful festivities. Do not forget my right hand, as I have not forgotten thee.[10]

The Yiddish poet reaffirms an altered pledge of allegiance. Poland is for him the crucible of Jewishness, and now that he is in exile, he has come to yearn for it as powerfully as his ancestors once longed for Jerusalem. The poet has already demonstrated his fealty to Jewish Poland by dedicating his right hand, his writing hand, to Yiddish its language, and he therefore prays for reciprocity—for continued inspiration from the source of his devotion. Jewish Poland is for the poet, as for the psalmist, both a geographic location and a symbol of peoplehood. Yash will reiterate a version of this pledge and prayer to Jewish Poland at the end of the second volume, in one of the few direct echoes of this book. Meanwhile, his journey ends at the station where his life began: Lublin!

III

But here is something strange. Despite the organization of this planned trilogy around the return of a native son to his home, Glatstein's emphasis falls on the caesura, on the empty place between the anticipation and the aftermath of homecoming. Home itself is missing. The curtain is drawn over Yash's reunion with his father and other relatives, leaving only the preview encounter with his mother's sister on the way to Lublin, and an account of his negotiations with the burial society when he has to

arrange for his mother's funeral. (Extortion at the hands of the
Jewish community is the price the native son pays for being an
American.) In the second book of the trilogy, *Ven yash iz gekumen,*
the narrator rests up from "several weeks in Poland" before returning to America. But he is no less marginal at Buchendler's Hotel
than he was aboard the *Olympic.*

Indeed, having tried to come back "home," Yash has a primal
memory of separation. Just as Yash at sea had been reminded of
Fishl Dovid in the rowboat, he no sooner stretches out on the grass
near the hotel than he remembers himself as a little boy in a navy
suit and a visored cap accompanying his aunt across a stretch of
sandy terrain to the military barracks where his father was serving as a recruit. They were bringing his father food that his mother
had prepared, during the stint of army service that marked the
first time the husband had ever left his sickly wife. Although nothing untoward happens during the visit, the little boy realizes that
he is suspended between parents who have come apart, and this
introduction to solitude then segues into the young man's memory
of arriving alone in New York. From the psychoanalytic perspective
that Yash provides, the trip to America reenacts the essential rift
in his life. Both separations were involuntary, his father's conscrip-
tion dictated by the czar, and Yash's emigration to America by Polish
anti-Semitism. Gentile powers have driven a wedge into the Jewish
body politic, separating the husband from his wife, the child from
his parents, the people from their European home.

What arises to span the vacuum is something Yash calls "the
eye," an adult consciousness that has replaced "Divine Providence,"
hashgokha elyona, and that never lets the child out of its sight:

> The eye truly did not take its eye off the boy or the aunt as he
> walked on and on alone in the bustling crowd. But now the young
> man was by himself, without his aunt, in a foreign city, elbowing
> his way alongside and among the others. Had it not been for that
> attentive young man's eye, no one in later years would ever have
> known that there had once been a boy in a dark blue suit and
> visored cap.[11]

Only poetry, the "poet's eye," can hold together the adult American
and the European child he once was. This is very different from the
image of the once firm center that William Butler Yeats evokes in
"The Second Coming;" different, too, from T. S. Eliot's once
flourishing Wasteland, and from Agnon's evocation of a prewar

Jewish golden age in Buczacz. Yash had never experienced his parents' Sabbath except as a voyeur. The Yiddish poet and his language were never rooted in a primary land or primary text. If Yash ever thought that homecoming would reroot him in his past, the way in which Zionists do when returning to Jerusalem, he now realizes that he was formed through the act of separation and that bridging the chasm between two places of exile will remain his whole life's work.

We have noted the images of the poet's ear and eye; this book opens with a voice: —Even from the gutter will I sing to you, O Lord—*Afile fun der blote vel ikh zingen tsu dir, mayn got, afile fun der blote.* Sounded in the Yiddish vernacular rather than in the original Hebrew, this *de profundis* delivers the actual *blote,* the palpable muck into which Polish Jews are sinking, and their reach for redemption without metaphysical powers. The man named Steinman who utters these words is holding a group of Jews spellbound, like some latter-day Hasidim around their rebbe, but the men are just a random collection of guests around the supper table of Buchhendler's Hotel, constituting only the modern tatters of the Jewish community of faith.

Buchhendler's is the Jewish version of Thomas Mann's great sanatorium. It specializes in arteriosclerosis, which signifies both the calcification of the arteries and a hardening of the brain. The physical and metaphoric properties of this illness stand in obvious contrast to the feverish tuberculosis of the *Magic Mountain,* a novel that had been translated into Yiddish in 1930 and that was widely discussed in American Yiddish circles.[12] Glatstein's sanatorium lies at the periphery rather than at the heart of Europe, with only a hill and a park nearby to add a dollop of nature. While the patients in Mann's novel are afire with all of the infections of modern Europe, Buchhendler's guests expect only palliative care. Yash could have vacationed in some livelier resort. Instead, he has gravitated like the hero of Mann's novel, Hans Castorp, to an asylum for a condition that knows no cure.

To his fellow guests, Yash is a Joseph, come from the land of plenty to benefit his brothers. Following the visit of a female cousin, Yash has a dream in which a young Jewish wife stretches out her arms to the character he is playing, crying "Joseph, Joseph, be kind to me, be unkind to me, be cruel, beat me, beat me hard, Joseph, Joseph." She is asking for his protection and for his sexual domination. Yash alias Joseph promises to run off with the unhappy woman, and to cut off his beard like a gentile so that he can function as her virile husband. The suppressed eroticism of Potiphar's wife cries out for release, but whereas the Bible applauds the rectitude of Joseph for denying her lust, Yash's dream-play finds him guilty for failing his responsibility. The Jewish husband offers his wife neither protection from the threatening Gentiles, nor sexual satisfaction. As if Yash's sense of unfulfilled obligation to his mother had extended to Jewish womanhood, he introduces a whole cast of Jewish daughters and wives who are unable to find love or companionship, intellectual challenge, or even a decent dancing partner among the Jewish men. Nor can this American Joseph provide for his brothers. The terrible poverty of Polish Jewry is dramatized through the appearance of twelve petitioners; "the community of the poor . . . their hands extended, addressing themselves not to me personally, but to me as the messenger holding out the promise of the mythical bread." Yash can do no more than lend them a golden ear—Ask my brother-in-law why he is letting us die of hunger. Tell my son I forgive him for letting me starve. Beg my wife's family in New York to send us a few dollars. See if my brother will send me a dowry. Instead of wasting words, just tell my son, *father, bread, eat, eat!* . . . But the Yiddish poet has no grainhouse, no political base behind him, and no higher faith. The stories he tells about suicides and accidental deaths in New York makes it seem less a place of rescue than an arbitrary hell. Yash becomes the conduit for Jewish suffering only through the medium of this book that demonstrates why he cannot become the Jewish rescuer.

The subtlest claims on Yash are made by a pair of would-be-redeemers who entrust him with their national ambitions. The aging Steinman is looking for a spiritual son to carry on his work of cultural transmission. He is one of those first-generation moderns, cast in the mold of Polish Jewish leaders like I. L. Peretz, or Zionists like Nahum Sokolow, Shmaryahu Levin, and Zalman Shazar, who try to transpose the religious vitality of Judaism into literature, and to fire up their coreligionists with a sense of their historic destiny.

Yash is also befriended by a sixteen-year-old Hasidic prodigy, a Micah Joseph Berdyczewski in religious garb, who is one of Glatstein's most inspired creations. This young visionary imagines a Jewish revival grounded in a protean new literature that eliminates Gentile influences and contains everything in itself:

[P]oetry, prose, philosophy, drama, psychology, astronomy, epigrams—everything. We have no use for neat little compartments. We must become a creative encyclopedia—do you hear me?—an encyclopedia, but a creative one. Do you grasp this colossal idea? Have you ever read a story of Rabbi Nahman of Bratslav? He is my hero among Hasidim. I am in love with him, I think about him all day long. He was an innovator and he loved Yiddish. Do you know what Yiddish is? What a marvelous language it is?[13]

The young visionary wants modern Yiddish culture to readmit even the so-called false messiahs, Sabbetai Zvi and Jacob Frank, who plead with him: "Just because we dreamed, do we deserve to be branded as false? . . ." The old and young neo-Hasidim recall aspects of Jacob Glatstein, who was composing a dramatic monologue about Nahman of Bratslav in tandem with these novels, and trying as an editorialist to inspire Jewish cultural revival.

But the glory of these redeemers is fading. As Steinman lies dying in the closing pages of the book, he can barely get the Jews around his bedside to overcome their embarrassment long enough to hum the "melody," the *nigun* he has taught them. And the young Hasid's parting words cast an even more ominous shadow on the future. Contrasting ethical Judaism with the corrupt behavior of other nations, he anticipates the day when all of the peoples of the world will acknowledge the moral radiance of the Jew, and he expects Christianity's homage to be the sweetest:

> "Yes, even my envious brother will have to come and bow before me," he said with a happy smile. "Sweet, sweet is the dream of Joseph—all the others will cross my threshold with their heads held high, but he will have to feel his humiliation. No matter how much recognition you get from strangers, it means little until your own sheaves come to bow before you. Joseph wanted to break the pride of the envious."[14]

The reader who has just seen Poland's Jews entrusting their lives to the American Joseph will weep at this imagined messianic reversal. Even more than the death of Steinman, this childish prediction of homage from the peoples of the world with Christianity at their head demonstrates the desperate irreality of the Polish Jew.

The biblical Joseph was able to feed his brothers. The contrast with contemporary politics crystallizes in the closing section of this book when Yash accompanies the novel's only well-to-do character, a retired lawyer named Neifeld, on an impulsive excursion to Kazimierz. According to legend it was in this town that King Casimir the Great (1310–1370) fell in love with a Jewish maiden and installed her in his palace. Yash's Jewish guide notes the subtleties of the myth:

[Our] people created a legend in defiance of boundaries—according to which one of our own daughters gets together with one of the others, a king, no less. There is not so much as a mention of marriage. Did Esther, the Jewish girl, marry the king, or did he possess her without the sacred vows? No Jew will touch upon the moral aspect directly. It is enough that we Jews have created the sense of its being possible somehow to become related to them, to the others—yet not with some ordinary Pole merely, but with the king, who needless to say, thereby becomes a lover of Jews.[15]

Neifeld enjoys the ambiguities of Polish exile. A perpetual minority, Jews need to "become related" to the others and to win the affection of the rulers, without intermarriage, without changing their names. But by 1934, the dangers of such accommodation have surpassed its charms. Under the impact of anti-Semitism, Neifeld has become a tourist in his own country, and he travels to Kazimierz the way in which Yash comes to Buchhendler's, for stimulating respite and "probably for the last time." Yash sees the wretched Jewish life at the foot of the palace hill, where Jewish artisans paint images of a dreamy past that belies the misery in which they raise their families. He knows that no modern Joseph or Esther will be enough to turn the political tide, and that unlike himself, the Jews of Poland cannot leave these "resorts" at will. The last thing Yash sees as he drifts into sleep at the dawn of his departure are the half-opened suitcases near his bed: "the sharpest and most solid objects in the room." These firm American grips will carry him back to safety, and separate him forever from the Jews of Poland.

Yash is as free as any Jew has ever been, the modern man free of Jewish observance, free from persecution, free to travel the world, and in this book, even freed temporarily from daily routine. Yash's freedoms are precisely the properties of Yiddish in America, liberated like him from religious discipline, collective responsibility, discriminatory laws, and from artistic conventions, just as the Introspectivists insisted, but therefore also divested of power, community, and God. The Yiddish poet in America has neither shored up the influence that once allowed Joseph to help his brethren in Egypt, nor invested the kind of trust in divine authority that would justify a prophecy of hope. It has been said that Glatstein could not complete his trilogy once Hitler unleashed his war against the Jews. If so, it was not because the horror had turned him mute. During and after the *khurbn*, the Holocaust, Glatstein wrote some of his most powerful poems of rage and quietude, poems of revolt and vengeance, an entire Holocaust Psalter. He wrote poems about America and Israel. What he failed to do was to complete the saga of Yash, his fictional self. The Joseph who discovers his irrelevance in Egypt did not warrant a sequel, and Glatstein was far too honest to invent for the American Yiddish poet a future he could not believe in.

IV

The reader who is familiar with Agnon's *Guest for the Night* will have noted, throughout the foregoing discussion, points of contrast between these comparable works.[16] Whereas Yash starts out as the consummate cosmopolitan, Agnon plunges his narrator into Jewish space and time:

> On the eve of the Day of Atonement, in the afternoon, I changed from the express to the local train that runs to my home town. The Jews who had traveled with me got out and went their way, while Gentile townsfolk, men and women, made their way in. The wheels rolled sluggishly between hills and mountains, valleys and gorges; at every station the train stopped and lingered, let out people and baggage, and started up again. After two hours, signs of Szibucz sprouted from both sides of the road. I put my hand to my heart. My hand throbbed against my heart, just as my heart throbbed under my hand.[17]

In the most charged hours of the Jewish calendar, the unnamed narrator approaches his city of origins that will be his residence for the ensuing year. The eve of Yom Kippur is for him not merely a date, but the core of moral time. The pace of movement slows, *rallentando,* as the heartbeat picks up. The city he approaches in Gentile Europe bears the Hebraized name Szibucz from the root *sh-b-sh,* "to make crooked," being the moralized version of Agnon's native city Buczacz.[18] The anxiety that overtakes Yash in his cabin at sea is here at the forefront of waking consciousness. For as Yash rushes across the globe to rendezvous with his mother's still beating heart, the Szibucz guest slows down for an appointment with himself. The missing ground of Glatstein's home is Agnon's exclusive location. The two Jewish narrators are not perched on the same axis: while the Yiddish writer balances on the horizontal tightrope between Gentile history and the Jewish experience of it,

the Hebrew traveler stands on a vertical axis, between a weakened
Almighty and a demoralized people. Already in the second sentence
he accepts the distinction between Jews and Gentiles in the same
uninflected way that he notes the gender separation between men
and women. Agnon's narrator never experiences the freedom from
Jewishness that liberates and then dooms his Yiddish counterpart.
His freedom and anxieties are of another kind.

To say that this "man," as Agnon refers to him, enters Jewish
moral time and space is of course not to suggest that he is returning to the shtetl, to the contained world of Tevye and his horse at
the dawn of modernity. Such a faithful Jew and his horse do appear
in Agnon's cast, but the horse Henoch and his master Hanoch freeze
to death in the winter of this novel, and pass into the realm of
myth. Mutation, not familiarity, greets the narrator from the moment he reenteers the Jewish sphere. The town's skeptics tell him
there may not be any suitable lodging for a Jew like him—one who
keeps his head covered. His guide Daniel Bach has lost a leg and
his faith, and gets along as well as he can with man-made substi-
tutes. That the narrator himself is not quite able to maintain the
traditional life of yesteryear is signaled by his arrival at the inn too
late to eat the prefast meal. Nevertheless, he is the most confident
Jew in town. Whereas Yash moves out of the Gentile cold into
temporary Jewish asylum, Agnon's narrator enters the cold of
present-day Jewishness. He is more intact than those who survived
the war in Europe, and because of his language of sanctity, and his
home in Israel, he doesn't readily gain the trust of his European
brothers. In modern Jewish life, social alienation is not the experience of the skeptics, but of the Zionist and the observant Jew.

Whether or not Agnon had *The Trial* in mind, his conception of
moral autonomy seems almost knowingly to contrast with Franz
Kafka's (in the same way that Buchhendler's hotel evokes Mann's
sanatorium). Yom Kippur is the Day of Judgment: Agnon's fully
cognizant Jewish narrator approaches the place and the moment of
his reckoning as an informed participant, indeed, as the controlling
author of his "process," his *prozess*. He fashions his own key to the
house of his fiction, he conducts his own prosecution and defense,
he spins his own parables, and provides his own commentary:

> Does the king refrain from putting the crown on his head because
> it is heavy? On the contrary, he puts it on his head and delights
> in it. The king's reward for the crown being on his head is that
> everyone exalts and honors him and bows down before him. What

good does this do the king? That I do not know. Why? Because I am not a king. But if I am not a king, I am a king's son and I ought to know. But this man has forgotten, he and all Israel his people, that they are sons of kings. The books tell us that this forgetfulness is worse than all other evils—that a king's son should forget he is a king's son.[19]

In K.'s paradox or parable, the ignorant man from the country waits a lifetime to be admitted to the law that could have been penetrated by himself alone. He does not exercise the free will that he was apparently granted. Agnon's narrator stands like the gatekeeper between the man from the country and the law, negotiating the traffic between them. The Jews as a people represent God's authority, and should they abdicate their privilege—forgetting that they are the sons of a king—they reduce the moral potential of the universe. The onus of Agnon's self-accusation falls heavier than Kafka's: when a Jew assumes the posture of a dog, or allows himself to be judged by anyone save God, *he* aggresses against the world, having doomed the possibility of human dignity and justice. K.'s anxiety is for himself alone. Far from diminishing anxiety, as some dull-witted moderns assume that religious allegiance necessarily does, the cognizant Jew recalls the anxiety of the Hebrew prophets, who throb with the anticipation of a national catastrophe that they have the means only to foresee, not to prevent. Kafka can be read as the moral forerunner of Agnon. The sequence does not work as well in reverse:

It takes an ordinary man a half hour to walk to the center of town; carrying baggage, it takes a quarter of an hour more. I took an hour and a half: every house, every ruin, every heap of rubbish caught my eye and held me.[20]

As compared with the radical indeterminacy of Kafka's prose, this narrator experiences each and every moment according to an implicit and known standard, whether he is setting the pace of his walk, determining payment for an employee, deciding whom he must visit and what tone he ought to adopt, expressing preference for a food or texture of clothing, or assuming the proper posture during study and prayer. Sometimes such passages are bolstered by intertextual Jewish references, and sometimes, as in this passage, they are not.

Those who emphasize Agnon's modernism point to his "use of paradox, the fusion of antonomies, the breaking down of logically marked categories, the revelation of chaos in the belief systems of apparently naive legends whose heroes appear to be models of mental and spiritual integrity, and the subtle reversal of readings that he himself has constructed."[21] Thus, in this passage, while the narrator's distinction between his slow pace and that of an "ordinary man" suggests the value of scrutiny over superficiality, the debased objects of his scrutiny—ruins and rubbish—contradict our concept of value, and complicate the meaning of scrutiny. Yet in our haste to situate Agnon among the modernists, we should not overlook his insistence on moral freedom that depends on a reliable narrator. When Agnon's narrator is invited to stop off for a glass of ale, he gives two reasons for accepting: first, to please his friend, and second, to assuage his conscience. (He says nothing about quenching his thirst.) A hundred pages earlier he had tipped the postman and told him not to squander the money on brandy, thereby inadvertently reducing the innkeeper's trade. So now he wants to make good that damage by going in for a drink. A man cannot excuse himself for the wrong he does one individual by the good he has done another, but the consciousness that is aware of multiple motives has a hard time achieving "the good." Moral prose does not imply moral certainty. The complication in Agnon comes precisely from *knowing* God's law, and knowing, therefore, that while human beings can never achieve pure justice or absolute good, their lives are the record of that attempt.

Agnon's narrator is not a tourist but a sojourner. He is neither resident nor stranger, but one who comes like a hero of the American Western to clean up the town because he feels some kinship with the residents. Like the old-timers, he remembers a better time: "when there was peace in the world, and joy, when a man had his victuals in plenty and his belly carried his legs" (43). But unlike the gun-toting Western hero, the European Jew cannot shoot up the town to restore the good. Politically handicapped and unarmed, he is limited to incremental cultural and economic improvements such as reopening the *beit midrash* (house of study), dispensing charity, boosting the economy by buying and ordering local goods, and by paying his upkeep at the local inn. All this time the surrounding "Indians"—the Gentiles—are sharpening their knives, and his money is running out. Recognizing from his own predicament that in order to stop being a guest one must have a house of one's own, he does what he can to inspire passion for the Land of Israel, even as he knows that most of the town will never reach it.

The phrase "a guest for the night" has at least three referents. Its plainest allusion is to the narrator, a tantalizing blend of fact and invention, whose arrival in Szibucz at the beginning of the Jewish year 5689 (autumn 1929) we have just noted, and whose return to *Eretz Yisrael* concludes the book one year and eighty chapters later. Thanks to the scholar Dan Laor, we know a great deal about the visit Agnon actually paid to his home city Buczacz between Tuesday, August 13, and Wednesday, August 20, 1930.[22]

Some of the narrator's activities in the novel correspond to passages in Agnon's letters of the time, for example, the visit to a *hakhsharah,* a preparatory farm of religious Zionist youth who plan to move to *Eretz Yisrael.* Slowing his narrative pace just as the guest does in the approach to Szibucz, Agnon turned this week's visit into what Gershon Shaked considers his fullest autobiographical work. Yet the presence of verifiable data is belied by obvious artistic changes in the representation of events, of which the manipulation of time is but the most obvious. Like Glatstein, Agnon is here interpreting himself as a character of fiction, and specifically as the visiting participant, transient proprietor, artistic bourgeois, sovereign subject of the Jewish God. Since this is the level of interpretation that has already been dealt with most thoroughly in earlier criticism, we will pass over it lightly here.

The designation "guest for the night" also emerges straight out of contemporary Polish Jewish political discourse. It characterizes the sociopolitical ambiguity of Jewish settlement on European soil. The Poles, eager for Jewish support of their reconstituted nation, yet uncomfortable with the sizable Jewish community in a modern Polish republic, tried to emphasize the generous welcome they had once accorded the Jews even as they expressed resentment of how much they had made themselves at home. The Zionist movement brought this ambivalence to a head: while Polish nationalists agitated against the Jews and even instigated pogroms as a way of driving them out, they simultaneously accused the Jews who promoted emigration of having treated Poland as a "guest-house for the night."

From the Jewish perspective, matters were equally complicated. Since the destruction of the Second Temple in 70 C.E., Jews had founded their sacred communities wherever they settled, and the narrator's magnetic attraction to Szibucz dramatizes this spiritual affinity to his Jewish birthplace. Far from producing a nomadic tribe of wanderers, the Jewish concept of exile had encouraged

the proliferation of autonomous communities, *kehilloth,* that substituted the *beit hamedrash* (house of study) for the *beit hamikdash,*
the "Holy Temple." Not disloyalty, but double loyalty was the Jewish problem, because the Temple in Jerusalem had proven no more
or less permanent than many a Jewish sanctuary in Asia and
Europe, and the Jew developed metaphysical as well as physical
attachments to whichever place housed his study and prayer. When
Agnon's narrator is persuaded to address congregants one Sabbath,
he elects to speak on the virtues of "the house of Israel," leaving
deliberately ambiguous whether his text points to the newly
reclaimed Szibucz house of study or to the newly reclaimed Land
of Israel.

The political crisis of modern Jewry is rendered in this novel
more complexly than in any other I know. Agnon's contemporary
Shimon Halkin described it as our new *Midrash Rabbah* commentary on the Book of Lamentations, saying that no work outdid it in
communicating the "physical and spiritual sensation" of the destructive process that culminated in the Shoah.[23] But whatever else
Eretz Yisrael means to the narrator, it does not yet figure as a
political haven: Daniel Bach in Europe may have lost his faith in
the Austrian trenches and his leg trying to earn a living in increasingly anti-Semitic Poland, but he is still alive, while his brother in
Ramat Rachel, near Jerusalem, has been murdered by Arabs. Zvi
the handsome pioneer is caught by the British police when he
jumps overboard from the ship that has brought him to *Eretz Yisrael,*
and sent back to Europe despite the narrator's intervention. The
characters are trapped between the catastrophe of World War I and
the catastrophe-in-the-making. And the narrator walks a political
tightrope between urging movement to Israel and cautioning against
messianic expectations.

Agnon's narrator passionately defends the Jewish settlement
in Palestine against the barbs of its orthodox critics and its dis-
illusioned idealists. He imports the fragrance of Palestine to
Szibucz through a crateful of oranges, and forwards to Israel—on
the grounds that there it will be more needed—a manuscript that
is said to have powers of easing the travails of women in child-
birth. All the same, the very premise of the book is that its narrator left his home in Jerusalem in the summer of 1929 because
it was destroyed by the marauding Arabs. Yes, it is far better to
leave Poland for *Eretz Yisrael* than to go on living in hate-driven
Europe, but, no, the narrator cannot guarantee greater safety in

the Jewish homeland. The return to *Eretz Ysrael* never before brought Jews political security, yet the realization that there is danger inside as well as outside the Land cannot weaken the confidence in Zion.

Without question, the book points in the direction of Israel. Indeed, for a writer who had acute problems with closure, the ending of this novel is astonishingly conclusive.[24] The narrator postpones his departure from Szibucz until the circumcision of the Freemans' son. He retraces his steps in leaving the city with almost ritual exactness. The return to *Eretz Yisrael* with his family is described as just that—a return to a permanent home:

> Now let us see what happened to that man who will live in Jerusalem and what he did in the Land; or rather—since he is settled in the Land and is only a tiny grain of its soil—who will deal with a single grain when the whole Land is before him?
>
> The story of the guest is ended; his doings in Szibucz are done.[25]

This ending is precisely what Glatstein the American Yiddish writer could not provide—the formulaic inclusion of the individual within a people, the people within a land, in a language resonant with precedent and promise. During his first return to Europe, in 1916, Agnon had composed a version of the legends "our fathers told us, how the exiles of Israel came to the land of Polin (Poland)." In quasi-biblical rhetoric, he rehearsed the story of how during their passage through the Polish forests, the Jews discovered a tractate of the Talmud incised on every tree, prompting those who seek for names to say: "This is why it is called Polin. For thus spoke Israel when they came to the land, 'Here rest for the night *[Po lin]*.' And this means that we shall rest here until we are all gathered into the Land of Israel."[26] Now the man who had supplied the earlier legend was providing its sequel, for the time of removal to the Land of Israel had urgently arrived. Nevertheless, as Agnon's narrator might say: "let us see" just how cannily he juxtaposes the fate of the individual with the perspective of a nation and of divine authority. The same person who is privileged *(shezakhah)* to live in Jerusalem becomes, in the destiny of the nation and from the divine perspective, no more than a grain of earth. The earth, being plowed by pioneers to feed the nation, is also our end. The book concludes at the point of maximal fragility rather than with pomp and strength.

V

But since the designation "guest for the night" refers ultimately neither to the narrator nor to the Jewish people, the nation's return to Zion does not exhaust the import of this book. It is the prophet Jeremiah who refers to God as "Guest for the night" in one of his serial visions of destruction. In chapter 14, prophesying the drought that will soon descend on Jerusalem as another confirmation of Jewish iniquity, Jeremiah reminds God that his reputation suffers when his people is in exile:

> Though our iniquities testify against us,
> O Lord, work Thou for Thy name's sake;
> For our backslidings are many.
> We have sinned against Thee.
> O Thou hope of Israel,
> The Saviour thereof in time of trouble,
> Why shouldest Thou be as a stranger in the land
> And as a *wayfaring man that turneth aside to tarry for a night?*
> (*oreyakh natah lalun:* the Hebrew title of the book)

Jeremiah resorts to the Jews' strongest defense against their avenging God, namely, the warning that if they are to be judged by the Almighty, He will also be judged by their fate. Agnon goes further. Author and narrator know that the Jewish God may be eclipsed by the destruction of the Jewish people, but He may also be rendered irrelevant by a political movement that says it is reclaiming Israel on its own. What is more, destruction, displacement, and exile have become so routine for the Jews that the threat of punishment has become ineffectual. After the catastrophes of his own lifetime, and after the neoprophetic responses they elicited from Chaim Nahman Bialik and Uri Zvi Greenberg, Agnon's narrator has no more outrage to expel either against the people who inhabit the cities of slaughter, or against their Guardian. He is not afraid of God but afraid *for* God. Nothing is as contingent in the modern world as its Eternal Judge.

Thus, everything depends on that man in the middle, the narrator who forms an organic link between the Jews and the King of Kings, using the historical language of their interaction to remind each of their interdependency. On the morning of Yom Kippur, the narrator notices that the Torah Scrolls had been stripped of their sacred ornaments during the war by the government that seized them to pay for guns and ammunition:

The Trees of Life, the staves on which the Scroll is rolled, protruded sadly, their faded color wringing one's heart. See how humble is the King who is the King of Kings, the Holy One, blessed be He, who said, "Mine is the silver and mine is the gold," but has not left Himself even an ounce of silver to adorn His Torah.[27]

A humanized God shares the humiliating fate of all Szibucz. Critics who argue over Agnon's relation to Jewish tradition would certainly note how the government's confiscation of synagogue property calls into doubt the fact that God "has not left Himself" the slightest adornment of his law. This ontological irony readmits God into the modern text on the only basis that the narrator honestly can, as an enfeebled authority no longer able to control political reality. Jeremiah anticipated this divergence between religious claims and political realities in his image of *orakh natah lalun* (the guest who tarries for the night), but whereas the biblical prophet remained in awe of God's power, Agnon's narrator awakens compassion for the King who has been stripped of glory. The narrator explains that he is *not* a prophet: "a prophet knows nothing by himself and is only the agent of the Almighty, neither adding to nor taking away from the Almighty's message, and since the day the vision was blocked, prophecy has been taken away" (114). For his part, the modern Hebrew writer comes to all knowledge on his own. Yet the denial that he is a prophet obviously prompts the question of his relation to the tradition of prophecy, else why would he make the distinction between the agent of the Almighty and himself? Although it is true, as Robert Alter reminds us, that fiction writers offer "no solutions to the problems of existence, only the imaginative and linguistic means for thinking about the problems, for seeing them with a depth of vision," what Alter subsumes under "only" becomes in Agnon a solution in itself.[28] Jewish religion is also, when all is said and done, less an answer than a means for living with questions, and Agnon's narrator persuades us by example, precisely through the texture of his book, what advantages accrue to the person who experiences his life within its framework. The advantage the narrator feels that he enjoys over the Jews of Szibucz (through his wealth and his home in Palestine) represents Agnon's advantage over readers who are not similarly situated within the great chain of tradition—and of its resonant literature.

I will bring only one example of the way in which Agnon fights for the divine spirit by attacking its enemies. There is no one in the

novel whom the narrator dislikes as consistently as Erela Bach.
His aversion for this young woman is the more remarkable because, as he himself admits, it is independent of her achievements and sympathies. She is not only the daughter of the Bach
family, otherwise the most sympathetic family in the novel, but a
teacher of Hebrew and a practical Zionist, both admirable from
the novel's point of view. What's more, she was unfairly jilted by
Yerukham Freeman, the abandoned orphan whom her mother had
raised, and who had promised to send for her when he left to
settle in *Eretz Yisrael*. Instead, while in Palestine he became a
communist, and when he returned in disillusionment to Szibucz,
he married Rachel Zommer, the hotelkeeper's daughter. Why, then,
does the narrator so strongly prefer Yerukham—and Rachel his
new bride—to Erela?

> Besides teaching the children Hebrew, Erela has a number of
> other merits. Nevertheless, I do not like her; first, because of the
> way she articulates her speech, for she slices up her words as if
> with a sword, and second, because of the spectacles in front of her
> eyes. After every word that comes from her lips she applies her
> spectacles to you like a plaster to a wound. It seems to me that
> her father's wooden leg is as nothing compared to her spectacles.
> Once Rachel asked me, "Why do you keep away from Erela, sir?"
> "Because of her spectacles," I replied. Rachel said jestingly, "And
> what can a person do if his eyes are weak? But I'm sure it's only
> for this—that spectacles are not mentioned in the Torah."[29]

By allowing himself to be twitted, the narrator draws attention to
both the apparent irrationality of his feelings and to their notice-
able intensity. But elsewhere he explains his dislike more plainly:
"[Erela] boasts that she has no concern with anything that cannot
be explained by reason alone." As the purest materialist in the
book, she is the narrator's greatest enemy, for the Hebrew she
teaches is deprived of its living resonance, and her rational scrutiny pretends to heal the wound that it actually inflicts. A deeper
truth lies behind Rachel's wisecrack, for, in fact, Erela's way of
looking at the world, her spectacles, *cannot* be found in the Torah,
and her pedagogical technique of slicing up the Torah into children's
stories guarantees the death of what was once a Tree of Life. Her
vision and style are the opposite of the narrator's. Agnon uses
Erela's spectacles and her clipped manner of speaking to designate
the kind of qualitative, characterological threat that the Jews cannot survive as opposed to all the other threats that they can and

will. The spirit will either live free and breathe or it will be pinioned by spectacles and sliced up by reason's sword. Besides finding a home for himself and the Jews, the narrator seeks one for God, and in that endeavor no one is as harmful as the ideological materialist who has taken up the sacred language only to pervert the soul of Israel's schoolchildren.

In Agnon's prose, which is the antithesis of Erela Bach's, there is no such thing as a strictly denotive sentence, and while we may distinguish different levels of a phrase as we have done with "a guest for the night," the text resists the separation of what is organically fused. What James Joyce does through stream of consciousness, by running together the various compartments of human thought, Agnon does through compression of symbolic, midrashic, homiletic, philosophical, and psychoanalytic levels of speech into the simultaneity of a single passage. Agnon can seem to do this "naturally" because of the long tradition of Hebrew exegesis that has read so many meanings into every biblical term. The style pits its congruence of spheres against the wreckage of postwar reality so that we experience the disintegration of a world in the language of integral fusion. Those who have a share in Agnon's tradition know that he has made ironic literary use of the rabbinic concept *hafokh ba v'hafokh ba,* the idea of delving into the mysteries of the Torah by turning over, and again turning over its every jot and tittle because *everything* is to be found in it.[30] The result of so much compression is not necessarily comforting. The reader who follows Agnon into his depths and into the heights must suffer God's agony of exile as deeply as the pain of the Jews and the anxiety of the narrator.

Because of the complexity of this project, Agnon's entire novel is organized around possession of a key—a worn metaphor with attendant meanings of "that which opens up, discloses, or explains that which is unknown, mysterious, or obscure." (According to the *Oxford English Dictionary,* Compact Edition, 1971.)

The story of this instrument begins shortly after the narrator's arrival in Szibucz, when he is cynically awarded the key to the House of Study because he seems to be the only one in town who cares about its viability: if you're so crazy about God's tent, why don't you take care of it? He ignores the insult to take up the difficult trust. He soon loses the key, and although he has a duplicate made, he finds it hard to maintain the building and harder still to gather a daily minyan. Perfectly plausible in realistic terms, the key opens as many meanings as the reader cares to admit, including the self-referential one, namely, that the author possesses the key to his book because no one else is equally keen to keep this study open.

The key becomes a central motif once again when the narrator is about to leave Szibucz. Who will become the guardian of the Szibucz House of Study once our guest returns to *Eretz Yisrael,* and what will the narrator do in *Eretz Yisrael* without the key to the House of Study? Now we see how the loss of the original key turns out to have been a blessing in disguise, since with the possibility of reproduction, the principle of exclusivity has been overcome. And, indeed, the experience of Polish Jewry had made it clear that Houses of Study had taken the place of God's lordlier Temple, whether or not the Jews returned to Zion.

So Agnon has laid the groundwork for a comprehensive resolution. In the most redemptive sequence of the novel, the narrator bequeaths the duplicate key to the newborn son of the Freemans at a circumcision ceremony that is cast in messianic terms.[31] The narrator who serves as *sandek* or "godfather" is associated with the figure of Elijah, and in the ceremony renewing the covenant between God and Israel, he transmits his legacy to his designated heir. Moreover, after the narrator returns to Jerusalem, his wife finds the original key in the crevice of one of his traveling bags. He places the key in a box that he hangs around his neck, and he repeats the same rabbinic saying that he quoted at the circumcision ceremony in Szibucz: "Synagogues and Batei Midrashim abroad are destined to be installed in the Land of Israel," adding, "Happy is he that has the key in his possession, so that he will be able to open them and enter in." The narrator's initial anxiety upon losing the original key seems to have been well compensated by the fact that there are now two keys in existence, one temporarily in the diaspora, and the other in his possession. We may take this to mean that the author's youthful neglect of religious learning has produced a redoubled investment in its worth. Or that the benefit of Houses of Study over the original Temple in Jerusalem is that Jews can live both outside Israel in a state of incipient redemption, and inside the Land of Israel, wearing the "key" to redemption against their flesh. Or that although there can be no single key to the knowledge of God, one is obliged to seek to know him everywhere.

Yet the most obvious thing to note about this dominant thread in the plot is that by the end of the novel there is no functioning Beit Midrash in either place. A key is no more than an instrument of potentiality, and a text can never do more than point a people on its way. We are back to the image of the gatekeeper who struggles to keep the traffic open. Agnon may have dusted off the approach to the mysterious place beyond the known, but no writer is powerful enough to keep the studyhouses open.

To the question: "what is Jewish Literature?" asked with increasing self-consciousness since Heine's day, these two literary odysseys of Glatstein and Agnon provide an exceptionally rich response. They plunge back into the constraining Jewish world not for its sake—much as they want to, they learn they can effect no rescue—but for their own. Having become moderns, they reverse their flight from the worldlier alternatives they once pursued.

More than one modern intellectual has quipped that "nothing is as parochial as a Jewish universalist": in their eagerness to ignore the fate of their Jewish birth, such would-be cosmopolitans ignore the main events of the century that had the Jews at their moral center. These two authors became convinced of the opposite proposition, that nothing is as universal as a Jewish parochialist. But the realization loomed differently for the Yiddish and Hebrew writer. Yash the Yiddish narrator discovers that the freedom he gained in America has cost him the power to use it. Agnon's Hebrew narrator finds the key to moral autonomy and becomes progressively humbled by the burden its possession imposes.

Notes

1. Jacob Glatstein, *Ven yash iz geforn* (New York: Farlag Inzikh, 1938). *Homeward Bound,* trans. A. Zahaven (New York: Thomas Yoseloff, 1969). *Ven yash iz gekumen* (New York: Sklarsky, 1940). *Homecoming at Twilight,* trans. N. Guterman, foreword by Maurice Samuel (New York: Thomas Yoseloff, 1962).

References will be to *Yash* I and *Yash* II, and to *Homecoming.* The translation of *Yash* I is partial and unreliable; translations from this book will be my own.

2. Benjamin Harshav, *Language in a Time of Revolution* (Berkeley and Los Angeles: University of California Press, 1993), p. 17.

3. Some recent discussions of the aesthetics of Inzikh and Glatstein can be found in Yael S. Feldman, "Jewish Literary Modernism and Language Identity: The Case of Inzikh," forthcoming, pp. 45–66; Benjamin Harshav, *The Meaning of Yiddish* (Berkeley, Los Angeles, and Oxford: University of California Press, 1990), pp. 175–186; Abraham Novershtern, "The Young

Glatstein and the Structure of His First Book of Poems," *Prooftexts* 6 (1986): 131–146; and David G. Roskies, "The Achievement of American Yiddish Modernism," in *Go and Study: Essays in Honor of Alfred Jospe,* eds. Raphael Jospe and Samuel Z. Fishman (Washington, 1980), pp. 353–368. The only book-length English study of the poet remains *Yankev Glatshteyn* by Janet R. Hadda (Boston: Twayne, 1980).

4. Abraham Shulman, "Yankev glatshteyn's kritik" [Glatstein's Criticism], *Unzer Shtime,* January 4, 1961, p. 3.

5. *Yash* I: 37. My translation.

6. *Yash* I: 39.

7. Yankev Glatstein, "Afn vaser," *InZikh* (3rd ser.), 4 (July 1934): 89.

8. Dan Miron, Afterword to *Kesheyash nasah,* translation of *Ven yash iz goforn* (Tel Aviv: Hakibbutz Hameukhad and Sifre Siman Kriah, 1994), pp. 205–221. Miron also compares and contrasts this novel with Agnon's.

9. *Ven yash is geforn,* p. 188.

10. *Yash* I: 222.

11. *Yash* II: 39–40, *Homecoming:* 39.

12. Isaac Baashevis Singer's translation of *The Magic Mountain* appeared in 1930.

13. *Yash* II: 159; *Homecoming:* 146.

14. *Yash* II: 299; *Homecoming:* 226.

15. *Yash* II: 266; *Homecoming:* 239.

16. Of the immense secondary literature on Agnon, I am particularly indebted to the articles on the novel by Shimon Halkin and Gershon Shaked, conveniently reprinted in *Sh. Y. Agnon babikoret haivrit, II: Parshanut laromanim* (S. Y. Agnon, *Critical Essays on His Writings,* Vol. 2: *Interpretations of the Novels* [Tel Aviv: Open University, 1992]), pp. 180–194 and 195–227; Arnold Band, *Nostalgia and Nightmare: A Study in the Fiction of S. Y. Agnon* (Berkeley and Los Angeles: 1968), pp. 283–327; and to Miron's discussion of the author in *Harofeh hamedumeh* [Le Medecin Imaginaire: Studies in Classical Jewish Fiction] (Tel Aviv: Hakibbutz Hameuchad, 1995), pp. 161–343.

17. Shmuel Yosef Agnon, *Oreakh natah lalun* (Jerusalem and Tel Aviv: Schocken, 1976), p. 7. All references will be to this edition and to the English translation by Misha Louvish, *A Guest for the Night* (New York: Schocken, 1968), p. 1. Henceforth *Oreakh* and *Guest.*

18. See Anne Golomb Hoffman, *S. Y. Agnon and the Drama of Writing* (Albany: State University of New York Press, 1990), p. 78, and the cited

discussion on which this is based on Barukh Kurzweil, *Masot al sipure Sh. Y. Agnon* [Essays on the Stories of S. Y. Agnon] (Jerusalem: Schocken, 1970), pp. 51ff.

19. *Oreakh:* 33; *Guest:* 30.

20 *Oreakh:* 8; *Guest:* 2.

21. Nitza Ben-Dov, *Agnon's Art of Indirection: Uncovering Latent Content in the Fiction of S. Y. Agnon* (Leiden, Netherlands; New York; and Köln, Germany: E. J. Brill, 1993), p. 15.

22. Dan Laor, *S. Y. Agnon: New Perspectives* (Tel Aviv: Sifriat Poalim, 1995), pp. 154–174. This information is on p. 156. [Hebrew]

23. Shimon Halkin, "Oreakh Natah Lalun," p. 192.

24. Miron discusses Agnon's problems with closure in "Domesticating a Foreign Genre: Agnon's Transactions with the Novel," *Prooftexts* 7 (1987): 1–27.

25. *Oreakh:* 445; *Guest:* 477.

26. Agnon's version of the legend stands as the motto of *Polin,* the annual of Studies in Polish Jewry begun in 1984.

27. *Oreakh:* 14; *Guest:* 8.

28. Robert Alter, *The Invention of Hebrew Prose: Modern Fiction and the Language of Realism* (Seattle and London: University of Washington Press, 1988), pp. 94–95.

29. *Orekah:* 143; *Guest:* 149–150.

30. Baruch Hochman leads to this conclusion in his evocative memoir "An Afternoon with Agnon," *American Scholar* (winter 1988): 99.

31. The occasion is so complete that even Erela comes, "that Erela who had been meant for Yerukham from the hour of her birth, but Yerukham had married Rachel, so Erela had been left without a husband." No one is excluded from this ingathering of the tribe, though at the realistic level of the plot, one must ask where this innocent child is likely to lead his flock.

CHAPTER NINE

The Conversion of the Jews and Other Narratives of Self-Definition: Notes Toward the Writing of Jewish American Literary History; or, Adventures in Hebrew School

Michael P. Kramer

We have no comprehensive histories of Jewish American literature, nothing comparable to, say, Emory Elliott's *Columbia Literary History of the United States* or Sacvan Bercovitch's multivolume *Cambridge History of American Literature*.[1] The histories we do have, such as Lewis Fried's *Handbook of American-Jewish Literature* or Allen Guttmann's *Jewish Writer in America,* deal primarily with the authors and writings of the last century, beginning with the large-scale Eastern European migration of the 1880s.[2] Scholars rarely look at the literature produced by Jews before then. The neglect is no doubt due, at least in part, to the sheer demographic dominance in the United States of Jews of Eastern European origins. It is their journey from "shtetl to suburbia" which (with a Holocaust subplot) has become the metanarrative of Jewish American literary history.[3] One exception to this exclusionary (and ethnocentric) rule is the work of Emma Lazarus, the born-again Sephardic poet of the "huddled masses yearning to breathe free." But she is so closely associated with the Eastern European immigrants she championed (I once heard a noted scholar refer to her mistakenly as an immigrant poet) that her exception emphatically proves the rule.[4]

Yet scholars have not neglected the early *history* of Jews in America. Most chronicles of American Jewry begin not in 1880 but in 1654, when "a group of Jewish families, fleeing Portuguese persecution in Brazil, landed in New Amsterdam."[5] (Some begin even earlier, with the "several probable marranos"[6] who sidestepped expulsion by accompanying Columbus on his first expedition to the

New World.) In fact, the American Jewish Historical Society's recent five-volume series, *The Jewish People in America,* devotes two entire volumes to American Jewry before 1880.[7] Within the larger narrative of American Jewry, the struggles and successes of the early Sephardic and German immigrants have been seen as paradigmatic of later developments. Each wave of immigration tells, at least in broad terms, the same encouraging story of survival in the American asylum of liberty. And whenever Jews have felt uneasy in America— during, say, the anti-immigration agitation in the early part of the century or, later, after the Holocaust—the early appearance of Jews in America has served as a source of comfort, proving, as Oscar Straus wrote during the xenophobic years preceding World War I, that the Jew "is neither a newcomer nor an alien on this continent."[8]

So why has the early history of American Jewish writing been neglected? I want to suggest that perhaps this narrower history is *not* similarly comforting, because it does not provide evidence for the story we want to hear. We can identify with, say, the battle of the early Jewish immigrants against the anti-semitism of Peter Stuyvesant. But Jewish American literary history challenges the imperatives of collective memory. For it begins with the conversion of a Jew.

The Jew I'm referring to is Judah Monis.[9] Born in Venice in 1683 to a family of Portuguese Marrano decent, Monis (reputedly) studied "in the Jewish academies of Leghorn and Amsterdam" and found his way to London and then to the New World. He served in religious posts of one sort or another (most probably as a Hebrew teacher) first in Jamaica and then in New York, where he was admitted as a freeman in 1715. By 1720, he moved to Boston, and his significance for Jewish American literary history begins to take shape. There, with his firsthand knowledge of Hebrew and Judaism and some pretensions of being a rabbi, Monis became something of a celebrity among the Old Testament-conscious and millennium-minded Congregationalist ministers in Puritan Boston. Benjamin Colman described Monis as "truly read and learned in the Jewish Cabals and Rabbins, a Master and Critic in the Hebrew." Cotton Mather noted in regard to him: "A Jew rarely comes over to us, but he brings Treasures with him." In recognition of his having composed "an essay to facilitate the instruction of youth in the Hebrew language," Monis was awarded an honorary Master of Arts by Harvard College—he was the first Jew to receive a degree from Harvard—and, under the influence of his Puritan admirers, he was converted to Christianity and baptized publicly on March 22, 1722. For the occasion, he preached a discourse "containing nine principal arguments the Modern Jewish Rabbins do make to prove the Messiah is yet to come; with answers to each, not only according to the Orthodox opinion but even with the authority of their own authentick Rabbins of old." This discourse, which he called "The Truth," together with two "short essays" ascribed to Monis, one called "the Whole Truth" and the other "Nothing but the Truth," were published in Boston in 1722. (The volume included as well the sermon Colman preached at his baptism and a preface by Increase Mather.[10]) Soon after his conversion, Monis became an instructor of Hebrew at Harvard—he was thus also the first Jewish faculty member there—and continued to work on his Hebrew grammar, which he completed in 1726 and published in 1735 as *A Grammar of the Hebrew Tongue*. These two books comprise his literary oeuvre and constitute, whether we like it or not, the beginnings of Jewish American literature.

True, he was an apostate. Although we have no way of knowing whether his conversion was sincere, we also have no evidence that it was not. From that day in March 1722, he appears to have lived and died as a Christian. He married a Christian woman and had Christian children. When he died, he left part of his estate to the Church. Still, he was born a Jew, the stock of Abraham, bone of the bone and flesh of the flesh. Moreover, he never rejected his Jewish identity, and it was never denied him by his neighbors. He flaunted (and traded upon) his knowledge of Hebrew and throughout his life idiosyncratically kept Saturday as his Sabbath. He was referred to throughout his life as a Jew (usually with the attached modifiers "Christianized" or "converted') and his tombstone bears the epitaph, "Here lie buried the remains of Rabbi Judah Monis, M.A." Furthermore, his writings reflect a substantial Jewish heritage—more than most unconverted American Jews of his time and ours—and these writings can be said, without exaggeration or undue irony, to have emerged out of his experience as a Jew in America, to embody that experience in the very fact that they represent his apostasy. One may even discern in them what Gershon Shaked calls "shadows of identity."[11] So if American literature can be said to begin with the Puritans, why not have Jewish American literature begin with the Jewish Puritan, Judah Monis?

I can't honestly claim that I'm surprised that no one has yet begun a history of Jewish American literature with Judah Monis. Most Jews—certainly those committed enough to be involved in Jewish Studies—find conversion offensive, a betrayal of people and past. Even in our postmodern age of fluid identities, conversion has not emerged as an acceptable mode of Jewish self-definition. True, Jewish literary historians readily embrace Heinrich Heine and bend over backward to make excuses for his apostasy. But Judah Monis is no Heinrich Heine: he leaves us neither signs of ambivalence concerning his conversion nor, more important, a body of poetry and prose admired by the *goyim*. And if we need not include him— let alone treat him as a literary forebear—why bother? Indeed, although general historians of American Jewry have known about Monis for some time—and they are not restricted by questions of literary form or subject to pretensions of discerning literary taste— few treat him as more than an oddity, a narrative aside.[12] And none suggest him as an origin of subsequent developments in Jewish American culture. (Indeed, Lee M. Friedman, who wrote two articles on Monis and is the source of much of what we know about him, chose not to include him at all in his 1948 saga of American Jewry, *Pilgrims in a New Land,* having relegated him to the antiquarian curiosities of his *Early American Jews.*[13]) There is one interesting exception however that, I think, proves the rule. For Anita Libman Lebeson, writing in her 1950 history of the Jews in America—she called it *Pilgrim People*—Monis is a tragic figure, a victim of Christian oppression who suffered from an extreme and debilitating case of double consciousness. (She called it "psychological dualism." Gershon Shaked might call it "the shadows within."[14]) "For more than forty years he walked a solitary path," she writes, "flanked by his past which he rejected and his present which he never fully realized." She reads (and in this case I think misreads) the Puritan insistence on calling him "Jew" and "Rabbi" not in honorific terms, not as their way of defining his role in millennial history, but as a sign of their unwillingness to accept him on equal terms. "Being a Christian did not help him much," she says. "He was never one of them." She goes on to caution that "the Monis episode is not isolated. It persists to our own day."[15] Thinking no doubt of Nazi racialist policies—she wrote *Pilgrim People* between 1943 and 1949—Lebeson casts Monis as the archetype of the haunted apostate (and perhaps of the unconverted but assimilated Jew as well) who must ultimately confront the folly of his betrayal. In short, historians attribute only anomalous significance to Monis's life. The conversion of the Jews is the story the *goyim* have scripted for us, they imply. It is not *our* story.

The same sort of cultural anathema that excludes Judah Monis's conversion narrative from Jewish American literary history underwrites the comedy of Philip Roth's short story, "The Conversion of the Jews." In that story, we recall, a preadolescent Jewish boy named Ozzie Freedman frustrates and angers his Hebrew school-teacher, Rabbi Binder, by asking naive but difficult questions. Most prominently—this in response to the rabbi's seemingly unprompted insistence that Jesus could not have been the product of a virgin birth because he was "historical"—Ozzie asks: if God could create the entire world, especially the light, why could he not cause a woman to have a baby without intercourse? Rabbi Binder cannot respond to this logic, accuses Ozzie of being a wise guy, and sends for his widowed mother. This is not the first time she has been summoned, and, out of weariness and frustration, for the first time in her life, she slaps her son. On the day of her appointment with Rabbi Binder, Ozzie is again hit, this time accidentally by Rabbi Binder after Ozzie shouts: "You don't know! You don't know any-thing about God!" Ozzie's nose bleeds. He runs, or is chased, to the roof of the school building, and feels a surge of freedom and power when he realizes that he can control Rabbi Binder, his mother, the old Jewish janitor, and the fire department—as well as please his classmates—by threatening to jump. So he forces them all to their knees and makes them declare, first, that God can make a child without intercourse, next, that they believed in Jesus Christ, and, finally—this directed specifically to his mother—that they would "never hit anybody in any controversy concerning the subject of God." Then he jumps; "right into the centre of the yellow net that glowed in the evening's edge like an overgrown halo."[16]

In this story, Roth dances at the border of Jewish self-definition and flirts with the Jewish taboo of conversion. The notion that a young Jewish boy would be so taken by the Virgin Birth and by the picture of a gathering of Jews accepting Jesus as their Savior are culturally absurd, outrageous—and hence funny. However, even more absurd and more outrageous than Ozzie's antics up on the roof are Rabbi Binder's antics in the classroom. It's odd that the rabbi feels that he needs to raise this issue of Christian theology altogether and preposterous that he insists on the logical basis of Jewish disbelief. Jews reject the virgin birth not because it is logi-cally impossible—this is what Ozzie has begun to discover—but because (for a variety of reasons, not least of which is the revulsion arising from Jewish collective memory) it is culturally untenable. It's just not part of our story, not emplotted in our corporate narrative of self-definition. Andrew Marvell knew it, which is why, in "To His Coy Mistress," he rhymes "the conversion of the Jews" with "refuse."[17] And Roth knew it, too. "It seems to me," he once explained (as it happens, to an audience in Israel), "that the Jews say this to the Gentiles, if only by their existence: 'We do not believe what you believe; we may believe nothing; we may all believe something different; but we just cannot swallow the central fantasy of Christianity.' "[18] (He describes that fantasy as "one woman [having] a child without first having the pleasure of intercourse.") We know that Jesus was historical. We know that Judah Monis was historical. We acknowledge the fact, but deny the significance. We may allow them to be part of our *history;* but we simply refuse to include them in our *story.*

So what *is* the Jewish American story? Through what narrative do Jews in America want to define themselves? Let me quote from a pamphlet called *The Essex Story: A History of the Jewish Community in Essex County, New Jersey.* It was produced by the local Jewish Education Association in 1955—the same year that Roth wrote "The Conversion of the Jews"—and it was intended for use in Hebrew schools as part of that year's celebrations marking the tercentenary of the arrival of the first Jews in North America in 1654. It should be noted as well that the largest and most well-known city in Essex County is Newark, birthplace of Philip Roth and, presumably, of Ozzie Freedman. Had they been in school in 1955, as it were, this is what they would have read. I quote from the foreword:

> Why a story of the Jewish community of Essex County?
> The annals of Jewish history contain the records of Jewish communities by the hundreds, if not by the thousands. Some of them existed two thousand years ago or earlier; others are as recent as our own, or still younger. Some, like Kai-feng Fu in China, Pumbeditha in Babylonia, Lublin in Poland, or Johannesburg in South Africa, are located in faraway places; others, like Charleston, S.C., Rochester, N.Y., or Mexico City, lie much closer.
> Their stories tell, in effect, a similar tale. For wherever Jews found themselves, they strove to maintain their own way of life. And this they accomplished despite all hardships, continuing to observe the same laws and customs, to offer the same prayers, and to dream the same dreams of justice and freedom.[19]

In short, the story that the Jewish Education Association wanted students to hear in 1955 was a story of exile, wandering, and survival—physical *and* cultural—against all odds. Wherever they lived, that is, Jews remained Jews. (Notice that, among the communities listed, neither Jerusalem nor Tel Aviv nor, say, Rishon Letzion is mentioned: they are apparently not part of this survival story. But this is another story.) This metanarrative could not include the Virgin Birth. It could not include the conversion of the Jews. And it could not include Judah Monis.

The foreword to *The Essex Story* suggests that the metanarrative of Jewish survival informs and authorizes the story it is going to tell just as it does all narratives of American Jewish history and, indeed, all of the accounts that comprise the larger history of the diaspora. The Jews in Essex county, like Jews always and everywhere, have observed the same laws and customs, offered the same prayers, and dreamed the same dreams. "And yet," the foreword continues without immediately elaborating, "our story is different in many respects." No doubt they meant in large part that in New Jersey their "dreams of justice and freedom" were realized, that, as they later explain, "New Jersey, unlike some of the other colonies, was known for religious tolerance from its earliest days."[20] It was the crucial difference, the defining difference—and not only for New Jersey. It had been a central motif of Jewish thought in America since the times of the early republic. "Deprived as we hitherto have been of the invaluable rights of free citizens," Moses Seixas wrote to newly elected president George Washington, "we now . . . behold a government . . . which to bigotry gives no sanction, to persecution no assistance, but generously afford[s] to all liberty of conscience and immunities of citizenship—deeming everyone, of whatever nation, tongue or language, equal parts in the great governmental machine."[21] It was a difference to be celebrated, especially in the wake of the Holocaust. And it *was* celebrated. But it was also a cause for concern. For over the course of the twentieth century in particular, many felt, the story of American Jewry was becoming *too* different. So different, in fact, that it threatened to overwhelm the Jewish story of survival, to transform it into a thing of the past. "That American Judaism has survived until now is no guarantee that it will thrive or even survive for another three hundred years," wrote Eugene Kohn frankly in a tercentenary retrospective. The question was not only whether Judaism had survived but "how [it had] survived?"[22] Had the Jews remained Jews in more than name only? Did they indeed observe the same laws and offer the same prayers? Or had they all but converted—not formally, perhaps, but virtually, through assimilation? It was a painful question to ask and it constituted a challenge in particular to Jewish educators. Perhaps this is why the authors of *The Essex Story* assert but do not elaborate the American difference in their preface. Perhaps they wanted to let the metanarrative of Jewish survival stand on its own for a while, to respect its integrity, to savor it, to allow it a formal primacy in the face of the American challenge. Perhaps they didn't quite know how to tell the American chapter of the story.

The Essex Story was written as a response to what was generally perceived at the time to be a crisis in Jewish education: "At no time since the origin of the New York Kehillah," wrote Judah Pilch in an overview of the period, "was there apparent a greater effort to consider Jewish education as a very important item on the agenda of American Jews."[23] Studies showed that many "Jewish young people [were] uneasy about their Jewishness and experience[d] a culture conflict" in their American environment.[24] "To be born into the Jewish inheritance, to grow up identified as a Jew in this Christian world," explained Horace Kallen, "is to be born into a future of outer hardship and inner conflict from which it is natural to seek escape even when escape is self-defeating and renders the hardship and conflict the greater."[25] The conflict was seen to have, first of all, an institutional base. In Eastern Europe, wrote Emanuel Gamoran, traditional Jewish institutions of education reflected and supplemented "the intensive life of a people steeped in Jewishness." But "a radical change took place in the new American environment."[26] "First of all," wrote Samuel Dinin, "specifically Jewish education now occupie[d] a secondary, even a minor role, in the total education received by the average Jewish child."[27] The primary role was given to the public school; Jewish education was relegated to a weekday afternoon or Sunday school. As a result: "Jewish education [became] a burden; it [made] demands on the time of the child and on the budget of the family."[28] Moreover, the lives of American Jews were no longer "steeped in Jewishness." The average Jewish student "comes from a home devoid of Jewish books and learning and often of religious ritual." The home "no longer fulfilled its historic functions *qua* Jewish home." Jewish education in America no longer supplemented Jewish life; it "substituted" for it.[29] Horace Kallen concluded that "Jewish parents delegate to it an insuperable task when they lay upon [the Jewish school] the entire burden of Jewish education."[30] To compound matters, there was a personnel problem. "If . . . one were to compare Jewish teachers with public school teachers in the seventy largest cities in which the vast majority of the Jewish population is concentrated," reported Dinin, "it would be found that their status is inferior as far as average salary is concerned, tenure, security, and even pedagogic training."[31] It was widely agreed that the problems of recruitment, retention, and training were critical, that "the future of our children and youth as Jews and the destiny of Jewish life in America" were hanging in the balance.[32] One writer summed up the general dissatisfaction this way: "All of us, in all types of Jewish schooling, are disturbed by the unsubstantial, elusive results of our efforts, by the lack of knowledge and lack of faith of so many of our graduates, by the comparatively little influence the best of us have on the generation of boys and girls that go through our schools, by the lack of relevance of much of our teaching to their life needs as American Jews."[33] Something, all agreed, had to be done. As it stood, however, it was clear only that Jewish schools in America as they were then constituted were certainly, in Dinin's words, not "produc[ing] children in great numbers who can be called *b'nei torah,* literate Jews."[34]

Strictly speaking, the loose translation of *b'nei torah* as "literate Jews" would have made Judah Monis an exemplary *ben torah,* which points to the deep-rooted problem that characterized Jewish educational thought in the midtwentieth century. On one hand, Jewish education (it was generally agreed) was supposed "to perpetuate our historic and religious ideals," to transmit to American Jewish children the same laws and customs, prayers and dreams that Jews had preserved in Kaifeng Fu and Pumbeditha and Lublin and Mexico City. This is how the Jewish story was supposed to be emplotted. "Jewish education is a serious business," all agreed, "if Israel is to survive in America." On the other hand, America was different, and Jewish education had to conform to the new American reality: above all, it was felt, Jewish education should never undermine what the students were learning in public school. In what seems like a desperate collective attempt to address the problem, Jewish educators produced endless variations on a theme of accommodation. One writer put it this way: "We must integrate our children into the lifestream of America in such a way as to make it dovetail with their Jewishness."[35] Another put it this way: "If we want our children to be better Jews . . . our philosophy of Jewish education must be rooted in some firm convictions about the democratic enterprise and *its* bearings on the interpretation of the Jewish tradition and the structure of Jewish community life."[36] To be Jewish and to be American were to be shown to be wholly compatible—even if that meant reconfiguring Judaism. (It was rarely suggested, however, that America had to be reconceived.) Mordecai Kaplan believed, for instance, that it was "a general principle both of common sense and of pedagogy that a teacher should not be expected to believe anything concerning God which contradicts or is out of keeping with what his pupils are taught in the [public] schools as generally accepted ways of thinking about the world and man."[37] In effect, the goal of American Jewish education came to be construed in paradoxical terms: at once to shape and to reflect the life of Jews in America, to "help the child realize his right to be different from his Christian neighbors" and at the same time to minimize the differences between them.[38]

One approach to the problem was to teach Jewish American history. We need to recall, however, that this chapter of the Jewish story was just then being written. Just as the postwar years constituted the "breakthrough" period of Jewish American literature—when "a large and impressively gifted group of serious American-Jewish writers ha[d] broken through the psychic barriers of the past to become an important, possibly a major reformative influence in American life and letters"[39]—it was also the period of the first flowering of Jewish American historiography, when Jewish historians were discovering and constructing their past. "How shall the history of the Jews in America be written?" Lee Friedman had to ask himself in the introduction to his *Pilgrims in a New Land*.[40] Writing in 1951, Jacob Rader Marcus bemoaned in Jamesian cadences the barrenness of the historiographical territory: "In this field," he wrote, "there are no biographical or historical dictionaries, no atlases, no auxiliary works, few collected sources, no satisfactory union list of Jewish serials, no genealogical tables, not a single complete history of the American Jew that satisfies the canons of modern methodology and criticism."[41] Certainly, Salo Baron had emphasized in 1949, "we have no adequate history of Jewish letters in America."[42] But this was all about to change. American Jews were beginning to look at themselves in a serious world-historical light. Four hundred and fifty years had passed since Columbus and his Marrano crew discovered the New World, three hundred since the first Jews settled in New Amsterdam. Moreover, the Holocaust had put an end to one chapter of Jewish history and the State of Israel had only just begun a new and still very tentative one. When the ashes of Auschwitz settled, American Jews found themselves to be in a very real sense what the first Jewish congregation on Manhattan Island had called itself, *Shearith Israel*, the "Remnant of Israel" (a realization that surely heightened as well the sense of crisis in Jewish education). "The time has come," Anita Libman Lebeson announced in 1950, "to write a full-length history of Jews in America." By narrating the past, Oscar Handlin explained in 1954, the Jewish American historian could help find meaning for the troubled present. "By enlightening the present," he continued, the historian could "aid all those who seek such meaning to shape their visions of the future."[43] During the tercentenary year, a major "Conference of Historians on the Writing of American Jewish History" was held, attended by, among others, Moshe Davis, Salo Baron, Ben Zion Dinur, Daniel Bell, Moses Rischin, Jacob Marcus, Allen Nevins, Lee Friedman, Charles Reznikoff, and Alfred Kazin. By the end of that year, Baron commented, "the growing awareness of their historical heritage by American Jews and its greater appreciation by their non-Jewish neighbors ha[d], for the first time, created a climate of opinion favorable to [Jewish American] historical investigations."[44] What had seemed to Baron's graduate students a few decades earlier as an uninteresting area for dissertation work now was considered, in Lebeson's purple prose, "a tale worth telling," a story whose "romance, excitement, adventure [were] ripe for a chronicler."[45]

The curricular revisions occasioned by the tercentenary incorporated the emerging history. Witness, *The Essex Story*. "Pupils," it was believed, "will need to know about the early arrival of Jews in this country, the reasons that motivated their migration here, the reception accorded them by those already settled in the land, the manner in which the immigrants earned their living, the growth of an organized religious and community life, and the particular contributions which Jews made to the progress of our nation of which they have been an integral part almost from the beginning of its history."[46] So ran an editorial in the periodical *Jewish Education*, and so, more or less, went the story told in works such as Lebeson's *Pilgrim People* and Handlin's *Adventure in Freedom*. The story of America's Jews, it was claimed, was the story of America. To begin with, they were virtually coextensive. "The Pilgrim Fathers had landed at Plymouth only 34 years before the arrival of the Jewish settlers at New Amsterdam in 1654," the authors of *The Essex Story* reminded their readers.[47] And if one counted the Marranos who sailed with Columbus—and many, such as Lebeson, were ready to count them—the Jews actually preceded the Pilgrims. (Emma Lazarus actually attempted to cast American history as a chapter of Jewish history, highlighting the coincidence of Columbus's voyage with the expulsion of Jews from Spain.[48]) Indeed, Jews could be shown to have played roles in all significant episodes of the American tale, from the discovery, through the Revolution and the Civil War, to World War II. More important was the suggestion that both stories shared a theme: religious persecution, exile, and the search for freedom. Jews, too, were Pilgrim people. In this, too, the Jewish story paralleled and exceeded the American. The Jews out-Pilgrimed the Pilgrims: "The [Jewish] trek had begun some 1600 years" before "reaching a peaceful haven on the shores of Manhattan Island," wrote the authors of *The Essex Story*. It was "when the Roman oppressor drove out their ancestors from their homeland" that the Jews "started their search for a place where they might be permitted to live in accordance with the teachings of the Torah and bring up their children in the faith of their fathers." Since then, "so great was the Jews' love of freedom and so deeply did they cherish their heritage that most of them never hesitated when faced with the choice of giving up their religion or going into exile all over again."[49]

The connection between Jews and Americans was shown to be even stronger than the Jewish contributions to American life and the similar patterns of Jewish and American histories. Historians and educators attempted to demonstrate as well "the intimate bond between Judaism and Americanism."[50] Not only was there, as Lee Friedman wrote in *Pilgrims in a New Land*, "an interpenetration" between the two, not only a "mutualism of Jewish life and tradition with Western philosophy and economics,"[51] but Jews and Christian Americans shared fundamental beliefs and values. Here, too, Jewishness seems to envelop America. For America, it was claimed, was founded on ideals borrowed from Jewish tradition. It was an argument first formulated in the nineteenth century by Reform rabbis such as Isaac Mayer Wise and Kaufmann Kohler and was reiterated consistently after the Second World War. I quote again from *The Essex Story:*

> While the Jewish pioneers who settled in New Amsterdam were but a handful, and their influence could not have been very great at first, Hebraic culture had come to the New World ahead of them, and was destined to play a most important part in the shaping of the American way of life. The Pilgrim Fathers were imbued with the spirit of the Bible, and in their flight from persecution in their native England they thought of themselves as the Israelites of old, fleeing from Egypt across the Red Sea to the Promised Land of Canaan. Once established in their new land, they decided to govern themselves in accordance with the Law of Moses. Their leaders learned Hebrew so as to read the Bible in the original, and Hebrew became a required subject at Harvard College which was founded a few years later. In that same spirit, they called their towns and villages by biblical names, such as Salem, Bethel, and Hebron.[52]

America was founded on Jewish values. No reason for Jewish students to feel uncomfortable, then, to feel different, to experience a "culture conflict." The Puritans were Jews; the Jews were Puritans.

(Lee Friedman, who, as I said, omits Judah Monis altogether from his history, begins the Jewish American story with Cotton Mather and his *Biblia Americana*.) What the authors of *The Essex Story* failed to mention, however, was that the Puritans were *not Jews*. They were Christians; their commonwealth was founded on "a model of Christian charity;" they learned their Hebrew at Harvard from a *converted* Judah Monis; they were interested in Jews only insofar as, in words preached at Monis's baptism, "Moses [was] a Witness unto our Lord, Jesus Christ."[53]

No wonder Ozzie Friedman is so confused; no wonder he asks so many questions. And no wonder Rabbi Binder has such trouble answering them. The intercourse question—though it frames the narrative, justifies its title, and provides its comedic punch—is really *only* a frame, drawing its full significance from the questions that Roth presents briefly in retrospect:

> What Ozzie wanted to know was always different. The first time he had wanted to know how Rabbi Binder could call the Jews "The Chosen People" if the Declaration of Independence claimed all men to be created equal. Rabbi Binder tried to distinguish for him between political equality and spiritual legitimacy, but what Ozzie wanted to know, he insisted vehemently, was different. That was the first time his mother had to come.
>
> Then there was the plane crash. Fifty-eight people had been killed in a plane crash at La Guardia. In studying a casualty list in the newspaper his mother had discovered among the list of those dead eight Jewish names (his grandmother had nine but she counted Miller as a Jewish name); because of the eight she said the plane crash was "a tragedy." During free discussion time on Wednesday Ozzie had brought to Rabbi Binder's attention this matter of "some of his relations" always picking out the Jewish names. Rabbi Binder had begun to explain cultural unity and some other things when Ozzie stood up at his seat and said that what he wanted to know was different. Rabbi Binder insisted that he sit down and it was then that Ozzie shouted that he wished all fifty-eight were Jews. That was the second time his mother came.[54]

With these questions—and Rabbi Binder's failure to answer them *to Ozzie's satisfaction*—we can place "The Conversion of the Jews" within the context of the crisis in Jewish education I have been sketching. Moreover, the story goes to the heart of Jewish American religious ideology at midcentury. Of all Jewish ideas, Will Herberg wrote in 1955, the Chosen People concept had become for American Jews "the most difficult to accept, perhaps even to understand."[55]

As a result, as Arnold Eisen has argued, the problem of chosenness was "the single most popular theme of discussion" among American rabbis of the second generation, between, say, 1930 and 1955.[56] (Roth was born in 1933; he wrote "Conversion of the Jews" in 1955.) Ozzie's question was their question. The rabbis of all denominations (though less so among the Orthodox) struggled with the idea. Some rejected it altogether. Most, however, reformulated it in an attempt to smooth its rough edges, to make it more compatible with American ideas, with what Jewish children were learning in public school. This is what Rabbi Binder was doing—or trying to do. The fact that Ozzie would not accept the distinction between political equality and spiritual legitimacy, that what he wanted to know was always different, points to Roth's sense that the entire discourse only obscured the underlying issue. What was it, at bottom, which constituted Jewish difference? And why did Jews have to insist on difference in America? Just as Ozzie wonders about the Jewish victims of the plane crash, so Roth asks his fellow Jew: "How are you connected to me as another man is not?"[57]

The underlying irony of "The Conversion of the Jews" is that, for all intents and purposes, the Jews had already converted. Not to Christianity, to be sure. Not formally. The Jews continued to reject Christ with "willfulness, zeal, and blood certainty." But "the strength with which Jesus continue[d] to be rejected [was] not equaled by the passion with which the God who gave the law to Moses [was] embraced."[58] Which is why Roth sends Ozzie to the roof and brings everyone else to their knees. It was all that was left. In all other ways, Roth felt, Jews were just like everyone else. Jewish polemicists railed about the "myth of the Judeo-Christian tradition," insisted on establishing exactly "where Judaism differed."[59] Meanwhile, rabbis and educators and historians labored to imagine a Judaism compatible with American conditions, and the substantive differences between Jews and Christians dissipated. More Jews than ever before belonged to synagogues and went to Hebrew school, but, as Roth saw it, Jewish values were pretty much the same as Christian values: "What a Jew wants and how he goes after it, does not on the whole appear to differ radically from what his Gentile neighbor wants and how he goes after it."[60] There was Jewish history, of course. But was that enough to define a people when "there is no body of law, no body of learning and no language, and finally, no Lord"?[61] (Judah Monis, at least, had learning and language.) And there were the *goyim*. But "the dying away of anti-Semitism in our country, its gradual ineffectiveness as a threat to our economic and political rights, further disoblige[d Jews] from identifying [them]selves as Jews."[62] What Jews had inherited, what distinguished them (besides their rejection of Christian mythology) was a vestige of Jewish culture and history, a way of thinking about themselves that, Roth said, could be "translated into three words, 'Jews are better.'" It was, however, "a psychology without content."[63]

In an address delivered at Bar Ilan University in 1983, Leslie Fiedler reiterated the oft-noted "paradoxical fact that the rise of Jewish American literature to a dominant position in the culture of the modern world occurred at a moment when the Jewishness of the Jewish American community had become problematical, and indeed its very existence was being threatened by intermarriage, assimilation, and cultural attrition."[64] For Roth, twenty years earlier, the reason was clear. Having inherited "a psychology without content," the Jewish American writer had to invent one, felt impelled to invent one. Assimilation, in other words, *generated* his creativity—just as it generated the creativity of Jewish educators and historians.

Fiedler noted a second paradox, too. He noted a pronounced "Jewish Christolatry" in the works of Jewish American writers, a prevalence in their works of Christian motifs and themes, even those works, like *Call It Sleep,* which to be seemed particularly Jewish. Fiedler explained the phenomenon as the result of the "brainwashing" he and his contemporaries received in public school, particularly in "literature classes aimed at persuading [him] that [he] was the cultural heir of Longfellow, Whittier, and Holmes, Shakespeare and Milton, Wordsworth and Dickens." And though he mumbled obscenities to himself rather than say the Lord's Prayer— "it was *their* Lord we addressed," he said, "not mine"—he nevertheless learned to call the Jewish Bible, "The Old Testament," and read it in the King James version.[65] This was an education that could not be counterbalanced—let alone be unlearned—in Hebrew School. When these writers (and educators and historians) sought to invent a content for their Jewishness, it was from this Christian American tradition that they naturally drew.

To varying extents, these writers and thinkers recognized the paradox. Certainly Fiedler did, when, in 1949, he published "What Can We Do about Fagin?" in *Commentary,* an essay that led to the symposium, "The Jewish Writer and the English Literary Tradition."[66] And so did John Hollander when in *Midstream* in 1958 he pondered the problematics of a Jewish poet's writing in English, a language whose "history is almost inextricably involved, until the eighteenth century, with the history of the Christian religion in England."[67] And so, in a more perverse way, did Alfred Kazin and even Fiedler himself when they joined the cult of the French Jewish philosopher Simone Weil, the "prophet out of Israel," who abandoned Marxism for Christianity before falling victim to the Nazis and who, they felt, *in her very apostasy* had epitomized the twentieth-century Jew.[68]

If Jewish American literature reaches its full maturity with the passionate embrace of American culture, with the blurring of distinctions between Judaism and Christianity, with the redefinition of Jewishness as apostasy, then why not begin its history with the conversion of the Jew, Judah Monis?

Notes

1. Sacvan Bercovitch, gen. ed. *The Cambridge History of American Literature* (Cambridge: Cambridge University Press, 1994—); Emory Elliott, gen. ed., *The Columbia Literary History of the United States* (New York: Columbia University Press, 1988).

2. Lewis Fried, ed., *Handbook of American-Jewish Literature: An Analytical Guide to Themes and Sources* (Westport, Conn.: Greenwood Press, 1988); Allen Guttmann's *The Jewish Writer in America: Assimilation and the Crisis of Identity* (New York: Oxford University Press, 1971).

3. See Sol Gittleman, *From Shtetl to Suburbia: The Family in Jewish Literary Imagination* (Boston: Beacon, 1978).

4. For recent work on Lazarus, see Shira Wolosky, "An American-Jewish Typology: Emma Lazarus and the Figure of Christ," *Prooftexts* 16 (1996): 113–125; Bette Roth Young, *Emma Lazarus in Her World: Life and Letters* (Philadelphia: Jewish Publication Society, 1995); and Michael P. Kramer, "Emma Lazarus Discovers America in '1492'" [Hebrew], in *Following Columbus: America 1492–1992*, ed. Miriam Eliav-Feldon, (Jerusalem: Zalman Shazar Center for Jewish History, 1996), pp. 159–171. One work that deals in detail with writers of the earlier waves of immigration is Diane Lichtenstein, *Writing Their Nations: The Tradition of Nineteenth-Century American Jewish Writers* (Bloomington: Indiana University Press, 1992). Lazarus is a central figure in this study.

5. Nathan Glazer, *American Judaism*, 2nd. edition (Chicago: University of Chicago Press, 1972), p. 12.

6. Howard M. Sachar, *A History of the Jews in America* (New York: Vintage Books, 1992), p. 10.

7. Henry L. Feingold, gen. ed., *The Jewish People in America*, 5 vols. (Baltimore: Johns Hopkins University Press, 1992). See especially, Eli Faber,

A Time for Planting: The First Migration, 1654–1820; and Hasia R. Diner, *A Time for Gathering: The Second Migration, 1820–1880.*

8. Oscar Straus, "America and the Sprit of American Judaism" (1911), in *The American Spirit* (New York: Century, 1913), p. 293. On Straus, see Naomi W. Cohen, *A Dual Heritage: The Public Career of Oscar Straus* (Philadelphia: Jewish Publication Society of America, 1969).

9. The short biography I provide in the following paragraphs is based on Lee M. Friedman, "Judah Monis, First Instructor in Hebrew at Harvard University," *Publications of the American Jewish Historical Society* 22 (1914): 1–24; George Foot Moore, *Judah Monis* (Boston: Massachusetts Historical Society, 1919); Jacob Rader Marcus, *Early American Jewry* (Philadelphia: Jewish Publication Society of America, 1951), vol. 1, pp. 106–110; and Marcus, *The Colonial American Jew, 1492–1776* (Detroit: Wayne State University Press, 1970), vol. 2, pp. 1096–1103.

10. In *Colonial American Jew* (1099) Marcus suggests that Monis may not have been sole author of his discourses. I do not find his arguments—that the texts are too well-written, too informed, and too anti-Catholic—particularly compelling.

11. See Gershon Shaked, *The Shadows Within: Essays on Modern Jewish Writers* (Philadelphia: Jewish Publication Society, 1987), pp. 61–62.

12. See, for instance, Sachar, *History of the Jews in America,* pp. 35–36; and Arthur Hertzberg, *The Jews in America: Four Centuries of an Uneasy Encounter, a History* (New York: Simon & Schuster, 1989), pp. 41–43.

13. See Lee M. Friedman, *Pilgrims in a New Land* (Philadelphia: Jewish Publication Society, 1948); and *Early American Jews* (Cambridge: Harvard University Press, 1934). Monis is mentioned briefly, and in passing, in Friedman's *Jewish Pioneers and Patriots* (Philadelphia: Jewish Publication Society of America, 1947).

14. See fn. 11.

15. Anita Libman Lebeson, *Pilgrim People: A History of the Jews in America, From 1492 to 1974,* rev. ed. (New York: Minerva Press, 1975), p. 85.

16. Philip Roth, "The Conversion of the Jews," in *Goodbye, Columbus and Five Short Stories* (New York: Penguin Books, 1986), pp. 112 and 120.

17. Had we but world enough, and time,
    This coyness, lady, were no crime.
    We would sit down, and think which way
    To walk, and pass our long love's day.
    . . . .
    . . . I would

Love you ten years before the flood,
And you should, if you please, refuse
Till the conversion of the Jews.

18. Roth, in "Jewishness and the Creative Process," *Congress Bi-Weekly* 30 (September 16, 1963): 61.

19. *The Essex Story: A History of the Jewish Community in Essex County, New Jersey* (Newark: Jewish Education Association of Essex County, 1955), p. 3.

20. Ibid., p. 10.

21. "Address of the Newport Congregation to the President of the United States of America," in *The Jew in the American World: A Source Book,* ed. Jacob Rader Marcus (Detroit: Wayne State University Press, 1996), p. 108.

22. Eugene Kohn, Foreword to *American Jewry: The Tercentenary and After,* ed. Kohn (New York: Reconstructionist Press, 1955), pp. v and vi.

23. Judah Pilch, "From the Early Forties to the Mid-Sixties," in *A History of Jewish Education in America,* ed. Pilch (New York: National Curriculum Research Institute of the American Association for Jewish Education, 1969), p. 176.

24. Aaron Soviv, "Self-acceptance of Jewishness by Young Jewish People: A Review of Qualitative and Quantitative Studies," *Jewish Education* 26:1 (1955): 31.

25. Horace Kallen, "Jewish Education and the Future of the American Jewish Community," *Jewish Education* 16:1 (1944): 11.

26. Emanuel Gamoran, "Jewish Education in a Changing Jewish Community," *Jewish Education* 23:3 (1952): 9.

27. Samuel Dinin, "American Influences on Jewish Education," in *American Jewry,* ed. Kohn p. 97.

28. Alexander M. Dushkin, "Towards an American Jewish Education," *Jewish Education* 13 (1941): 18.

29. Gamoran, "Jewish Education in a Changing Jewish Community," p. 9; Dinin, "American Influences on Jewish Education," p. 117; and Pilch, "From the Early Forties to the Mid-Sixties," p. 125.

30. Kallen, "Jewish Education and the Future of the American Jewish Community," p. 11.

31. Dinin, "American Influences on Jewish Education," p. 113.

32. Edward A. Nudelman and Zalmen Slesinger, "The Personnel Problem in Jewish Education," *Jewish Education* 26:1 (1955): 6.

33. Dushkin, "Towards an American Jewish Education," p. 20.

34. Dinin, "American Influences on Jewish Education," p. 118.

35. Gustave Klausner, "Changing Requirements of the Jewish Educational Program in the American Communities," *Jewish Education* 13 (1941): 15.

36. Jack J. Cohen, "New Emphases in Jewish Education," *Jewish Education* 26:1 (1955): 16. Emphasis added.

37. Mordecai M. Kaplan, "The Belief in God and How to Teach It," *Jewish Education* 12 (1940): 103.

38. Mordecai Halevi, "Divergent Formulations of Objectives in American Jewish Education," *Jewish Education* 25:3 (1954–1955): 16.

39. Irving Malin and Irwin Stark, Introduction to *Breakthrough: A Treasury of Contemporary American-Jewish Literature* (New York: McGraw-Hill, 1964), p.1.

40. Friedman, *Pilgrims in a New Land*, p. 8. See also Friedman's several addresses to the American Jewish Historical Society, issued by the society in pamphlet form: "The Significance of American Jewish History" (1949); "Know Thyself: A Program for American Jewish History" (1950); and "E Pluribus Unum: Unity in Diversity" (1951).

41. Marcus, *Early American Jewry*, vol. 1, p. vii.

42. Salo Wittmayer Baron, "American Jewish History: Problems and Methods," in *Steeled by Adversity: Essays and Addresses on American Jewish Life*, ed. Jeanette Meisel Baron (Philadelphia: Jewish Publication Society of America, 1971), p. 66.

43. Oscar Handlin, *Adventure in Freedom: Three Hundred Years of Jewish Life in America* (New York: McGraw-Hill, 1954), pp. viii–ix.

44. Baron, "Some of the Tercentenary's Historic Lessons," in *Steeled by Adversity*, p. 473.

45. Lebeson, *Pilgrim People*, p. ix.

46. Edward A. Nudelman, "The Tercentenary and the Jewish School," *Jewish Education* 25 (fall 1954): 4.

47. *Essex Story*, p. 5.

48. See Kramer, "Emma Lazarus Discovers America in '1492.' "

49. *Essex Story*, pp. 3 and 6.

50. Klausner, "Changing Requirements of the Jewish Educational Program in the American Communities," p. 15.

51. Friedman, *Pilgrims in a New Land*, p. 3.

52. *The Essex Story*, p. 5.

53. Benjamin Colman, *Discourse Had in the College-Hall at Cambridge, March 27, 1722 Before the Baptism of R. Judah Monis* (Boston, 1722). Colman's discourse was entitled, "Moses a Witness unto Our Lord, Jesus Christ." Monis's discourses are included in the volume.

54. Roth, "Conversion of the Jews," pp. 108–109.

55. Will Herberg, "The 'Chosenness' of Israel and the Jew of Today," *Midstream* 1 (1955): 83.

56. Arnold M. Eisen, *The Chosen People in America: A Study in Jewish Religious Ideology* (Bloomington: Indiana University Press, 1983), p. 4.

57. Philip Roth, "Jewishness and the Younger Intellectuals: A Symposium," *Commentary* (April 1961): 46.

58. Ibid., p. 46.

59. See Arthur A. Cohen, *The Myth of the Judeo-Christian Tradition* (New York: Schocken, 1971); and Abba Hillel Silver, *Where Judaism Differed* (New York: Macmillan, 1957). See also, Trude Weiss-Rosmarin, *Judaism and Christianity: Their Differences* (New York: Jonathan David, 1943).

60. Roth, "Jewishness and the Younger Intellectuals," p. 46.

61. Roth, "The Jewish Intellectual and Jewish Identity," *Congress Bi-Weekly* 30:12 (September 16, 1963): 21.

62. Roth, in "Jewishness and the Younger Intellectuals," p. 46.

63. Roth, in "The Jewish Intellectual and Jewish Identity," p. 21.

64. Leslie Fiedler, "The Christian-ness of the Jewish American Writer," in *Fiedler on the Roof: Essays on Literature and Jewish Identity* (Boston: David Godine, 1991), p. 59.

65. Ibid., pp. 66 and 69.

66. Fiedler, "What Can We Do about Fagin: The Jew-Villain in Western Tradition," *Commentary* 7 (1949): 411–418.

67. John Hollander, "The Question of Identity," *Midstream* 4 (1958): 85.

68. See Alfred Kazin, in *The Writing of American Jewish History*, eds. Moshe Davis and Isidore S. Meyer (New York: American Jewish Historical Society, 1957), pp. 440–441; and Leslie Fiedler, "Prophet Out of Israel" and "On Living With Simone Weil," in *To the Gentiles* (New York: Stein and Day, 1972), pp. 5–35.

CHAPTER TEN

The African American and Israeli "Other" in the Construction of Jewish American Identity

Emily Miller Budick

In 1975 in *Commentary*, a Jewish American historian named Stanley Elkins published an article entitled "The Slavery Debate," a review of twenty years of scholarship in the field of black history.[1] As important as the subject of the article is the fact of its appearance in *Commentary*. Inaugurated in November 1945, explicitly in response to the Holocaust, as "an act of faith in our possibilities in America," *Commentary* was primarily a forum for contemporary Jewish concerns.[2] Nonetheless, it distinguished itself during the 1950s and 1960s and well into the 1970s with an uninterrupted flow of more than seventy articles concerning race prejudice, civil rights, and, toward the end of that period, black-Jewish relations in the United States. No other topic, save Jewish ones, receives the same kind of extensive treatment as the situation of the American black. Moreover, until the period of black-Jewish tension in the late 1960s, most of these articles, written by Jews, refer very little, if at all, to Jews. Except for black journals such as *Crisis,* the journal of the NAACP, no other journal of the period expressed such a direct commitment to exploring and eradicating racism in the United States. Nor, I must add, are the many prestigious contributors to *Commentary* the only American Jewish intellectuals who involved themselves in issues of race and racism in the years following the war or who, in various ways, marked their interest in race as having something to do with the Holocaust.

I emphasize, from the start, the sterling contribution of the Jewish intellectual community to the issue of civil rights because what follows constitutes, not so much a criticism of that contribution, as an attempt to trace some of its consequences for the construction of Jewish American identity, at least among a certain segment of the Jewish American population. I also want to put up front that, just as my critique proceeds according to the cultural assumptions of my contemporary time and place, so the writers and intellectuals who concern me functioned according to the assumptions of theirs. This means that they wrote out of the spirit of 1960s America, which focused on assimilation for Jews and integration for blacks. I, on the other hand, write, not only at a remove of thirty years, under the sway of American identity politics, but having crossed over from that culture to another culture. As we shall see, the African American "Other" in the construction of Jewish American identity has direct implications for the relationship between some groups of American Jews and the State of Israel.

The Jewish interest in race, as in human rights generally, preceded World War II by several decades. It had as much to do with the Jews' European experience as with their emerging lives in the United States. Many of the original founders and supporters of the NAACP and *Crisis,* as well as many of the most active proponents of unionism, socialism, and communism in the United States, were Jews. And from the start, such Jewish activism had to do with issues of Jewish self-expression. As Irving Howe put it in relation to one of those areas of Jewish endeavor: "socialism, for many immigrant Jews, was not merely politics or an idea, it was an encompassing culture, a style of perceiving and judging through which to structure their lives. . . . Unacknowledged motives were also at work, having less to do with Marxist strategy than our own confused and unexamined feelings about Jewish origins."[3] Involvement in issues of race and black civil rights provided similar outlets for the expression of Jewish values outside the confines of traditional Jewish affiliation, in a process of assimilation hardly unfamiliar to world Jewry.

But as the Holocaust brought the horrors of racism to the forefront of international consciousness and, more problematically perhaps, cast the Jews as *the* victims of racism, and, as at the same time, because of the extermination of six million fellow Jews, the Holocaust produced a pressure on American Jews not so willingly to give up their specifically Jewish identities and cast their lives into some other "encompassing culture," a very particular process of Jewish intellectual self-expression began to emerge in the United States. This self-expression in some measure crystallized around the experience of the American black. A vivid example of this was Stanley Elkins's 1959 study entitled *Slavery,* the defense of which largely inspires his 1975 *Commentary* piece, and which, like his later article, deals with black, not Jewish, history.[4] *Slavery* makes a move in relation to Jewish history that reflects many similar Jewish moves and that becomes decisive for black-Jewish relations in the United States and for Jewish self-identity: it deals indirectly with Jewish issues by dealing directly with black issues.

Elkins's book was intended as nothing less than a major address to the issue of black civil rights. It set out to lay to rest, once and for all, any romantic defense of plantation slavery. In an effort to achieve this purpose Elkins recovered the myth of the black "Sambo." "Sambo," he attempted to show, was not a feature either of African biology or even of culture. Rather it was the direct result of what Elkins called the "dehumanizing, infantilizing effects of plantation slavery." In order to validate this point, Elkins educed an analogy to the Nazi death camps of the Second World War. This analogy sparked the controversy that turned the motives of Elkins's study virtually on their head. Rather than a voice allied with blacks in the struggle against oppression, Elkins's book was viewed as one more indecorous assault against blacks by white and, in particular, Jewish intellectuals. Had Elkins's analogizing between slavery and the Holocaust remained purely academic, perhaps the consequences would have been less severe. But Elkins's insights were immediately taken up by Daniel Patrick Moynihan in what became the extremely controversial "Moynihan Report." They punctuated as well several major civil rights addresses by President Lyndon Johnson, starting a chain of black and Jewish entanglement that evoked the wrath of quite a number of prominent black intellectuals. Elkins's book placed the Holocaust at the center of American thinking about racism. More problematically, perhaps, it placed it at the center of a form of Jewish thinking about Jews.

Part of the problem for blacks was simply the slight offered in describing them as infantilized and dehumanized by what was in Elkins's view their camplike experience. This is like the offense (also inspired by Holocaust analogizing) offered by Norman Podhoretz in the article which, in Podhoretz's words, had something in it to offend everyone. In "My Negro Problem, and Ours" Podhoretz wonders aloud whether Jewish survival was worth the life of a single Jewish child in the Second World War. He concludes that, while he could understand why once Jews wanted to maintain their separate identity, he was no longer *sure* he saw the reasons in the United States and he could certainly not see *any reason whatsoever* for blacks to maintain racial integrity. His solution to the problem of racism (it was Norman Mailer's, Leslie Fiedler's, and Hannah Arendt's as well) was miscegenation, intermarriage. Blacks, he suggests, must disappear as blacks, an idea that was as distasteful to blacks as the analogous argument, made famous in contemporary intellectual history by Jean-Paul Sartre, was to Jews.[5]

But more fundamentally what blacks are responding to in the Jews putting the Holocaust at the center of their thinking about civil rights—and this is the major black insight into processes of Jewish self-definition—is the implicit assumption that the example of the Jews is more primary and basic to understanding racism than the example of the blacks, even in America. This assumption, on the parts of Jews, reaches back into the long history of Jewish universalism, which sees the Jew as the prototype of human suffering. Take the following apparently inoffensive statement by Bernard Malamud, which expresses the perspectives of quite a number of American Jewish intellectuals: "I try to see the Jew as a symbol of the tragic experience of man existentially. . . . I try to see the Jew as universal man. Every man is a Jew though he may not know it."[6] Such a statement contains more than a little of what Ralph Ellison, in relation to a statement of Irving Howe's, labels "Olympian authority." Under the guise of universal brotherhood, "Jew" becomes the essential, transcendentalized category of the human. Indeed, Malamud is also reminding his readership that the original figure of the suffering Christ, which appears everywhere in Malamud's writing and is implicit here as well, was a Jew, not a Christian. Judaism preceded Christianity. It produced it.

Malamud's universalization and transcendentalization of the Jew, in other words, hovers very close to a claim of origination and priority. It turns the Christian universe upside-down or, perhaps, simply, restores it to what is, from the Jewish perspective, its proper balance. If the Christian move in relation to Judaism is supercessionist, the Jewish move is the reassertion of its originary status, a reclamation, in revised form, of the idea of the Chosen People. Jewish Marxism, even in its aesthetic rather than political version, concealed similar assumptions of chosenness, now brought to bear, in the period of the civil rights struggle, on black as well as white Americans.

The problem with this kind of Jewish rhetoric is not simply, as the black intellectual Harold Cruse had already pointed out in the 1960s, that while "one cannot deny the horror of the European Jewish holocaust . . . for all practical purposes . . . *Jews have not suffered in the United States.*"[7] Rather, what it comes down to for

Cruse and others is, as James Baldwin puts it, that "the Jew's suffering is recognized as part of the moral history of the world and the Jew is recognized as a contributor to the world's history: this is not true for blacks. . . . The Jew is a white man, and when white men rise up against oppression they are heroes: when black men rise they have reverted to their native savagery. The uprising in the Warsaw ghetto was not described as a riot, nor were the participants maligned as hoodlums."[8] Baldwin's formulation at least slightly overstates the case, especially since what was emphasized in the immediate postwar period was not Jewish heroism but victimization. Nonetheless the legitimacy of his insight, particularly as it pertains to Jewish self-perceptions, is born out by, one would have to say, an uncharacteristically thoughtless moment in Elkins's otherwise very cautious study of slavery. The moment occurs as Elkins is trying, quite valiantly, to quell the incredulity of his readers that a mere institution (even as horrible a one as slavery) could produce such personality-transforming consequences as he is observing in African Americans. Therefore, Elkins produces the image of the camp Jews to testify to the possibility of such dehumanization and infantilization. The Jews of Europe, Elkins asserts by way of explanation, were "people in a full state of complex civilization, . . . men and women who were not black and not savages."[9]

This assumption of Jewish superiority, in a text dealing with black civil rights, in which a Jewish scholar marks himself as Jewish, *not* through explicit self-reference, but though using examples from Jewish history in order to talk about black history, lies behind many Jewish American intellectual assertions in the 1950s and 1960s. This includes one of the most famous and indeed stunning moments in black-Jewish relations, when Irving Howe, in defense of Richard Wright as the quintessential black writer, enters into dialogue with Ralph Ellison in such a way as to produce from Ellison the charge that Howe, the Jew, speaks with just the presumption of white superiority that Howe's Jewish liberalism is supposed to oppose. The point of Howe's article "Black Boys and Native Sons" is that black people have no choice but to write as blacks: "How could a Negro put pen to paper," asks Howe, "how could he so much as think or breathe, without some impulsion to protest, be it harsh or mild, political or private, released or buried? . . . To write simply about 'Negro experience'," he continues, "with the aesthetic distance urged by the critics of the fifties, is a moral and psychological impossibility."[10]

One might think that Howe's position is purely the expression of his political, Marxist aesthetic. Ellison, however, understands otherwise. He realizes that Howe's insistence that blacks speak as blacks and about blacks, at the very moment that he, Howe, is demonstrating through his own writing, in this article and elsewhere, that Jews no longer need to speak as Jews or about Jews, produces an asymmetry that itself expresses racial bias, the same asymmetry expressed in the decision of a Jewish historian like Elkins to write about slavery rather than about the Holocaust in terms that nonetheless compare slavery to just that Jewish event: "My reply to Howe," Ellison writes in the second of his installments in their four-part exchange,

> was neither motivated by racial defensiveness nor addressed to his own racial identity. It is fortunate that it was not, for considering how Howe identifies himself in this instance, I would have missed the target, which would have been embarrassing. Yet it would have been an innocent mistake because in situations such as this many Negroes, like myself, make a positive distinction between "whites" and "Jews." . . . I feel uncomfortable whenever I discover Jewish intellectuals writing as though *they* were guilty of enslaving my grandparents, or as though the *Jews* were responsible for the system of segregation. . . . The real guilt of such Jewish intellectuals lies in their facile, perhaps unconscious, but certainly unrealistic, identification with the "power structure." Negroes call this "passing for white."[11]

Howe later affirms that "in his exchange with Ellison he was not approaching their discussion from any Jewish standpoint." Still, Ellison is wrong on one account. He imagines that Howe wants to pass for white. Howe, however, is not so modest. He is, rather, staking a claim of superiority to whites and blacks both, and he is staking this claim for cultural authority on the place he occupies outside of and above American or even Western culture. For this reason Howe, who is, of course, Jewishly identified elsewhere, ends his part of the exchange with Ellison by supporting his arguments with the example of Yiddish writers. Like Elkins, however, the choice to go to Jewish materials is precisely *not* grounded in any self-identification on the part of the writer of the essay: "It is not, after all," Howe concludes his piece, "as if these problems were unique to the Negro writers. In Yiddish literature, the main tradition has, for obvious reasons, been one of national outcry, humanist expression, social protest. . . . The great themes of writers," Howe goes on, "are not those which they choose, but those which choose them." In the exchange between Ellison and Howe (as in the fictional restaging of it in Malamud's novel *The Tenants*), the struggle between intellectual blacks and Jews in America is for a position of cultural authority, where one is finally permitted to speak without hyphenation in, or as, the voice of, the culture itself.

But there was, as I have already suggested, another pressure on American Jewish intellectuals in the 1950s and 1960s, which exactly mediated against their dissolving the specificities of their Jewishness, even to transcendentalize them. And this other pressure, the pressure not to permit Hitler's Final Solution to succeed even on the cultural level, produced a further attraction to African Americans and to their culture. The result was a further problematizing not only of black-Jewish relations but also of the construction of Jewish American identity. Though most readers will likely not remember Philip Roth's 1959 *Goodbye, Columbus* this way, the book, like a large number of Jewish-authored fictions reaching back into the 1940s, is virtually obsessed with the American black: "Over the next week and a half," Neil tells us concerning the major events of the book, "there seemed to be only two people in my life, Brenda and the little colored kid [in the Newark library] who liked Gauguin."[12] Once one has noted (or recalled) the novel's deep investment in the African American experience, it becomes fairly easy to interpret the ostensible intention of the novel's references; and this intention nicely corresponds to the dynamics evidenced in Elkins's and Howe's relation to the black experience. What attracts Neil to the little boy, as to the Patimkins' black maid Carlota, with whom he feels a deep "kinship," is the position of outsidership and powerlessness that Neil feels himself to share with them (67). Following this line of thinking, Roth constructs the novella in such a way as to produce an image of the Jewish American as, like the American black, a marginalized outsider. Insofar as the novella participates in a tradition of such American literary representations of alienation and outsidership, this means that Roth is also claiming for the Jew, rather than for the black, the role of prototypical American antihero. Ironically, this is the position that black writers will reclaim for themselves, sometimes in explicit opposition to the Jews, in the 1970s and 1980s.

For if there are similarities between the black and Jewish situations, there are also, this novella knows, significant differences. These differences permit, indeed they produce, a transcendentalization of the Jewish position, an implication, verging on an insistence, that the Jewish experience constitutes the paradigm of which the black experience is a lesser reflection. Barely has the novella begun when Neil phones that first and most famous proto-type of the Jewish American Princess Brenda Patimkin and launches into his "you-don't-know-my-name-but-I-held-your-glasses-for-you-at-the-club" "speech." Naturally enough, Brenda asks Neil what he looks like, producing the following exchange between them: "I'm . . . dark," he answers; "Are you a Negro?" she responds. "No," he replies. Pages later the conversation repeats, in even more trun-cated form. Asked what his cousin looks like, he responds: "She's dark—" "Is she—" "No" (14–17).

This "No" is as painful as it is decisive. On the one hand, and quite admirably, it registers, among other things, what the novella elsewhere recognizes as well: the assimilationist advantage pos-sessed by the Jews. This advantage obliges them to sympathize and assist blacks in their struggles. For this reason, Neil devotes himself in the library to making sure that the little colored kid is accorded all rights and privileges, quite over the racist objections of his non-Jewish superior. But, on the other hand, it is exactly this advantage, predicated on the racial consanguinity between whites and Jews, and their shared historical and cultural backgrounds, which produces problems for Jews, both in their relationship with blacks and in their own self-definition.

For Jews their likeness to whites (culturally as well as ge-netically) constitutes the basis for their losing ethnic specificity. At the same time, it forms the basis for their superiority over blacks, and, as importantly, their attraction to them: for blacks do not have to worry in the same way as do Jews about losing their ethnic or racial marker. It is the paradox of the possibility of assimilation that must be resisted that locates the special cul-tural work performed by the black Other in the construction of American Jewish intellectual identity. Anticipating what has now become a commonplace in understanding black-white relations in the United States, Roth exposes the phenomenon that Ishmael Reed has called "cultural tanning."[13] This is the desire of white people to fantasize themselves as racially Other, and thus to partake of what they perceive to be the physical prowess of the racial Other, at the same time that they vigorously deny this desire and devalue it. Following is Neil's (I'd say it's Roth's as well) description of Brenda and of her fellow Jewish suburbanites, which captures, and thereby critiques, just this desire for, and denigration of, blackness:

[Brenda] wore a black tank suit and went barefooted, and among the other women, with their Cuban heels and boned-up breasts, their knuckle-sized rings, their straw hats, which resembled immense wicker pizza plates and had been purchased, as I heard one deeply tanned woman rasp, "from the cutest little *shvartze* when we docked at Barbados," Brenda among them was elegantly simple, like a sailor's dream of a Polynesian maiden, albeit one with prescription sun glasses and the last name of Patimkin. (19)

Roth's insight into, let's call it "Jewish racial consciousness," is powerful. Yet Roth's novel participates in exactly the dynamic of cultural tanning it exposes. Even in this passage, the purpose of the novel's critique is as much to produce the positive portrait of Brenda as a "Polynesian maiden" (at least from Neil's point of view) as it is to satirize the New Jersey suburban matrons. More importantly, as Roth sets up the story, the African American child in the library, in love with the pictures of Gauguin, represents, not only to Neil, but within the structure of the novel itself, a vitality absent from white America, and most especially from Jewish America.

In this process of cultural tanning, for Jews and non-Jews both, African American vitality is an aspect of color, which is to say physiology, which is why the novella can so easily blur differences among African Americans, Native Americans, Polynesians, and so on. Indeed, this vitality is more than physical; it is expressly sexual, enabling Roth to slip easily from Neil's appreciation of the child to his infatuation with Brenda, and also serving to link Roth's book to a line of such thinking about the relationship between Jewishness and sexuality, reaching back to Ludwig Lewinsohn and Isaac Rosenfeld. The significance of this for the Jews is that the difference of color is precisely *not* cultural. It is not like the difference that the American Jewish community, as represented by the Patimkins, halfheartedly attempts to maintain through a smattering of Yiddish words and the lukewarm celebration of a few leftover Jewish holidays. For Roth, as for many other Jewish American writers, African Americans served as a vehicle of Jewish ethical commitment in the United States. They *also*, however, marked a vitality and authenticity that Jews not only might emulate but to which they might in some sense apply in order to reinvigorate themselves as Jews. But since "black" was a physical or racial, rather than a cultural or religious category of difference (which is what causes the African American backlash; for blacks in the 1950s and 1960s color is as much a political construction as a biological fact), Jews could, by identifying themselves with black Americans, constitute themselves as a biological, genetic, *racial* group. Like universalism beforehand, this enabled them to bypass some of the more perplexing issues of Jewish identity, such as the relationship to Jewish history or tradition or, increasingly after 1967, to the State of Israel. At the same time, however, it prevented their sacrificing the specificity of their ethnic Otherness. As a racial designation, "black" was a difference that both didn't matter and that wouldn't disappear, guaranteeing the perpetuation both of the Jews as a people and of Jewishness as a moral position, with little conscious, individual effort to preserve such difference, which adherence to something like a faith or even a historical continuity might demand. As one Jewish American intellectual, who also wrote about blacks and Jews in the context of the Holocaust, put it, a Jew is as unalterably a Jew as a pigeon is a pigeon.

Almost in defiance of Nazi racial policies, then, some American Jewish intellectuals took upon themselves a racial definition. But, by linking it to their ethical commitments in the United States, they transformed the racial definition into a moral rather than a physical category. And through identification with black Americans they Americanized that image, making of America the natural habitat for the universal, genetic Jew. Not accidentally, therefore, the racial image of the Jew goes along with an idea of diaspora, as in Isaac Rosenfeld's *Passage from Home* or Malamud's *Tenants* or, most painfully, perhaps, Saul Bellow's *Mr. Sammler's Planet*. This idea of homelessness has direct implications for the Jewish American relation to Israel.

The concealed assumption of Roth's *Goodbye, Columbus*, its idea of the Jew as racial Other, transcendentalized into a universal moral principle of difference, comes clear in Bellow's *Mr. Sammler's Planet*, through the book's astounding reversal of the major dynamic of most prior Jewish American fiction concerning blacks. Like *Goodbye, Columbus*, *Mr. Sammler's Planet* evokes the twin features of the Jewish relationship to blacks: the secular, humanist, ethical commitment; and the shared raciality. Sammler, we are told, is not European but Asian; unlike the Germans, who try to murder him, he is expressly *not* white. But in *Mr. Sammler's Planet* the black character—a pickpocket who, in what is probably the novel's most memorable and disturbing scene, exposes himself sexually to Sammler—in no way represents what Jews must identify with or aspire toward. Also atypical of

Jewish American fiction, Bellow includes on the scene of the novel's action an Israeli character.

The joint appearance of black and Israeli is no coincidence. Both represent what the Jewish American protagonist must resist. Indeed the black pickpocket-sexual pervert and the violent, mentally imbalanced, wife-abusing Israeli function as counterparts both of each other and of Sammler. And they both, at various points in the narrative, serve to recall the Nazis as well, whose violence Bellow thus understands to have evolved from the desire of the Germans after the First World War to rise up from and put to rest what they perceived as their former victimization. Of central importance to Bellow's novel is the question whether surviving persecution in any way produces morally superior human beings, a question especially directed, in this and other of Bellow's writings, at that nation of survivors whose very claim to legitimacy and whose defense of its political and military policies (especially post-1967) depended on its survivor status. The novel's resounding condemnation of 1960s American black power and post-'67 Israeli militarism recovers a Jewish American identity in which the distinctive mark of the Jews is their loyalty, not to nation or people, but to an abstract moral code (still a mark of Jewish superiority) evolved out of the specific conditions of Jewish powerlessness and dependent on an idea of homelessness.

And this returns me to Elkins's 1975 *Commentary* article and to his defense of his book on *Slavery:* "Judging from what others have published over the last few years," writes Elkins, "Ralph Ellison . . . has clearly carried his point on black culture": that it was produced, brilliantly, despite slavery and racism. But, he continues: "culture, under such conditions as those of slavery, is not acquired without a price; the social and individual experience of any group with as little power, and enduring such insistent assaults . . . is bound to contain more than the normal residue of pathology. Any theory that is worth anything must allow for this. It must allow, that is, for damage."[14] Leading into this point, and to lend his sympathy once more to the black cause, Elkins turns again to the example of the Jews. Reviewing a recent lament on the failure of slave insurrection by Orlando Patterson, he suggests that Patterson, "rather like a young Israeli tank sergeant of a decade ago commenting on the Holocaust, is demanding to know why they capitulated, why they were not more heroic."[15]

That Elkins should once again derive his analogy from Jewish history, though this time, post-'67, including Israel in the calculation, reinforces and extends the pattern of his 1959 book, once again applying the example of the Jews to the blacks, making that example more primary and basic, and, at the same time, expressing Jewish consciousness through the expression of sympathy with black history. Indeed, Elkins's point here concerning damage raises important questions concerning Jewish history, which undercut Elkins's methodology: if culture under such pressures as those of slavery or persecution is produced disfigured, then how could Jewish culture have avoided such deformation? How, then, do Jews presume to provide a model for blacks? Here one must point out that a part of the reason why Elkins's and others' analogizing between slavery and the Holocaust goes askew is that these are not, as had been pointed out, comparable events. Slavery took place over generations, with the intention, not of exterminating a people but of destroying their culture and appropriating them for economic benefit. The Holocaust transpired over a short period of time with relatively few designs on the people *except* to annihilate them.[16] When Elkins turns to Patterson and to the Israeli tank sergeant he is completely missing Ellison's point, which has to do with cultural formation, not with armed resistance.

Or, more precisely, perhaps, he is revealing his own major anxiety as a Jew, and his own motivation in turning to black history. This has less to do with understanding black culture than with comprehending the annihilation of a people—his people. For once Elkins has made his point concerning Patterson, one feels obliged to inquire whether a similar desire to understand a lack of Jewish heroism during the Holocaust might not have motivated Elkins's own investigation into plantation slavery, and whether then his conclusions, emphasizing damage rather than resistance, might not represent his own coming to terms with the Nazi extermination, producing something of a reversal of the black critics' cultural perspectives. Certainly, one consequence of Elkins's study, which replicates in terms of Jewish history what African Americans objected to in terms of its presentation of blacks, is that it presents Jews as Sambos, incapable of asserting or defending themselves. Since one traditional anti-Semitic portrayal of Jews represents them as weak in precisely this way, Elkins's unintentional slight against the Jews as deeply reinforces ingrained prejudices as does his unintentional slight against the blacks.

What does Elkins have to gain from the portrayal of a people, either blacks or Jews, as damaged? There is, of course, the reason Elkins himself claims: that to ignore damage is to blind ourselves

to how horrible slavery or anti-Semitism really were. But, especially as the Holocaust comes to epitomize the centuries' long experience of anti-Semitism, and as Elkins himself establishes himself,
through his book, as a force of (Jewish) morality on the American
scene, in part as a consequence of anti-Semitism and the Holocaust, what begins to emerge is just the equation that Bellow is
formulating in *Mr. Sammler's Planet:* that suffering produces moral
consciousness *only* when the next step, the step toward the assertion or claim of power or even resistance, is put aside.

Though it isn't his subject, Elkins produces between the lines
of his studies of slavery an image of the Jew as physically powerless, which has the effect of locating Jewish moral power, the power
that enables Elkins himself to write his book on slavery, in the
Jewish experience of catastrophe. Jewish defeat during the Holocaust emerges for Elkins in the acceptance of damage, which the
Jewish American intellectual now brings to the task of recasting
and reconstructing American history. Elkins, like Patterson, might
want to understand why his people didn't resist. But, unlike
Patterson, he finally wants to celebrate their passivity, in much the
same way that Hannah Arendt does in *Eichmann in Jerusalem* (a
major subject of Bellow's novel), where she first takes the *shtetl*
Jews to task for their powers of organization, which, in her interpretation (as in Bruno Bettelheim's), played directly into Nazi hands,
and then tops off her critique with a denunciation of the State of
Israel for its aggressive legal and military apparatus.

By placing the analogy between the Holocaust and slavery on
the scene of popular debate in the United States, Jewish intellectuals not only prepared the ground for the competition, which
continues today with the Nation of Islam and with members of
the Native American population as well, as to whose holocaust
was worse; they also established the grounds for viewing the assimilated, successful, post-Holocaust Jew as victimizer rather than
victim. In Elkins's text, as in Bellow's, and in Arendt's, and many
others, the Jews function as the repository of moral knowledge
only so long as they preserve their status as victims, without
power, and, significantly, without nation. Though many African
Americans imagined Jewish solidarity in the United States as
having to do with shared Zionistic aspirations, Jewish American
intellectuals, from the early part of the century onward, consistently distanced themselves from the Zionist option. After the
1967 war, the popular Jewish American position vis-à-vis Israel
shifted dramatically. But rather than produce greater solidarity

between Jewish intellectuals and Israel, this move by the community at large forced a more visible, more reasoned resistance to Zionism. Even Irving Howe, who, he tells us, couldn't "suppress a thrill of gratification that after centuries of helplessness Jews had defeated enemies with the weapons those enemies claimed as their own," adamantly maintained that he and the other editors of his journal *Dissent* were "not Zionists; or Jewish nationalists; or by any means uncritical of the state of Israel."[17]

In the years following the ascent of Afrocentricism in the United States and renewed Jewish nationalism in Israel, opposition to black power *and* to Zionism allowed Jewish Americans to assert their national allegiance to the United States as the place that would preserve for racially or ethnically different groups (like themselves, like the blacks) the possibility for their continued existence outside the violent politics of nationalism, as had once, devastatingly, erupted in Nazi Germany and, in their view, now characterized post-'67 Israel. Of course, African Americans did not accept the idea of the United States as outside such politics of nationalist violence, and this becomes in the 1970s and 1980s a major basis for black-Jewish disagreement. The idea of homelessness or diaspora comes to mean radically different things to blacks and to Jews. Jews celebrate their homelessness in an America that made of homelessness a perfect kind of home for Jews. Blacks, however, continued to experience their homelessness as their exclusion from the home that was rightly theirs and that they would reclaim, violently if necessary. Another way of putting this is to say that, first identifying with the black Other, then transcendentalizing that Otherness as inherently Jewish, and finally rejecting in their self-definitions both literal blacks and, significantly, Israelis, who no longer represented to American Jews powerlessness but power, American Jews produced a self-definition of the "Jew" as a condition of radical self-Otherness, in which the essential "Jew," the authentic Jew (like Alain Finkielkraut's "imaginary Jew") is defined by the position of victimhood.

What this means for ex-patriot American Jews like myself, as we reread the familiar texts of our own constructions of Jewish identity, is not only a different relationship to our Israeliness but a revamping of our Jewish Americanism as well. What is the Jew in her nonvictimhood, indeed, in the position of national entity, even conqueror or over other peoples? How does one preserve the rich diasporic heritage of the Jew, so beautifully, if comically expressed by Philip Roth in a novel like *The Counterlife,* and still accede to the possibilities, and problems, of power? How, in other words, does one begin the process of Jewish self-definition, not in analogy to other peoples and their compelling and informative histories, but from within something like autonomy and integrity of Jewish history itself? Though I do not have definitive answers to these questions, isolating the phenomena that account for my own construction of American and Israeli Jewish identity seems to me one place to begin. And this chapter is one contribution to that ongoing, private, and collective, effort.

Notes

1. Stanley M. Elkins, "The Slavery Debate," *Commentary* 60:6 (December 1975): 40–54.

2. *Commentary* 1:1 (November 1945).

3. Irving Howe, *A Margin of Hope,* pp. 11–14 and 47. Writes Grace Paley, "I . . . really felt that to be Jewish was to be a socialist"; quoted in Ezra Mendelsohn, *On Modern Jewish Politics* (New York: Oxford University Press, 1993), p. 94, who also discusses the similar attitudes of Alfred Kazin, Lionel Trilling, and Sidney Hook (93–103). In the same vein see Alexander Bloom's discussion of the New York intellectuals generally in *Prodigal Sons.* In *Writers on the Left: Episodes in American Literary Communism* (New York: Octagon Books, 1979), Daniel Aaron quotes an editorial from a 1927 issue of the *New Masses* (Mike Gold's publication) which depicts the artist in just the kind of Jewishly resonant terms that suggest the transfer from religious to secular identity that I am suggesting: "Are artists people? If you prick an artist does he bleed? If you starve him does he faint?" Aaron also cites Arthur Koestler's comment that Marxism is the extension of the Judeo-Christian tradition. See also Aaron's 1965 essay in *Salmagundi,* 1, pp. 23–36: "Some Reflections on Communism and the Jewish Writer."

4. Elkins, *Slavery: A Problem in American Institutional and Intellectual Life* (Chicago: University of Chicago Press, 1959).

5. Norman Podhoretz, "My Negro Problem—and Ours," *Commentary* 35:2 (February 1963): 93–101.

6. "Interview," *Jerusalem Post Weekly Overseas Edition* (April 1 1968); quoted in Edward A. Abramson, *Bernard Malamud Revisited* (New York: Twayne Publishers, 1993), p. 2.

7. Harold Cruse, *The Crisis of the Negro Intellectual* (New York: Morrow, 1967), pp. 482–483.

8. James Baldwin, "Negroes Are Anti-Semitic Because They Are Anti-White," in *The Price of the Ticket* (London: Michael Joseph, 1985), p. 428.

212 *Emily Miller Budick*

9. Elkins, *Slavery,* p. 89.

10. Howe, "Black Boys and Native Sons," in *A World More Attractive: A View of Modern Literature and Politics* (New York: Horizon Press, 1963), pp. 98–122.

11. Ralph Ellison, "The World and the Jug," in *Shadow and Act* (New York: Vintage Books, 1972), pp. 107–143, originally published as "The World and the Jug: A Reply to Irving Howe," *New Leader* (December 9, 1963): 22–26 and "A Rejoinder," *New Leader* (February 3, 1964): 15–22.

12. Philip Roth, "Goodbye, Columbus," in *Goodbye, Columbus and Five Short Stories* (London: Penguin, 1986), p. 42. Further references are incorporated in the text.

13. *"Writin' is Fightin' "*: Thirty-Seven Years of Boxing on Paper* (New York: Atheneum, 1988), p. 7.

14. "Slavery Debate," pp. 53–54.

15. Ibid., p. 49.

16. Laurence Thomas, *Vessels of Evil: American Slavery and the Holocaust* (Philadelphia: Temple University Press, 1993).

17. Howe and Stanley Plastrik, "Comments and Opinions: After the Mideast War," *Dissent,* pp. 387–384, quoted on p. 387.

CHAPTER ELEVEN

Schizolingua: Or, How Many Years Can Modern
Hebrew Remain Modern?
On the Ideological Dictates of the Hebrew Language

Yitzhak Laor

Zionism as Canaanism

If we did not know the story of the struggle for the revival of
the Hebrew language, and if we were not in fact witnesses of this
revival, we would find it astonishing that, out of a language used
for generations almost exclusively for liturgical purposes, a literary
language should emerge. According to more than one account, the
story begins with Shalom Abramovitch (1835–1917), or as he called
himself, Mendele Mokher Sefarim (Mendele the Bookseller). After
using Hebrew for some time he decided in 1863 to return to Yiddish, because, as he put it, he was "disgusted with the artistic
insincerity of using Biblical Hebrew for expressing the thoughts
and actions of the ghetto Jew." When in 1886 he resumed writing
in Hebrew, the Hebrew he wrote was, according to Haim Rabin,
utterly transformed. Equally important, when he began once again
to employ his special admixture of biblical Hebrew and later Hebrew from the period of the Mishna, there were on the scene of
Jewish writing quite a few other writers, most of them sitting in
Odessa, who were ready to follow his lead. One can begin the long
story of modern Hebrew literature with this event, Mendele's return to the Hebrew language. And one can trace its development in

In memory of my mother, Minna Laor, neé Friedman (1918–1976) the fact that modern Hebrew literature invented not only its language, but its speakers, the Hebrew-speaking Israelis who would come to dominate the scene of Hebrew writing.[1]

So overwhelming was the commitment by the end of the nineteenth century and the beginning of the twentieth century of the new Hebrew writers to the language itself that, for example, in all of his Hebrew poetry Haim Nahman Bialik used only one Yiddish word, and only on two occasions. This is so, notwithstanding the fact that he spoke Yiddish, which was his mother tongue, and that a good deal of his spiritual life took place in Yiddish. He even, on occasion, wrote poems in Yiddish for children. But, while he spoke Yiddish with his wife, for his beloved mistress he sat down and translated his Hebrew poems, word for word, into Russian. He also wrote poems for her in Hebrew, which she did not in the least understand. On one of the two occasions in which he did incorporate a Yiddish word into his Hebrew poetry, he solicited the advice of Ahad Haam, asking his permission to use the impure Hebrew verb *leshnorer* (to beg), taken from the Yiddish *shnorr*. Bialik wrote sublime musical poetry in Ashkenazic Hebrew. He produced a rich language, and a great poetry. And he did this in resistance to his own, more natural, language.

As this example begins to illustrate, the relations between Hebrew as the written language of Jewish culture and the literary language of its writers are complex and ridden with conflict. Equally manifold and contradictory are the relations between modern literary Hebrew and the other languages of the different cultures in which Jews lived and wrote. In the spirit of extreme struggle, the Hebrew that has, over the course of years, emerged as victorious, has cleansed itself of any evidence of the rich heterogeneity upon which a culture, any culture, is built. The decision regarding Hebrew, in other words, was accompanied by a cleansing and purification of the language of all foreign elements. Even after Hebrew had become a spoken language, a large segment of writers still bore feelings of suspicion toward the language of the streets. To put a somewhat tragic spin on this situation, Hebrew literature, we might say, inherited a rift between its cultural and spoken languages that it has been unable to repair. The writers have been incapable of incorporating into their writing spoken language itself, even though, as part of the dominant elite, they took part in constructing and imposing that language.

Take, for example, the attitude to Agnon of the authors belonging to *Dor Hamedinah*, the "State Generation," the writers who began to write and to publish their literature after the founding of the State. If there is one thing that they did not want to or could not learn from Agnon, it was his linguistic heterogeneity, which incorporated the richness of both the Mishnah and Talmud alongside that of the Bible. The result, notwithstanding the revered position held by Agnon in the cultural canon, was a situation in which there is no real continuity between his language and subsequent Hebrew literature. Instead, the literature returned itself to a language freed of linguistic hybridity. It resumed the biblical Hebrew upon which the new grammar of the language of Israeli culture was itself being modeled.

Unanswered Questions

Is the inability (within literature, the press, and the academy) to come to terms with Hebrew speech as it exists, in practice, today, unique to a particular kind of author of a certain social stratum, or to a particular genre? Is it characteristic primarily of mainstream prose fiction, because such fiction, by virtue of its commitment to realistic representation, finds it difficult to integrate into the language of literature the language of speech, which is a kind of compromise between the presumably highborn or pure-bred language of culture and the various languages that have been defeated by it? Are there nonlinguistic reasons that have determined this alienation in Hebrew prose from spoken language? Is there a connection between the ideological position implicit in the struggle to revive the Hebrew language and the predominantly purist position within the Hebrew literary community with regard to the *kulturkampf* that is to be waged against the enemies of this language (enemies, e.g., "exilism" [diasporism], "ultra-orthodoxy," *tchachtchachism* [roughly: the speech of the "uneducated" Sephardic Jews from the working and the lower middle class], "American rot," and so on)? Is Hebrew literature (and not only the academic discipline known as Hebrew Literature) imprisoned within an ideological prison house of words, which is the lot of the linguistic elite in all modern societies, as if the literature were compelled to perform a particular political and cultural function; as if to say, "since the people need to speak a proper language, we will educate them in the course of writing among ourselves, and we will write an 'educated' language not only for purposes of precise communication among ourselves, but because a boorish people is a danger to culture," and so forth? In a society that is so heterogenous, so multilingual, so multi-accented, is not the *cultural* Hebrew of the media, as a bastion in the cultural war, the enemy of literature? Can literature ignore the abundance of speeches surrounding it?

I have no intention of answering these significant questions. I do think that "Enlightenment Hebrew," that is, the high-cultural, written Hebrew as it was produced from the period of the Enlightenment on, had good reasons to blur the boundaries between Eastern European Hebrew literature and the Hebrew literature that migrated to, and took root in, Palestine. The construction of a continuity between the two Hebrew literatures, or two phases in the writing of Hebrew literature, provided the only reasonable justification for seeing this literature as a single canon or tradition, which could be taught, for example, as a university discipline known as Hebrew Literary Studies. In terms of the continuity of Hebrew literature, Eastern Europe predominates as the place from which Hebrew literature takes its origins. This includes even medieval Spain, which Bialik, the Russian Jew and great reviver of modern Hebrew literature, who quit writing once he arrived to Palestine, included within the tradition.

It is in light of this background that one needs to consider, for example, the painful peregrinations, including linguistic ones, of a Sephardic writer like A. B. Yehoshua. Born in Palestine in the 1930s, Yehoshua nonetheless had to "emigrate" to the (Ashkenazi) State of Israel in 1948. Many other Israeli writers of his age, who were also born in the 1930s but of a different, Ashkenazi, background, did not have to go through that emigration. On the one hand, the native-born writer has to adapt himself to the national literature. On the other hand, precisely because the continuity of Hebrew literature is secular, linguistic, and not racially or nationally determined, anyone can join it, given their willingness to adopt its basic linguistic principles. Natan Zach and Yehuda Amichai, Hebrew poets born in Germany, as well as natives of Palestine, both Jews (Yehoshua) and Arabs (e.g., Anton Shammas), can all write literature in the same "victorious" Eastern European Hebrew and thus enter as full-fledged members in the canon of Hebrew literature. The history of those writers who emigrated from Arab countries to Israel and could never adapt to the dominant version of the literary tradition has yet to be written.

The accusation of Canaanism that the national religious circles so much loved, even in the 1970s and 1980s, to hurl against the secular culture, was not a completely baseless fabrication. The manner in which Hebrew chose its separation from diaspora Jewish languages (including traditional Hebrew) and from the language of the uneducated masses was very close in spirit to the real core of Canaanism. The biographical connection of some of the major writers, at one or another phase of their formative years, with the Canaanite movement is only one aspect of the subject. Such writers include Benjamin Tammuz, Yehoshua Kenaz, Amos Kenan, Amos Oz, and A. B. Yehoshua at the beginning of their paths (note also the Canaanite end of Yehoshua's novel *Molcho;* translated into English as *Five Seasons*). What was created as the cultural center in Tel Aviv of the 1930s, the "place" that would define the new culture, was transplanted directly from Eastern Europe. It brought with it a Hebrew that had been renewed in a very specific way, which had first of all an almost uninterrupted link with *Haskalah* Hebrew (Enlightenment Hebrew). The "place" of Hebrew literature is sometimes called "Israel" and sometimes *Eretz Yisrael* (The Land of Israel). Sometimes it is referred to by the name "the national homeland" and sometimes by the claim that there is no other place (*ein makom aher*), notwithstanding the fact that there are other places, even within the geographic unit known as Israel, not to mention in the west and the east of the Jewish people, from Oman to Brooklyn and Berkeley, via Casablanca. The historical study of this "place" has remained in its infancy for too long a period of time, and not by chance. What remains as an open wound in the writing is the inability to produce, within Hebrew literature, a Hebrew that renews itself with the help of the folk languages that exist or were imported to the "place" where the literature took root. What the literature lacks is the richness of a living language, produced by compromise and the bridging between the Hebrew of the Enlightenment and the languages it defeated, such as Arabic, Spanish, Yiddish, Romanian, Polish, and Russian.

The following are some explicitly Canaanite statements by Amos Oz:

> Like any other language, Hebrew has a certain integrity which I'm keen to preserve and protect from modernization. For example, in Hebrew the verb usually sits at the beginning of the sentence. This reflects a form of cognitive hierarchy. What's more important? Ever since the Bible, actions have taken priority: before we discuss where, why, to what end, and to whom you have done something, let's first establish what you actually did. Languages reflect in a very profound way a certain cultural ethos, a system of values. I believe that the Hebraic value system is a good one and I'd like to preserve it.[2]

This essentialism not only exudes the bad odor of nationalism of the type so much loved by nineteenth-century Europe (e.g., Ernest Renan). It also postulates a separate (national) existence for the language, independent of its speakers. During all those long years between the Bible and the establishment of the State of Israel, a unique Hebrew ethos waited for the Jewish people to come and make use of it. This conservatism is, of course, pleasing to the Western ear. One can respond to its romantic longings, even its nationalist demands. In addition to seeing Hebrew as evidence of the miracle of return, one can also experience it as some sort of superior script, analogous to the language of the aristocracy or of the high bourgeoisie. It may also be connected with the concept of Hebraism developed by Matthew Arnold.

But this aristocratic, miraculous language landed in inhabited territory, populated by real, living, speaking people, who dominated the scene with a concert of human voices. Thus, after he declares his intent to preserve "the ethos" of the ahistorical, biblical language, specifically by means of literature, Oz makes these sociological and aesthetic comments:

> This system is under threat not only of modernization and from foreign languages. Hebrew is like a person with loose morals: it has slept around and been influenced by Aramaic, Arabic, Russian, German, Yiddish, English, Polish, and what not. And all these influences have the effect of giving it enormous flexibility. . . . When I write . . . dialogues, I'm just a bystander and I always try to be a truthful bystander. But when it comes to a description or a philosophical or narrative passage, I feel responsible for using and preserving the integrity of the Hebrew language and the values which I believe are inherent in her deeper structure.[3]

Language is gendered here; it "has slept around." In the final analysis she emerges pure, "her deeper structure" preserved by the male author.

More than a decade earlier, at the beginning of the 1970s, Oz had published similar ideas:

> The New Hebrew is—so to speak—a slut in heat. Today she is entirely, so to speak, with you, and yours, and at your feet, ready for any adventure, rejoicing in any daring innovation— and then, in the twinkling of an eye, you are thrown behind her, spread-eagled on your back and slightly absurd, and she is off prowling for new lovers. . . . But she never forgets, not even for

a moment, the prophets and the tannaitic Sages. In all of her goings she betrays them with every passerby . . . and from all her paths they gaze from afar, in the background, like the mountain and the sea.[4]

Here the sexual connotations of Hebrew as a whore stand out even more strongly. In both cases the (male) writer's function is to guard the purity of the language. He is the master, who determines when he will allow the language "to become soiled" and when he prefers that it be "cleansed." It is the phallocentric function of the writer as educator that is paramount. As Jacqueline Rose once put it:

> Oz defines one of his tasks as writer as the preservation of the [sexual] integrity of Hebrew against the dual threat of modernization and foreignness. . . . To read Oz in English is therefore to read a translation of a translation. Or to put it another way, you can already be a translator in your own tongue.[5]

More Questions without Answers

Is there available to the young State of Israel, whose leaders define their task as building the nation, either through aliyah or through the revival of Hebrew, an alternative version of secular Zionism, something other than the Canaanite model? Is there something other than the Ben-Gurionist idea of "a biblical nation that originated in this country" and "our ancient Hebrew to which we must return," which was first expressed in the decision to use the so-called Sephardic pronunciation, and thereafter in the systematic uprooting of everything that was not considered true to purist, biblical Hebrew? Is not the building of a nation "from above" accompanied by a similar construction of a language "from above"? Amos Oz says the following in the continuation of his article:

> Spoken languages are all poor and reedy. Most of the people around me use an active vocabulary of 1000 to 1500 words, and even this little bit is enchained to idiomatic patterns and fashionable expressions that come from overseas. . . . It is my hope that written literature will gradually enrich the spoken language. In the final analysis, the limits of language are [absolute] limits, and what you cannot express in words you are also unable to conceive clearly. The opportunity to express complexity and nuances is [also] the opportunity to enrich life and to live it according to a fine and complex rhythm.[6]

But spoken languages are not all "poor and reedy." This description is perhaps true—due to specific sociological reasons—of the language of the Israeli elite, with all due respect to its military and economic achievements. Further on Oz says: "It may perhaps be possible to run a factory or a tank brigade or foreign policy using only six hundred 'active' words." On the other hand, in the spoken language "it is impossible to court, to argue, to influence the other." Are all spoken languages as impoverished as the Hebrew of the factory or the army?

Twenty years prior to Oz's *Beor hatekhelet haaza* [In the Daring Blue Light], Natan Zach had launched a violent attack on Alterman's poetry, which can help shed light on the problem reflected in Oz's assumptions concerning the Hebrew language. Preferring T. S. Eliot, Ezra Pound, Rainer Maria Rilke, and Georg Trakel over the Russian French symbolism and constructivism that had reigned supreme in the days of Shlonsky and Alterman, Zach, as Gershon Shaked describes it, defined a new poetics characterized by no four-line verses; a more fluid column; irregular rhyme; a free meter; less rigidity in the architecture of the verse; no excessive figurativeness; deflation of the poetic image; opening up to the objects, views, and landscapes of the modern world; a more informal language; rejection of highflown rhetoric; attention to "unrepresentative" side-aspects of a given situation—that is, avoidance of its standard signs and symbols; a tendency to disrupt formal balance; a preference for imaginary and incomplete tensions; a preference for small lyrical forms; the aspiration to make the poetry express some rapport with reality—the poet's biographical reality or his surroundings; continued use of biblical material (but not posture!), sometimes in novel contexts that completely alters its signification; and objection to groups writing in an identical style (regardless of the "stylistic climate").[7]

Zach's assault against Alterman was intended to implicate more than his poetry. Literary Hebrew reached a certain conclusion with the removal from the stage of the Shlonsky-Alterman old guard. This is not the place to discuss the extent to which the "Zachian revolution" was important in terms of what happened to Hebrew poetry from the linguistic viewpoint. But one important aspect of this attack, which has been unfortunately neglected, is relevant to our purposes here: his pointing to the difference between official and unofficial language, and his highlighting of the importance of the latter. Alterman's linguistic innovations, according to Zach, had to do only with Alterman's use of official language:

> We are speaking here primarily of "official" words, without conno-
> tative richness, freshly coined in the workshops of the committees
> for military terms and the language academies, which have found
> themselves a place in the daily press and in military orders-of-
> the-day. Alterman does not hear the way that people actually talk
> in the street, or does not see fit to put it in his poetry.[8]

If this is the significance attached by Oz to the danger of modernization of the language, then he has fallen victim to that same
modernization. Like Alterman, he only agrees to linguistic innovations that come from above. Ironically enough, given Zach's indictment of Alterman, Zach can be seen, in his translations of the
poetry of Allen Ginsberg, to commit almost the identical sin, even
in cases where the Hebrew could easily accept Ginsberg's slang
vocabulary.

Zach's distinction is extremely pertinent for reading the Hebrew prose of "the State Generation," including that of Oz himself.
Oz's spoken language oscillates between the high language in which
it is possible, as he puts it: "to court, to argue, to persuade others,"
and the spoken language, in which it is only possible "to administer
or to command" (i.e., to be part of the ruling elite). From this point
of view, the central Hebrew authors, and not only Amos Oz, have
not deviated from the tried and trusted path: they are only able to
speak of the world through the language of culture, the language
of the library, and of a selective textual continuum.

The spoken Hebrew recorded in literature (dialogues within
prose, or the language used in realistic drama) and Hebrew itself
as a narrative language find it difficult to create what we might
designate a spoken literary language (these distinctions, and more,
I owe to Prof. Itamar Even Zohar). When it is created, it insists
upon being the high literary language of the narrator, which makes
use of four or five types of characters from the low mimetic mode,
who speak poor Hebrew (Oriental Jew/Arab, new immigrant, child,
old man, and recently also the *Shenkinists* [the urban pseudobo-
hemians associated with Shenkin Street in Tel-Aviv]). The rest of
the novel's dialogues—if they are not carried on among these minorities—are generally far removed from the Hebrew spoken by these
same people in the real world. How does a technician, a journalist,
a bank clerk, a writer, a teacher, and a professor in his fifties, speak,
if he is not one of those minorities who speak broken Hebrew?

It is very hard to say on the basis of the literature, for apart
from short comments, answers to questions, and telephone responses,

we do not get this speaking. It is difficult, apparently, for the Israeli self to speak in a natural way in Hebrew literature, beyond brief sentences. In order to speak, she needs to be in the stance of the narrator-writer, which enables them to speak elegantly without sounding improbable, because they are speaking the language of writing. But real people don't speak that way. The readers of American literature among us cannot but envy the tremendous efforts that were expended during the short years of this literature in the construction of languages, and not of a language. It is doubtful whether the democratic revolutions of Europe were as wise in preserving the dominant style in literature as was the American revolution, in creating a "democratic aesthetic obligation": from Mark Twain and Walt Whitman and Herman Melville, via William Faulkner, and through Allen Ginsberg and Raymond Carver and Toni Morrison—the polyphony of languages is certainly connected with a democratic approach unknown to Israelis. The country, not to mention the State, belongs to its citizens.

One Needs to Have Some Small, Modest Loyalty to One's Own Language

Even though the victory of the *Maskilic* Hebrew[9] within Hebrew literature is generally widely hailed, it is important to remember three things:

1. The Hebrew spoken by Israelis is not the same Hebrew as that in which Hebrew literature is written (this is an extreme case of what is generally true of literature worldwide).

2. The victory of "our" Hebrew was, and still is, connected with the uprooting of the languages spoken by Jews (the various forms of Yiddish, the Judeo-Arabic of Iraq or Syria, the Moroccan Arabic, Ladino, and of course the vernacular, spoken languages of their countries of origin).

3. The victorious Hebrew—that is, that version that is predominant in Hebrew literature, which is referred to as correct Hebrew (and from which I myself make my livelihood due to its hegemony in the press)—finds itself involved in an unending struggle against the folk languages, which were never entirely eradicated. This struggle is described in ideological terms by

those charged with the purity of the language. It is, therefore, designated as protection against corruption or against extinction or against levantinization or against Americanization.

At the beginning of his book about Hebrew drama during the period of the national renascence, Gershon Shaked notes the connection between language and ideology. A writer who decided, from the 1880s on, in favor of the Hebrew language, and chose it, from among the various possible competing languages (i.e., Yiddish and/ or foreign, European, languages) as his primary tool, identified with the nationalist, Zionist, movement. The return to the Land was associated with the return to the language. The linguistic tools, which had been prepared by the *Haskalah* (Enlightenment) writers for other purposes, now came to serve this end. From now on, those works that were written in Hebrew, whether their authors identified openly with Zionism or whether they remained outside of its boundaries (like David Frischman), became national assets. Even though this literature was at its best not an ideological literature, and in its poetry and short stories separated itself from any didactic approach, nonetheless it became ideological in practice, as Shaked points out, by its very existence as a living, linguistic, testimony to the rebirth of the nation.[10]

Even More Unanswered Questions

Even today many ordinary human activities in Israel take on (as they also did in the past, as Shaked point out) ideological significance. Hikes in the countryside, for example, are not just hikes, nor is working the land an ordinary sort of labor. The same holds true for paving roads, protecting nature, being victorious in a soccer game, and so forth. Even good-mannered behavior abroad has an ideological function. Can we say with regard to the Hebrew language that the sense of writing in Hebrew as being the fulfillment of some sort of obligation has ceased? And if so, what Hebrew ought to be spoken by those who are mobilized for Hebrew? If Hebrew has a function, what is that function? Does not its function end with the providing of an entrance ticket to Israeli nationality, by means of *Ulpanim* (Hebrew schools for immigrants and other foreigners) and other preparatory courses, which enable people to secure a livelihood in the country? And what is the function of the recruiters who recruit people to this language? Who are they? And has not the cultural elite imprisoned itself within a linguistic garrison just like every other cultural elite?

Rather than answering these questions, I would like to posit a certain assumption: that there is a direct, almost paradoxical, but logical, line connecting the revivers of the language, that is, the writers of Hebrew in Eastern Europe, and their heirs in contemporary Hebrew literature. This is equally true of those who promote *MILEIL,* in which the stress is predominantly on the penultimate syllable, characteristic of the traditional Ashkenazic pronunciation, and *MILRA,* in which the emphasis is on the ultimate syllable, characteristic of the neo-Sephardic pronunciation. Hebrew has obviously changed, and there are descriptions (albeit inadequate ones) of this change. But the revival of the language means that we write in a Hebrew that was revived on our behalf. And this means that Hebrew as a cultural language, that is, as the authentic language of a living culture, remains a cultural rather than a living language. What has become the spoken language remains remote from that cultural language and from the literary language as well.

There are certain absurd aspects to the struggle on behalf of Hebrew. It is enough to listen to children's programs, to animated films, or to radio or television advertisements to experience the absurdity. In the overall context of a language that is filled with non-Hebrew nouns and names of products, or within sentences whose tone is already completely slang, the old rules of Hebrew pronunciation, such as the rules governing weak accents, are quite without rhyme or reason adamantly insisted upon. One can enumerate hundreds of such contexts in which Hebrew acts as if it were still struggling for its very survival. One can even find explicit arguments on behalf of the protection of the language (and on behalf of institutions that exist to protect it) on the Internet. The enemy that occasions such active protection of the language is not the Americanisms, for example, which have penetrated into every language of the world, and that occasionally elicit anger. These Americanisms, in fact, seem to fit in quite well among at least part of the Israeli elite, as well as outside it, whether in the ubiquitous use of the "anyway" form, or "OK" or "bye" or even "yallah, bye," or in the tiresome repetition of "at the end of the day" or "the bottom line" (translated into Hebrew, of course). The enemies of the language that necessitate fierce defense are not those who toss in an occasional colloquialism from outside the language, but, rather, those who do not speak "proper" Hebrew in the "proper" way.

Ironically, this struggle for the already victorious Hebrew language is waged, not specifically among the ultranationalists, but, rather, among avowed liberals. Israeli liberals are extremely sensitive to governmental interference in the private affairs of the nation's citizens or members of the business community. They are far less concerned about official involvement in the (even more private) realm of language. This is no paradox. One is dealing here with cultural legacy. Therefore the presumed owners of this legacy behave in a proprietary fashion, as if a foreign culture among us constitutes a danger to their power. Hegemony in a given society is not acquired by means of money or political power alone. Just as the property owner is afraid of taxes being imposed on his property, so the owner of cultural goods fears a challenge to his power, which is the power to define the culture.

Nily Mirski is a very well-known and outstanding translator. Among her famous works are translations of Anton Chekhov, Nikolay Gogol, Fyodor Dostoevsky (from the Russian), Thomas Mann, Fontane (from the German), and several other French writers as well. From this point of view, she is an emblematic figure. Her work is, without doubt, deserving of great praise. I love her translations from nineteenth century literature, which exhibit a great talent for finding Hebrew equivalents for other languages. Yet Mirski is a representative of the younger generation of Hebrew purists, and her work, which includes translations from three languages, may be described as a corpus of *Maskilic* Hebrew. She inherited this Hebrew from the generation of the national renascence, and she has devoted much time and energy to perfecting it.

In the September 20, 1996 issue of *Ha'Ir*, the local Tel Aviv weekly, she gave an interview in which she expressed her opinion concerning the cultural situation in the Netanyahu era. Most of her expressions and experiences were, or so it seemed from reading the interview, the result of watching news on television. Among other things, together with some rather racist comments concerning Oriental Jews, Mirski made several rather categorical comments about the Hebrew language. Referring to secular culture, she complained quite rightly of the automatic television images that juxtapose yeshivas against the coffeehouses and discotheques of the secular community. But thereafter, when asked to express her opinion of religious culture, she rapidly passed over what is understood by the *Haredim* [Ultra-Orthodox] themselves as their own culture, indeed, did not even take an interest in it, and quickly went on to condemn their world for failing to meet the test of linguistic correctness:

> When I hear Hebrew spoken by Yeshivah students, and not only by [newly religious] "penitents," but even by rabbis and people who grew up there—my stomach turns over. People who sit all day studying the sources—it's true that they deal mostly with the Talmud, which is written in Aramaic, but thank God the Mishnah is written in Hebrew and the Bible is in Hebrew—so perhaps this is a wonderful value to which to be devoted. . . . One ought to have at least some small and modest loyalty to one's own language. What about that? When they open their mouths what they speak is quite simply incorrect Hebrew, filled with errors, poor, with a small vocabulary, a non-existent store of imagery, and with primitive arguments, if you'll pardon me saying so. Most of what you hear, I won't say all of them, there are people there from whom one can learn something, but that is the dominant speech there.

Let's ignore the moment where her stomach turns over. In the first part of the essay Mirski protested against the stereotypical images provided by the media: "they" learn and "we" sit in coffeehouses. Now things are turned around: "they" are inarticulate and we, the secular, are the people with a rich Hebrew. Does this include our politicians? Or the academicians, who need to be rewritten for publication?

Mirski's remarks in the other parts of the interview express patience and sensitivity with regard to strangers, non-Jews, and Palestinians. But here, as everywhere else where the liberal Israeli discourse is dominant, there is also exposed, as the flip side of the coin, lack of tolerance toward those Jews who are not one of us. One can see here the hatred of the Israeli liberal for heterogeneity. Whatever is not us is tolerated only when it does not threaten our cultural monad. But whatever belongs to us (i.e., Jews-Israelis) is required to meet very strict criteria, in order not to spoil the rich identity that we have attained, apparently, over the long cultural process of our history.

There was good reason for Mirski's failure to enumerate the corpora from which she expected the rabbis and yeshiva students to learn Hebrew: Bible, Mishnah, and Talmud. These are the corpora that were used by official modern Hebrew in the order in which Mirski was taught that they should be learned. And not for naught did she fail: first, because Dostoevsky, or Gogol, or Marcel Proust, or James Joyce, or Thomas Mann, play a more important function than the Baal Shem Tov or the Maggid of Mezerich in our cultural schizophrenia, in our complex vacillation between East and West, and between the concept of secularism and the (Christian) concept of the West, whether secular or not; second, because a large portion of the religious, or ultra-Orthodox, corpus did not at all grow out of what is called correct "Hebrew," that is, the Hebrew of the *Haskalah*. Rather they belong to the history of Hebrew as a language based upon the Mishnah and the Talmud. One needs a great deal of arrogance and prejudice, and very little modesty, not to hear in the language of the rabbis and the *Haredim* (even if they say the most outrageous things in relation to democracy or equality of women and/or Palestinians) the long tradition of *Halakhic* Hebrew, which was generally speaking rejected by the Hebrew of the *Haskalah*, and thereby relegated to the realm of the foreign.

Precise illustrations of these competing Hebrews and their formal elements are, of course, impossible to render in English translation. But it may be sufficient to bear in mind that modern Hebrew, like biblical Hebrew, is very strict about gender agreement between the noun-phrase subject and the verb of the predicate and agreement also between a noun and its adjective. *Haredi* Hebrew is not consistent in terms of gender agreement, especially in written texts. The noun subject might be in masculine whereas its verb is in feminine, and vice versa. This Hebrew, as we have said, does not belong to the version of Hebrew that we use. But it is part of a culture which, to our good fortune, has not been lost. From the viewpoint of linguistic heterogeneity, it is part of those languages that do not belong to our language, whose grammar is poor. But when scholars of Hebrew literature trouble to emphasize the continuity of Hebrew literature between Abraham Mapu and David Grossman—and the curricula of Departments of Hebrew Literature and of teachers' seminaries run along the span of this continuity—when they say that the formula of literary Hebrew as we (both writers and readers) use it today, that selfsame reasonable and correct sort of language employed by Mendele, M. J. Berdyczewski, Aharon Reuveni, Y. H. Brenner, S. Yizhar, Amos Oz, and David Grossman, was created along this continuum, they are saying, essentially, three things:

1. Whatever does not belong to the flow of belletristic literature does not belong to the flow of Hebrew literature, and therefore the stories of wonder workers, Hasidic literature, homiletic and

ethical literature, the later (i.e., high medieval and later) *midrashim,* and other texts that were written in Hebrew over the course of many centuries, do not really belong to Hebrew literature.

2. The break in this continuum, between those born abroad and those born in Palestine (*Eretz Yisrael,* i.e., the Land of Israel), between Europeans and Israelis, a break connected with immigration, that is, with the establishment of the State (and with the creation of Israeli literature, from the 1930s on), is not sufficiently important to learn from it several of the things connected with this break; as a result, the problematics involved in a new language are swept under the rug. This is the case, for example, with the issue involved in the so-called Sephardic or *MILRA* pronunciation (i.e, with stress on the ultimate syllable), which turns a great deal of Bialik's poetry—which is accepted as a part of Hebrew poetry but is written in Ashkenazi Hebrew—into poetry utterly lacking in music. To the myriads of students who do not at all know that poetry—whether rhythmically balanced or not—is syntactic music having a verbal content, and not a monologue in short lines, Bialik's poetry can only produce a painful grating of the ears.

3. Jews, such as the Oriental Jews, who developed another language (and/or any other version of Hebrew), had to join a language that had undergone other processes of revification of a different nature. Hence they too needed to join Hebrew literature as if from outside it. Their language became a different language within Hebrew literature, reflecting as well their image within the literature, when they were reflected in the literature at all, as also being different.

"Against the Study of History"

Hebrew is not the only language that originated in a cultural language and whose great achievement lay in its transformation into a spoken language. Italian, for example, is also a young, synthetic language. The Piedmont liberators of Italy were unable to speak to those whom they liberated. Some even claim that Mazzini's impassioned speeches were delivered in French. Italian was expeditiously built up as a spoken language by breathing life into the Florentine dialect. Even though the liberators and their armies were Piedmonts and their dialect was far removed from this dialect, the Tuscan of Florence was specifically chosen for the purposes of the new language because it brought with it tremendous cultural capital. The works of Francisco Petrach, Boccaccio Boccaccio, and Dante all utilized the spoken Tuscan of Florence. Thus a corpus of literary texts underlies the synthesis we know as proper Italian, even though anyone listening to Italian knows that this synthesis produces strange linguistic consequences for the nation, such that even buying a watermelon in Rome (literally rendered: "bring a watermelon after you finish work") needs a different vocabulary in Padua or Torino. The dominant, victorious version of language is that of political society, of the communication media, and of the news and advertisements on the commercial channels.[11]

Fascism attempted, with all its strength, to suppress the languages that were spoken by the modern Italians between Sicily and Piedmont. Is there a connection between the purist demands on the part of the Fascist regime to speak only Italian, and the general political ideology of fascism? Is there a connection between the prohibition, in Franco's Spain, against using the dialects of Galicia, Andulasia, Catalan, and the Basque region, with the concomitant imposition of the Castellan tongue upon all Spaniards, and other elements of Francist ideology? Here, too, I do not intend to answer my questions. But there is no doubt that there is a relationship between such political ideologies and the establishment of an ahistorical ideal language, placing the nation—that same placeless abstraction with that selfsame language lacking a throat to speak it—above the lives of individuals and above the speech of actual human beings, who talk, stutter, and prefer the language of their father above that of the judge or the officer of the region.

The historian Eugen Weber has remarked that the Third Republic "found a France in which French was a foreign language to half of the population."[12] Still in 1728, the Academy at Marseilles announced that it could not hold public meetings because the public did not understand French.[13] But already by then the middle class in the cities spoke French, and here too French (Parisian) literature, primarily that of the seventeenth century, performed an important function in transmitting *the* language and in uprooting the nonofficial languages. The archives of the modern French state, says Weber, are filled with complaints by regional police supervisors, supervisors of the Ministry of Education, and school principals, testifying to their impotence in Paris' confrontation with the

various different languages. On the other hand, none of these languages succeeded in standing up against the center. Modernization
eradicated the various folk languages.

And indeed, French was the language of the Declaration of the
Rights of Man and of the Citizen, as fixed by the National Assem-
bly itself in 1792, and by virtue of those same principles of human
and citizen rights, the French language was imposed upon all the
citizens of France, from the French Revolution on. One who wishes
to do so may find within this contradiction the same break found
by the critique of totalitarianism (by Theodor Adorno and Max
Horkheimer) or by the French poststructuralists vis-à-vis modernism: the imposition of a particular center in the name of a democratic universalism. In any event, language instruction became an
important aspect of French acculturation. Only since the end of the
First World War, claims Weber, have the last three great dialects—
Provencal, Flemish and Bartonist—disappeared. Even more important is his description of what took place with the victory of French:

> Notably in the center and the south there developed a whole series
> of compromises between official or school French, on the one hand,
> and the local speech, on the other: buffers between patois and French,
> drawing on both, applying the structures and accent of patois to
> French, changing the meaning of terms in order to use them in
> vernaculars that ran from frenchified patois to patoisant French.[14]

The ignorance of the native-born, Hebrew-speaking Israeli of
the tension between dialects and their origins as different languages that were annexed by the dominant language, is connected
with the complete ahistoricity of the discipline of cultural studies
in Israel, at least insofar as it is concerned with the discussion of
our Israeli culture. At a certain stage of idealization, even in Europe, where the unification of a national language is also still new,
and where the battlefield is still full of culture-corpses (e.g., in
France), sociolinguistic theories were formulated that attempted to
explain dialects as break-offs of the dominant language, and not
the opposite, a kind of Babel anarchism that took place sometime
in the dawn of the nation.

The denial of the languages that lie beneath the national language is not characteristic of only one culture. Nor it is to blame
simply for the uprooting of human languages. It is guilty of far
more serious crimes as well. The nation is composed of many denied, eradicated places: villages and minorities as well as languages,

which are in truth the very soil upon which the modern nation grew. To avoid catastrophe and ensure the existence of the nation, the historian and philologist Ernest Renan ordered the French to forget. "Forgetting," wrote Renan more than a hundred years ago:

> is a crucial factor in the creation of a nation, which is why progress in historical studies often constitutes a danger for [the principle] of nationality. Indeed, historical inquiry brings to light deeds of violence which took place at the origin of all formations, even of those whose consequences have been altogether beneficial. Unity is always effected by means of brutality.

He continues:

> Yet the essence of a nation is that all individuals have things in common, and also that they have forgotten many things. No French citizen knows whether he is a Burgundian, an Alan, a Taifale, or a Visigoth, yet every French citizen has to have forgotten the massacre of Saint Bartholomew, or the massacres that took place in the Midi in the thirteenth century.[15]

Weber wrote at a distance of nearly one hundred years from Renan's nationalist preaching on behalf of forgetting. He has eloquently described what has been lost to the various languages of Europe, that is, what their speakers have forgotten and also what remains to them. Does the writer who lives and writes Hebrew in Israel, even if he belongs to the elite and identifies with the language that erases the others, gain anything by turning a deaf ear or a dull tongue to the languages that have been made to disappear?

One way or another, these former, virtually forgotten languages reemerge, albeit with great difficulty, within the literature. Some writers make extensive use of Oriental images, in which they allow themselves to build up inarticulate or funny dialogues (Amos Oz in *Kufsah Shkorah* [Black Box] and Yehoshua Kenaz in *Hitganvut Yehidim* [Heart Murmur]). A. B. Yehoshua circumvents the subversive Sephardism of *Molcho* by means of free and indirect speech. This is the most widely used means in modern Hebrew literature, its purpose being to bypass the deep split between the lack of a written form of spoken language and actual spoken language. Yaakov Shabtai's *Zikhron Devarim* [Past Continuous] is written entirely in such free and indirect speech. In contemporary women's writing extensive use is made of spoken language that drips with irony, at times excessively so. Until recently largely excluded from the tradition, this group of writers tries to struggle free from the linguistic, cultural bind in which it finds itself, without breaking loose from the tradition altogether.

It is difficult, in an article written in English, to bring examples of the truly interesting linguistic breakthroughs of contemporary Hebrew literature. Translations cannot convey the great mosaic of lost languages that appear in the text as a kind of return of the repressed. I can only remark that Sammi Michael's Arabic mother tongue intimately inhabits his best-selling novel *Victoria*, whose Hebrew is its strongest feature. And I have no doubt that Anton Shammas's impressive translation from Arabic into Hebrew of the last novel of Emil Habibi *[Saraya, Bat Hashed Hara]*, published in Hebrew in 1993, may provide Hebrew readers with some impression of the power contained in that cultural, linguistic memory against which nationalists like Renan warned.

The nation loves one story. Human beings love many stories. The nation speaks one language. People speak many languages. All this is far removed from the images of stone and the (desired) purity of Amos Oz, said Avot Yeshurun, at the Brenner Prize ceremony in 1967,

> when the Hebrew language becomes mixed with forbidden metal, and you suddenly feel: the hour of the language is coming, this happiness, that it is permitted to look at every place, to touch everything with your eyes, as the bee that touches with its music against every flower.[16]

Lost in translation is the mixture of languages—whether it be Arabic, Yiddish, Polish, or (more than anything else in Israeli Hebrew) the real Hebrew of the real Israel—that the great modern poet always uses, such as Yeshurun himself spoke when receiving his prize on that winter day of 1967. Later, in one of his poems, playing on tender shifts from right and wrong uses of Hebrew, which sometimes sounds like a translated Yiddish, sometimes like Polish-in-Hebrew, he praised that language, the simple language of the streets. It is fitting, I think, to end this chapter with Yeshurun's words, however much the English translation fails to render the linguistic richness of his words:

> God of Abraham, you who know tongues
> who spoke with my mother in ancient Yiddish,
> when you went out on the Sabbath
> among the stars.

My Hebrew is not clean
My Hebrew is makeshift, and speaks makeshift and silly things,
for it is not enough.
I am the one who goes out at night in the garden, in the
square, and in Dizengoff, in a darkness of words
that is impossible.

You, who hear speech in seventy translations
At night, in the garden, in the square, in Dizengoff.
See: "What did you buy?" "Moth balls for the closets."
"I also want." The tongue of our days.
To tell you what? That this is what we have.[17]

Translated by Jonathan Chipman

Notes

1. Haim Rabin, "The Revival of the Hebrew Language," *Ariel* 25 (1969): 31.

2. Amos Oz, *Israel, Palestine and Peace* (New York: Vintage, 1994), p. 54.

3. Ibid., pp. 54–56.

4. Oz, *Beor hatekhelet haaza* [In the Daring Blue Light] (Tel Aviv: Sifriat Poalim, 1979), p. 27. [Hebrew]

5. Jacqueline Rose, *State of Fantasy* (Oxford: Oxford University Press, 1996), pp. 36–37. This brilliant scholar does not read Hebrew and thus misses the militant, phallocentric dimension of Oz's stance in relation to Hebrew.

6. Oz, *Beor hatekhelet haaza,* pp. 27–28.

7. Gershon Shaked, *Modern Hebrew Fiction,* trans. Yael Lotan, ed. Emily Miller Budick (Bloomington: Indiana University Press, 2000), pp. 197–99.

8. Nathan Zach, "Reflections on Alterman's Poetry," *Akhshav* 64 (1996): 11. [Hebrew]

9. This is the Hebrew developed during the so-called Russian *Haskalah,* the secular and nationalist-oriented "Enlightenment" among Eastern European Jewish intellectuals during the latter half of the nineteenth century.

10. Shaked, *The Revival of Historical Hebrew Drama* (Jerusalem: Mossad Bialik, 1970), p. 12. [Hebrew]

11. The status of Proper Italian, as a reductive language, was discussed by the director and poet P. P. Pasolini. Among other things he dealt with the

wealth of other dialects, in *Lutheran Letters* (Manchester, 1983) and in *Scritti Corsari* (Torino, 1975).

12. Eugen Weber, *Peasants into Frenchmen* (Stanford, Calif.: Stanford University Press, 1976), p. 70.

13. Ibid., p. 71.

14. Ibid., p. 89.

15. Ernest Renan, "What Is a Nation," in *Nation and Narration,* ed. Homi Bhabba (New York: Routledge, 1990), p. 11.

16. Avot Yeshurun, "Hebrew Literature Will Conduct the Service," *Kol Haketavim* I, (Tel Aviv: Siman Kriah, Hakibbutz Hameuhad, 1995): 280. [Hebrew]

17. Yeshurun, "Got Fun Avrom," *Kappela Kolot* (Tel Aviv: Siman Keriah, 1977), p. 40. [Hebrew]

CHAPTER TWELVE

Betrayal of the Mother Tongue in the Creation of National Identity

Nili Rachel Scharf Gold

Fourteen years ago my family and I traveled through Europe. Italy did not smile on us. We were cheated at a Venetian restaurant and at a gas station outside Milan. We arrived in Florence during a terrible heat wave, and when we fled to the Italian Alps, our car hit a large rock and we were stranded for five hours before our rescuers arrived. No one spoke English or French; we spoke no Italian. Battered and bruised we crossed the border to Austria. A great sense of tranquillity came over me. Magical bliss. As if there had been no Holocaust, as if my father had not vowed he would never again set foot in the country that had spit him out. I tried to understand the tenderness engulfing me. I heard: Apfelstrudel *(apple strudel)*, Eisekaffe *(Iced coffee)*, *bitte sehr* (please), but did not yet know that the caress I felt came from these familiar syllables. A few hours later, we left for Paris.

Years passed. Yoel Hoffmann's *Bernhard,* which I read in New York, aroused a similar thrill. I understood the non-Hebrew words in the text without looking in the margins for their translation. When Aunt Magda from *A Christ of Fish* whispered on the phone the magic words *stell dir vor; ausgezeichnet; eigentlich,* I felt them, licked and tasted them. The shiver they sent through my flesh tied me to Aunt Magda and to her little nephew, to Katschen and Bernhard, with threads that pulled me back into the lands of my childhood. This time, unlike after that brief stay in Austria, I decided to follow the voices. The work of unraveling began with the words I found in Hoffmann: "And sometimes Bernhard too hears the sound of his dead mother Clara's voice. He thinks: 'All the voices in the world are coiled together like the threads on one

235

bobbin (that's invisible) and the bobbin turns and turns and the voices are heard'."[1]

I was born in Haifa. My mother, a native of Bukovina, came to Israel as a pioneer; my father as a refugee from Vienna. German was their secret language, the language of their love. They read the German-language newspaper *Yedioth Hadashot* and spoke German with their relatives, acquaintances, and customers. With us they spoke only Hebrew—because of the Nazis, they said. I never spoke German at home, but I had heard its sounds even before I came into being. It was my mother and father's tongue, the language of songs hummed in the kitchen, the buzz coming from the living room. In the years that followed my distant childhood in Haifa, I rarely had the chance to hear German. The desire to listen to it, now, became a fascinating voyage of research, one that has not yet reached its end.

The purpose of this research is to retrieve the sunken remains of a forgotten mother tongue hidden in the sea bed of Israeli works of Hebrew literature, to listen to the sounds dwelling within the depths of the central, dominant narrative. My assumption is that literary works that were not written in the author's mother tongue contain traces of the sounds that the fetus heard before birth and that the infant suckled along with his mother's milk. Many Hebrew texts conceal—perhaps repress—the notes and echoes of a different verbal past. Bringing these lost notes to the surface, acknowledging their existence, will, hopefully, lead to a more complex and complete reading of Hebrew literature and its representation of Israeli identity.

The rhythms and fluctuations of a mother's voice and speech penetrate the nervous system of the fetus beginning with the fifth month of pregnancy, when the development of the ear is complete. Through the amniotic fluid and the mother's spinal cord, the unborn child hears the music of the language that is to be his mother tongue. Evidence of this phenomenon has been provided by physicians and ear specialists, such as Alfred Tomatis and Paul Madaule, and by neurologists and scientists studying fetal development, such as Jacques Mehler and William P. Fifer.[2] In an experiment conducted in the United States, Fifer and Christine Moon tested babies twenty-five to fifty-six hours old and found that they always preferred their mother's language, even when it was not spoken by the mother herself.[3] Similar experiments in Europe confirmed that newborns show a strong preference for their mother's tongue. In his book *The Secret Life of the Unborn Child,* Thomas Verny quotes a radio interview with the orchestra conductor Boris Brott:

> As a young man, I was mystified by this unusual ability I had to play certain pieces sight unseen. I'd be conducting a score for the first time and, suddenly, the cello line would jump out at me; I'd know the flow of the piece even before I turned the page of the score. One day I mentioned this to my mother, who is a professional cellist. I thought she'd be intrigued because it was always the cello line that was so distinct in my mind. She was, but when she heard what the pieces were, the mystery quickly solved itself. All the scores I knew sight unseen were ones she had played while she was pregnant with me.[4]

Even if we consider the musician's story as no more than an anecdote, the scientific facts remain: first, the ear is the only prenatal means of communication with the outside world, and second, the first sound that the fetus absorbs, remembers, and prefers is the voice of the mother and the melody of her language.

One must ask, it seems to me: what is the lasting power of these early sounds for those who would eventually write in a different tongue? Does the language heard in the womb and during the first year of life leave traces in the adult's work, or does the turn toward a new language sever the umbilical cord completely? Is, perhaps, the music of the mother tongue the core of the literary work? Moreover, the role of the mother's speech is not limited to teaching the language and its melody. Along with this first language, even before knowing the difference between inside and outside, self and other, the baby learns to love and to hate. These primary experiences are powerful and extreme: good experiences lead to the blissful merging of self and other, bad ones to a threatening and painful relationship with the other. The words and rhythms of the mother's tongue, therefore, carry an enormous emotional weight, infused as they are with the force of the first pregenital conflicts and primeval chaotic feelings.

The Babel of the Unconscious, written by the psychoanalysts Jacqueline Amati-Mehler, Simona Argentieri, and Jorge Canestri, is the first and only work that examines the place of the mother tongue in the psychoanalytic dimension.[5] According to the authors, language is absorbed by the baby as it nurses. The first linguistic experience, in other words, is concrete and corporeal. The mother's voice is the voice of the nascent superego. It caresses and nurtures, but it also commands and forbids. Adopting a new language, then, may help the individual forge an independent identity. It can serve to defend, repress, and assist in the processing of traumatic experience. However, severing ties with the mother tongue may also be destructive, since the memories of that wondrous merging with the mother and the immediate conjunction of "word" and "thing" are woven into this first language. The writer who, out of necessity or choice, attaches new signifiers to his signifieds, relinquishes that vital kinship of word and thing that is essential for the verbal creator. Amati-Mehler, Argentieri, and Canestri question whether the step-language is capable of translating primary experience. They wonder what occurs in the creator's internal "workshop": how the individual assimilates the loss of the first language. They also ask which emotional needs are met by the change from mother tongue to second language.

This issue strikes a chord deep in Hebrew literature. The majority of literary works written in Hebrew, both before and after the move to *Eretz Yisrael* (the Land of Israel), were written after a long series of departures from mother tongues, a kind of betrayal of the mother committed, for the most part, by male writers. Literary critics, like most of the writers themselves, viewed writing in Hebrew as an expression of national revival, a return to the Jewish people's ancient heritage, as well as to normalcy. It was also, as Amalia Kahana-Carmon says, an expression of solidarity with "the enterprise of the Jews in the Land of Israel."[6] Hebrew was a kind of linguistic "draft notice," a circumstantial necessity that often also served the deep emotional need to construct a new self. Much research has been devoted to the elaborate network of cultural connections and intertextual relations extending back to the writers' countries of origin, and the subject is still being studied by critics. The study of the primary sounds is a different matter. The effect of the early residues of learning and of verbal development has not yet been examined in the context of the author's passage from the mother tongue to another language.

Out of the many Hebrew writers who had not been born into the Hebrew language, I was particularly drawn to those whose origins, in one way or another, were German, whether those from the peripheral areas at the far ends of the former Austro-Hungarian Empire, or those who had been born in Germany itself. These were "young immigrants who joined the native-born Israelis," as Gershon Shaked puts it.[7] They came to *Eretz Yisrael* in the 1930s and 1940s, their ages upon arrival ranging from two to sixteen, having re-

ceived, at best, only a partial German education. Though I am aware
of the unbearably heavy shadow that the Holocaust casts over any
such discussion, I will not be focusing on it. For the children who
had grown up in German-speaking Jewish homes, this was the
mother tongue, their verbal home. My goal, therefore, is to identify
and analyze the indirect methods consciously or unconsciously used
by writers in order either to commemorate or to repress their verbal
past in the Hebrew texts. Echoes of the mother tongue can be heard
in works by Aharon Appelfeld, Yoel Hoffmann, Natan Zach, Yehuda
Amichai, Dan Pagis, Tuvia Rübner, and others. There are, however,
great differences in the accessibility of these echoes to the reader's
detection. Some of the writers obscure, either intentionally or unin-
tentionally, verbal traces of the earlier language. Some may not
even be aware that such echoes exist in their writings.

The melody of German, the forgotten language of childhood, is
knowingly and explicitly woven into the text of Yoel Hoffmann's
first story, "Katschen." Hoffmann is one of the harbingers of Israeli
postmodernism, even though, according to his biological age, he
belongs to the same gereration of writers as A. B. Yehoshua and
Amos Oz, the established writers of *Dor Hamedinah*, the "Generation of the State." Before making his debut as a writer in his late
forties, he translated selections of Zen-Buddhist philosophy, which
he titled *Where Did the Sounds Go* and *The Sounds of Earth*.[8] It is
as though he was already trying to follow the footprints of lost
sounds but was looking for them too far away. It may also have
taken the literary community—editors, critics, and readers—until
the late 1980s to be ready for the conscious unveiling of the other
language within the Hebrew text.

"Katschen" is a kind of journey inward, into the labyrinths of
language and the unconscious, into an infantile or even fetal thinking that cannot distinguish between word and thing. This journey
binds together the child Katschen's longing for his dead mother
with his yearning for the sounds of her language:

> "Mutti," said Katschen. But when the sound of his voice reached
> his ears, it seemed as though the word had not come out of his
> mouth. "Mutti," said Katschen again, but it was as though his
> lips were not his own. "Howw," blew the wind, "waa," blew the
> wind. Katschen listened to the sound of the wind and remem-
> bered Avigail's song. "Howwa" is the sound of the wind and
> "howwa" is the name of the wind, thought Katschen. When the
> wind blows you hear its name and when you hear its name it

blows. "Wi—ind," said Katschen. "Wi—ind," and this word too sounded to Katschen like the sound of the wind.

And as things and the names of things became one, the fear in Katschen's heart disappeared. "Mutti," he said for the third time, and this time the voice was his own and the lips were his own. "Have you lost your way, my son?" Katschen heard Margarethe say. "Ja," answered Katschen, "I have lost my way." But there was no doubt in Katschen's mind that he would soon find his way, and follow it until he reached the cow. And the cow would look into Katschen's eyes and say, "There, you have found your way, *mein kind,* and you need never stray so far again."[9]

The thirst for the *m* sound, the sound that connects mother and nursing child, is almost compulsively repeated in the stories— "Mutti," "Margarethe," and *"Mein Kind"*—the link between the cow, who is the source of milk, and the dead mother, emphasizes even further the preverbal connection, which is made so concrete in the text. For Hoffmann the longing for the mother merges metaphorically with a Proustian awareness in a place where sounds are forever preserved:

> Katschen saw a shell. Once his mother Margarethe told him that shells contained the sound of the sea, and even if the shell was far away from the sea, in the mountains, or the desert, the sound of the waves is always in it. Katschen lifted the shell to his ear. The sound of the sea came out of the shell and seemed to Katschen to be saying "bei mir, bei mir."[10]

Just as the sound of the sea continues to reverberate within the shell, so the voice of the dead mother continues to resonate in her son's consciousness.

Hoffmann takes a sensual pleasure in reviving the musical notes of his childhood. Nursery rhymes are quoted in the original, like the teddy bear who died in *Bernhard,* for example, or the dog and the egg in "Katschen": *"Ein Hund Kahm in die Küche."* Anne Birkenhauer, the gifted translator who translated Hoffmann's children's book into German, recited for me a German nursery rhyme: *Jaguar und Neinguar / treffen sich im Februar.* In this German verse, February becomes a meeting place for jaguars and their made-up ontological opposites (as if there are "yes-guars" and "no-guars," the *neinguar).* Is it a coincidence, then, that Hoffmann's Hebrew children's book is called *It's a Good Idea to Buy Elephants in February?*[11] As she translated this book, Birkenhauer also discovered the hidden resonance of the line: "a man who cries becomes an owl." *Eule* is the German word for "owl," *heulen* means "to cry." Therefore, a crying man becomes an owl, or, in Birkenhauer's translation: "*dass ein Mensch, wenn er heult, zur Eule wird.*"

German reverberations are evident in verses in which Hoffmann mixes eye and ear. "Onomatopoeia" in German is *Lautmalerei* (literally, sound-drawing, from *laut* [sound] and *malerei* [drawing]). This may be the source of the line: "one can draw the picture of a sound" in one of Hoffmann's nursery rhymes. Such sound-drawing is more elaborately developed in "Katschen." A conversation Katschen has with his mentally ill father, Ernst, provides a wonderful example of Hoffmann's artistic craftsmanship, which retains the vitality of the primary experiences and their dependence on the mother tongue:

> "Before my eyes," said Ernst suddenly, "there is glass and a bird pecking at it all the time." Katschen looked at his father's face and saw that his eyes did not see what was in front of him. "Before my eyes," said Ernst again, "there is glass and a bird pecking at it all the time." The picture took shape in Katschen's mind. The bird approaches the glass, its eyes getting bigger and bigger. Then he heard the sound of the beak pecking at the glass. The sight and the sound emerged in German and Katschen was filled with wonder that even a picture needed a language to draw itself. If Ernst had spoken Hebrew, thought Katschen, he would have looked through the glass without seeing it and the bird would have flown elsewhere. "Vater," said Katschen, "Warum sprichst du nicht Ivrit?" ... A distant memory came back to Katschen's mind. Margarethe is asleep in her bed, her face to the wall. His father lifts him out of the cradle and brings him ever so slowly towards his face. And through the lenses of Ernst's glasses Katschen sees the eyes of his father coming closer and closer.[12]

Thus *Lautmalerei* becomes one with the language of love, the only place where image and sound, child and parents, can fully merge with one another.

Hoffman's art of reconstructing the vanished sounds is accompanied by the graphic design of Hoffmann's texts. While in the first version of "Katschen," translations of the foreign words appeared at the bottom of the page, as is customarily done, by the second version, the German had already moved to the side-margins.[13] *Bernhard* and later works feature brief texts placed in the center of the page, surrounded by white and wide spaces. Only a few

German words and their Hebrew translations occasionally dot the very wide white margins. It is as if these margins contain only the translations of those German phrases that have succeeded in breaking through the wall of repression. The page graphically represents the separation of conscious from unconscious, of that which can be spelled out in black print and that which cannot be said at all.

The effort to revive the sounds heard in childhood, to reproduce German words and phrases and a *Yekke*-accented Hebrew, is characteristic of Hoffmann's work between 1985 and 1991, between "Katschen" and *A Christ of Fish*.[14] This latter work is the most densely packed with the attempt to find the "correct music," as Hoffmann himself calls it.[15] The text abounds with references to ears, songs, musical pieces, and instruments. A cembalo, a trombone, a contrabass and a piano, Beethoven's Ninth and Amalia Rodriguez, Marlene Dietrich singing, and a thousand birds: "My father, Theodor Weiss, ear, nose and throat specialist, said, I remember, 'sinusitis.' "[16] And elsewhere:

> my father's body in the water. A thin man. A white soundbox. A slender violin for the reform of the world. A doctor for the vocal chords . . . did he hear the beating of birds' wings in the woods of Moldavia? Had he seen, in some old medical textbook, a picture of the inner ear.[17]

Human beings, it seems, are in fact walking sound-boxes, and the doctor listens not only with his stethoscope but also with the inner ear, capable of hearing those vanished sounds that the self remembers, re-creates, plays with:

> I love words like *"Papagai"* or *"tinte."* A French aunt (Coquettish. Her body gives off whiffs of cheap scent.) is called *"tante."* But a German aunt (full-bodied) is called *"Tante."* When a German aunt dusts the table and knocks over a bottle of ink, they say *"Schau"* (i.e., "Look"), *Tante* spilt the *Tinte*.[18]

A Christ of Fish is a living musical monument to the sounds of childhood and to the emotions with which they are laced. This work brings repressed acoustic materials to the surface, appearing to complete the work of mourning. It is no coincidence, I believe, that the books that followed *A Christ of Fish* are distant from the world of the earlier works. The self is at last liberated so to speak, free to move on and leave the sounds of the past behind.

The works of Natan Zach, Aharon Appelfeld, and Dan Pagis move in the opposite direction. While the language of childhood is treated with striking tolerance in Hoffmann's first story and only relinquished in his later works, Pagis and Zach began by writing in purified, restrained, at times hermetically sealed Hebrew, from which the veil is finally lifted only in their much later works. The language and plot of Zach's last volume of poems attest to the presence of "a choir [. . .] in dead people's language, people who are no longer my parents."[19] Although we will never know what direction Pagis would have taken in his writing, there is evidence in his cycle of prose poems "Father," which is supported by comments made later by his widow Ada Pagis and by Eleazar Benyoetz, that, as the years passed, his childhood and its language demanded an increasingly greater portion of his consciousness.[20]

As I was leafing through Pagis's manuscripts, it for a moment seemed to me that Pagis had done privately that which Hoffmann had done openly. The Hebrew poem was typed or handwritten at the center of Pagis's page, while in the wide, white margins faint traces of penciled German could still be detected. It was as though Pagis's intimate language, the one he used with himself, was a different one: *Noch immer zu süss* (still too sweet), he debated with himself. *Oder ohne Kristal* (perhaps without the word *crystal*)? And, at the bottom of the page, a simple *Ende* (the end). The German, however, never made it to Pagis's readers. It remained concealed. The single exception is the German title of one poem: "Ein Leben," a life. The poem, which overflows with longing for the mother, is the only one crowned with her language.

However, the sounds of Pagis's first years can be heard even outside the margins of his archival manuscripts. The double-verbal existence maintains, so it seems, its own code: words, symbols, and images that emerge from the very depths of consciousness. Like Zach hearing "the language of dead people," so Pagis's Robinson Crusoe, far away from his birthplace, hears the "ticking of his dead, and their alarms."[21] The speaker of another poem is a patient who complains of "a shriek in the ears / the shrill whistle between two rival radio stations."[22] The ear, Hoffmann's favorite organ, is also frequently found in Pagis's poetry, as are the seashell conch and the sound of the sea. In Pagis's libretto for a young people's concert, for example, the various musical styles, from Bach to jazz, are introduced by a figure named *Benkol,* whose name in Hebrew means "echo," or, literally, "son-of-sound." Even though he could play many different tunes, Pagis writes: "Benkol himself was very lonely" and lamented not having a melody of his own. Suddenly, "from heaven, (or who knows, perhaps from his heart)," *Batkol, echo,* or *daughter-of-sound* tells him: "they are all still with you, you are one, one who is all of them / you are the sum of your memories / your voice bursts forth through the echoes of their voices."[23] Pagis himself seems to have been searching for the correct melody, a tune of his own. But he also knew that the voices of the past, though concealed, could be found within the music of the present.

The quintessential symbol for the multiplicity of languages and the suffering it causes is the Tower of Babel. Zach in his later poems confesses: "To speak four languages by the time you are six is also confusing / A kind of wobbly tower of Babel, barely walking, could lead you to a psychiatrist."[24] Pagis is more enigmatic in his poem "The Tower": "quick-fingered memories / . . . were mixed in the tumult of strange tongues without a translator for myself, unfinished."[25] The multiplicity of languages, says Pagis, prevents wholeness. One must always translate; no single language can say it all. The simple connection between word and thing is lost.

The "footprints" in Pagis's great poem by this name are usually (and rightly) interpreted as the world's painful scars and as an ironic description of the remnants—the invisible remains of the Holocaust victims who perished in the flames. "Footprints," however, is far more relevant to the issue we are considering than an initial reading might suggest. One of the poem's many intricate verses says the following:

> Too many tongues are mixed in my mouth. But
> at the crossing of these winds,
> very diligent, I immerse myself
> in the laws of heavenly grammar: I am learning
> the declensions and ascensions of
> silence.[26]

These lines describe the process of learning Hebrew. The word for "Semitic" in Hebrew is *shemit.* The word for "heavenly" is *shmemit.* In referring to the language he learns as *shmemit,* the poem's speaker indirectly points to the Semitic language i.e. Hebrew, as the language he studies.

"Very diligent," Pagis writes of himself in the poem—and this, indeed, is how he is described by his teachers, friends, and wife. Hebrew is learned as a means of staying silent. It is a speech that preserves inner voices unspoken. Furthermore, the poem's motto and pseudorefrain—"from heaven to the heaven of heavens to the heaven of night"—is a quotation from Yannai. As it turns out, the verse is taken from a *kerovah (piyyut)* Yannai wrote to introduce the biblical story of the Tower of Babel. [28] "Footprints" is a cynical, macabre exegesis of Yannai's *piyyut.* While Yannai's angels "become men/become women" for the purpose of their mission, the men and women in Pagis's poems become angels. These people are mere footprints of their past existence. They themselves have become *seraphim,* gone up in smoke.

The word *seraphim,* often translated as "angels of fire," contains a pun: the Hebrew root *s r ph* means "burn." In the poem, however, the angels of fire are burned people, who went up in smoke.[27] This gloss, however, does not exhaust the meaning of the image. The footprints left behind are also those of the long-gone child. Toward its end, the poem offers an autobiographical detail dating back to the time before the smoke: "Maybe what remained of me / were little gliders that hadn't grown up: / they still repeat themselves in still-clouds, glide." According to Ada Pagis's biography of her late husband, *Lev Pitomi* [Sudden Heart], when Pagis was a child he liked to dress up in a pilot's uniform and to collect model airplanes. What motivated this hobby, writes Ada Pagis, was that he "longingly associated airplanes with his father." The gliders in "Footprints" are therefore the footprints of the four-year-old boy pining for the father who had gone to Palestine. The longing for the father, according to the biography, became the young Dan Pagis's main hold on life.[29] Is there a connection between these gliders and the study of the heavenly Semitic language, Hebrew?

Sidra Ezrahi, aware that writing in Hebrew was an act of choice for Pagis, interprets this act as the deliberate construction of a barrier between himself and his past.[30] I believe the motives for this linguistic choice are more complex. Although I am well aware of the pitfalls involved in basing a literary reading on biographical data, I nevertheless wish to claim that, in the little boy's mind, airplanes and Hebrew merged and became a ticket to *Eretz Yisrael,* to Daddy. Pagis had a Hebrew tutor in Bukovina: "It is unclear how much he actually learned," writes Ada Pagis, but the tutor did dictate a Hebrew letter to him. "My dear father! How much I, too, would like to go to *Eretz Israel* and to see you."[31]

There is no doubt in my mind that the internal connection between Hebrew and the yearning for the father was formed at this early stage. The father, however, remained unattainable even when Pagis did come to Palestine. When, after the inferno of the war, the boy finally arrived, he was once again rejected by his father and sent to live on a kibbutz. Pagis clung to the promise that "he would stay on the kibbutz only until he had learned a little Hebrew," and he threw himself into the study of the new language with all the might of his talent.[32] Although he might have found a convenient role model in Tuvia Rübner—his older friend at the kibbutz, who was then writing poetry in German—Pagis began to write Hebrew poems even before he had completely mastered the language.[33] His teacher in Merchavia, Avraham Goren, said that Pagis's way of learning Hebrew was one of the wonders of the human mind. It seems to me that this was also the wonder of a soul yearning for its father.

Pagis became a leading scholar of medieval Hebrew literature and Hebrew poetry. However, he never really parted with German, his mother's tongue. Gershon Shaked says that he "lived in German," and Ariel Hirschfeld further argues: "It is clear that the central drama of [Pagis's] poetic world is played out on the foreign landscapes of German culture, which to him is not at all foreign: for Pagis, it is both home and homeland, in the most fertile sense of these two words."[34] While Hirschfeld's primary interest is cultural influence, his words also convey the sense of German language as Pagis's home, perhaps even in the maternal sense of the word. In her essay "Dan Pagis Übersetzen" [To Translate Dan Pagis] Anna Birkenhauer recalls: "As I worked on the translation, I sometimes had the impression that I was putting some parts of the poems back into the language in which they had originally been conceived. . . . Some of these poems . . . actually present Dan Pagis to the reader in a sharper and purer form when they are translated into German. The added value of this translation, which stems from Pagis's mother tongue and the first few years of his existence . . . ." and so on.[35] German, Birkenhauer believes, is not a foreign landscape but rather the very fabric of Pagis's poem.

It is only when the poem "Draft of a Reparations Agreement" is translated into German, Birkenhauer rightly argues, that the full meaning of its central image is revealed. Unlike the Hebrew word for reparations, *shilumim* (payments), the German word *Wiedergutmachung* means "to make good again," the word *wieder* meaning "again." This concept of *again* reverberates throughout the poem, producing a more chilling text than either the original Hebrew or the English translation: *Alles kommt wieder an seinen Platz* (everything comes again to its place), as if "the scream [could again go] back into the throat / The gold teeth back to the gums."[36] Another example of how the Hebrew text is "returned" to its "original" German is the translation of the poem "Fossils." The poem's core sentence is focused on that favorite subject, ears and hearing. The ear in this poem is a seashell: "The arch-shell is an ear that refuses to listen." The sound of this line in the Hebrew original and in Mitchell's English translation is unremarkable, the "arch shell" all but swallowed within a catalog of fossils: arch-fly and archer fish. Only the German translation, through its clarity, highlights the centrality of this line to the poem as a whole: *Die Urmuschel ist ein Ohr, das sich weigert zu hören.* "The Arch-shell is an ear which refuses to hear." In German, the line plays on the puns: *hören, ohr, ur* (hear, ear, arch-).

The conches or seashells that repeatedly appear in Pagis's poetry are reminiscent of Hoffmann's "Katschen." The shells guard and protect primeval sounds, which may be the voices of childhood. The shells remember, even though the sea, at times, "forgets their beauty," as Pagis writes in an early poem, "White Are the Sea-Conches of Silence."[37] The work of preserving the sounds of the 'writing seashells' is a multifaceted art, and listening to them at times requires an intuitive third ear. Translating their whispers into the language of the sea—the language of the first sounds—may illuminate many texts whose writers betrayed their mother tongues, not only in the case of Pagis and Hoffmann, and not only in the case of German and Hebrew.

Little detective work is necessary to discover the German footprints in Natan Zach's volume of poetry, *Because I'm Around,* a remarkably candid and self-aware work. Here, the German pronounciation, a trademark of Zach's actual speech, leaves traces on the page. It is a testimony, perhaps, to a dual linguistic loyalty. The absence of a translation for the German rhyme emphasizes the alienation of the poem's speaker as well as that of its author. The German-sounding vocalization of foreign words appears in Hebrew print: *joongle* (jungle) as opposed to the normative Hebrew pronunciation *joongel; Aushvitz* (Auschwitz) rather than the Hebrew *Oshvitz.* A genuine German rhyme closes one whimsical poem: *ein Stern/Danke gern* (a star/thank you). Through its use of vowels and rhythms or, occasionally, the Latin alphabet, Zach's book boldly confronts its acoustical heritage. It reveals the pain behind the sounds without any attempt to camouflage it.

In retrospect, one might claim that Zach's early poetics also stemmed from the same sense of alienation so visible in the later poems. Zach's poetic doctrine to avoid the collective "we" voice and to prefer the "I" was also a refusal to join the national Hebrew chorus. His early verbal economy, restraint, and caution were symptoms of repressed memories and sounds. In rereading Zach's wonderful opening to his early poem "One Moment," one may hear a precursor of the later poems: "One moment. Quiet please. I beg of you. I want to say something."[38] This is the voice of a stranger pleading for permission to speak in a language he at one and the same time masters and doubts. Only in the latest volume of poetry does the dam fully burst. The terrors of the past are accompanied by the discordant sounds of childhood trauma:

> And since then I long . . . not for her
> And surely not for Haifa of the British Mandate—
> And surely not for the pharmacy
> Which the Italians, may their name be blotted out . . . blew up.
> And my mother was also Italian, and they used to force us
>   to get off
> The buses when we spoke Italian
> And German was even worse in the buses of Haifa,
> And since then I have a problem with buses and with
>   languages.[39]

This confessional poem reveals the scars, or footprints, left by languages and humiliations. Those are intertwined in Zach's poetry and both still live in "the distant fields of then, perhaps." When scrambled, the letters of the Hebrew words for then *(az)* and perhaps *(ulay)* reverberate with the German conjunction also (pronounced *alzo*). The repeated use of meaningless conjunctions, such as the Hebrew *az, ulay,* and the German *also* (pronounced *alzo*), or the English "so," is in keeping with the poem's stuttering confessional tone. The Hebrew title "In the Fields of Then Perhaps" *[Bisdot az ulay],* also evokes other traumatic homonymic associations, which are outside the scope of our current discussion.[40]

A visit to Germany recalled in another poem succeeds in "waking the dead" even more than the Haifa buses mentioned in the previous quotation:

> And what about the food Mr. Zach?
> I am asked in German by the maid.
> And what shall I answer her?
> That suddenly I'm hearing voices. . . .
> Only *I* know that I'm truly hearing. . . .

"Why don't you stop this nonsense?"
"Who could possibly deal with you?" [i.e., who has strength
      for you]
"When will you finally finish eating?"
Or, "so young and so bad already!"
A choir is heard . . . from a very distant past
In dead people's language, people who are no longer my parents.[41]

German, then, is a language whose commands are cruel, a language of discipline, prohibition, and punishment. Writing in Hebrew most likely served as a defense mechanism for Zach, keeping the threat at bay. Hebrew reduced the pain of rejection by a refugee-father, who never spoke a loving word because, in German, "they do not speak this way to children."[42] Private family Holocaust merges with the larger, national one: "Forgive me," says Zach, "Hitler is still running through my veins, he is still alive."[43]

The cruel education provided by history is also described by Yehuda Amichai in "The Travels of Benjamin the Last, of Tudela":

History is a eunuch, / Looking for mine too / To castrate, cut with paper sheets / Sharper than any knife, to crush / To block my mouth forever / With whatever she cut, / As a desecration of the war dead, / So I sing only an impotent chirp, / So I learn many languages / And not one tongue of my own, / So I am scattered and dispersed, / Not a Tower of Babel rising to heaven.[44]

Such violent vocabulary is uncharacteristic of Amichai.[45] Yet he uses it to relay the horrifying process of teaching new languages to refugee children. Like Zach, Amichai, who emigrated in the 1930s, had to leave Germany behind.

For Amichai—whose diction exposes his country of origin, even though he adamantly declares that he has been speaking Hebrew since kindergarten—emigration was like a castration, a form of verbal brutality. Nevertheless, the Hebrew of the synagogue, with which he is intimately familiar, was transformed in his poetry into an elastic and playful mother tongue.[46] Amichai's poetic model is revealed in his late poem "Summer Rest and Words":

I shut my eyes / And return to the words of the rabbi in my childhood / On the *bimah* of the synagogue. . . . He changed / The words of the prayer a little, he did not sing and did not trill and did not sob. . . . But said his words with a quiet defiance, demanded of God / In a calm voice that accompanied me all my life.[47]

Like the rabbi, Amichai somewhat changes the words of Hebrew Scripture and prayer in his poetry; like him, he does not trill and does not sob.

I asked Amichai about the rabbi.[48] His name, he said, was Hanover; he preached in German, and the rhythm of his words came not from rhyme and verse, but from within the words themselves. The music that the child Amichai internalized and later wished to reconstruct in his Hebrew verse was the lilt of German sermons. Rabbi Hanover, Amichai told me, brought the music of Hebrew into German; I, he said of himself, am returning that music to its origins.

In his book *Two Pools in a Wood,* Shimon Sandbank recounts an experience of which Aryeh Ludwig Strauss wrote under the heading "A Psalm Returns to Its Rightful Place."[49] In an English-speaking film, which Strauss saw in Israel, a minister delivered a sermon: "Yea, though I walk in the valley of the shadow of death I will fear no evil for thou art with me." Strauss, who glanced at the Hebrew subtitles, suddenly saw the biblical phrase as it was originally written: "The movie was probably shown in other countries," Strauss later wrote, "and everywhere the clergyman's words remained what they had been: a translation, and everyone knew that they were a translation. But here in Israel they suddenly returned to their rightful place. . . . [T]he modest accompanying text, the subtitles, became the real thing. The type blazed with mysterious power. . . . For a moment, the translation became the original, and the original became translation." Sandbank compares Strauss' Hebrew writings to Psalmic transformations of this sort.

Unlike Pagis's competing radio stations, in Amichai's poetry Hebrew and German peacefully coexisted almost since infancy. The Hebrew of the ancient Scriptures, the language of the maternal father, blends with the German, the mother tongue, the language of home. Rabbi Hanover poured Hebrew into German; his spiritual son restores the words to their Hebrew original while retaining their German melody. Yet in this unique melting process, the Hebrew alone is visible on the page. However, German traces can clearly be detected in Amichai's pseudo-autobiographical novel, *Not of This Time, Not of This Place.* One of the book's detective-style subplots focuses on the search for Rabbi Manheim's lost speeches in Germany. This search constitutes an indirect admission that the novel indeed originates in the realm of childhood and its sounds: "And this, approximately, is Dr. Manheim's sermon, which he would give every Sabbath in German: Our father in heaven, blessed be your people and all that they have and all those whose souls rest in Eden. And bless also those who found a new life in the land of our forefathers."[50] Though the language is typical Amichai, it seems to resonate with the elevated tone, rhythm and syntax of the German original.

Yoel, the novel's protagonist, has a split self. He is embarking on a winding journey into the depths of his Jerusalem-German consciousness. Another novel similarly dominated by pseudo-delusional, pseudodetective elements, is Shimon Sandbank's *Targil Bimehika* [Blotting Out Exercise], whose speaker reveals that his subconscious speaks in German.[51] A more distant variation on this theme can be found in Aharon Appelfeld's 1978 *Tor Hapelaoth* [*The Age of Wonders*]. However, the chapters of Amichai's early novel, are unique in that, they move in two realms simultaneously (to the extent that any linear text can transpire in two places at once). Although *Not of This Time, Not of This Place* is written in Hebrew, its Würzburg revenge plot is played out in the German language, which dominates many pages. The Hebrew text is inlaid with German words, even whole sentences, which appear in original German type. Furthermore, my conversations with Amichai himself and with the editor of his novel, Dan Miron, revealed that when the novel's manuscript was edited in the 1960s, a hundred or so pages containing entire German passages were cut out.[52] Had the novel been published in the climate of the 1990s, these passages might well have been retained. In any case, unlike in Hoffmann's divided text, the translations of German words are woven into the Hebrew with Amichai's characteristic nonchalance.

At the end of the novel, the archaeologist—hero of the Jerusalem love plot—is killed. His other half was the man who set out to close a door in his life. He wanted to uncover the footprints of his dead childhood sweetheart and seek revenge on her behalf. Now, he is on an airplane, his future is vague, but his chances of an integrated existence are far greater than those of the Jerusalemite, who has opted for absolute repression. In the cases of both Hoffmann and Amichai, the early literary "work of mourning" seems to have permitted a later turn in new directions. After *A Christ of Fish*, Hoffmann abandoned the German-speaking milieu that dominated his writing up to that point. Amichai never wrote another novel after *Not of This Time, Not of This Place* nor did he utter a German word in the many poems that followed. The conclusion drawn from

Amichai's novel may apply to both author and protagonist: only the readiness to hear the melody of the past enables one to move beyond it. Only the "Yoel" who returns to Germany is aware of this truth:

> That is why I came here. To measure distances. To remember and to recall and to remind, to hear again the sounds of childhood by which I could measure the true distance to that time and that place. The voice of dear Ruth and the voice of Henrietta, still alive. . . . I heard these voices and I wasn't sure whether I was calling to them or they to me.[53]

The sounds are made tangible in the names of characters such as Henrietta, Heinz, and Siegfried, in the names of places, such as *Parade-Platz* (Parade-Square) or Weinburg; in the songs and in the words spoken by the locals: *Blut and Boden . . . Kraft durch FREUDE* [Blood and soil! Strength through joy!], which in the Hebrew original appears as German words in Hebrew alphabet, interspersed within the otherwise Hebrew text.[54]

Amichai's idiosyncratic etymological thinking is at play in the novel even in German. The word *Hexenschuss*, for example, in common usage is a neck "ache". Amicahi prefers to interpret it literally, "a witch hit me." (Hexe = witch in German.) In moments of grace, German also serves as the language of love: *Komm, Kleine. Komm her. . . . Bald geh' Ich von hier weg.*[55] The sentences appear in the original German. They are neither transliterated nor translated. When the narrator is overwhelmed with love, he bursts out in un-Hebraized German. The language erupts unexpectedly, speech flowing from within, welling up from some unknown internal source. Glimpses of German burst forth in incorrect usages of Hebrew (intentional or unintentional) as is the following: "Where is the good Mrs. Minster?" In Hebrew the adjective follows the noun. The sentence ought to read, "Mrs. Minster the good," but in the novel the order of words is reversed to match the German grammer.[56] A more significant error (particularly for this discussion) occurs in the descriptions of Yoel's return to St. Augustine Street, where he was born. Although the modern Hebrew word for "street," *rechov,* is masculine, Amichai's text refers to it in the feminine, as it is in German.[57] The street where the narrator emerged into the world is indeed a feminine one, sharing, perhaps, the gender of the mother. The German mother tongue, in this case, overrules the laws of

Hebrew grammar. Dan Miron told me that Amichai vehemently opposed a suggestion to "correct" the "error." This novel of divided return concretizes in its plot the duality of languages and the hold of the mother tongue even over the man who—perhaps more than any other—did assimilate himself to Israel and to its language.

The kind of reading, or rather listening, that I have proposed is a challenge to the critic: can one hear the faint sounds of the writer's early linguistic self, which seem to have gotten lost? The footprints of the old are engraved in the new. German continues to speak within Hebrew, through Hebrew, as do other mother tongues. If we redefine the goals of reading, a rift between past and present in the fabric of Hebrew literature may be mended. In other words, in many instances we must read Hebrew literature with an ear inclined to listen to the vanished sounds of (m)other tongues.

The reader's ability to hear and to access these other voices in a text that on the face of it is purely Hebrew may liberate its repressed materials. As a result, Hebrew itself might emerge as a more integrated entity. Modern Hebrew does not exist in linguistic isolation. Rather, it harbors other remnants, old notes, remote tunes. If we hear this subterranean music, we might better understand the "other" within us. Contrary to the beliefs of the first generation of Israeli writers and their critics, Elik was not "born from the sea."[58] He had a long line of ancestors and even many of his contemporaries were born on other shores into myriad languages. The attempt to repress or erase their remnants prevents a full and integrated reading of Hebrew and Israeli literature.

For myself, I wish to hear Hebrew in a comprehensive manner, which recovers the mother tongue concealed within it. I want to receive the sound waves of other hidden selves and to liberate their phantom voices.[59] So reading, we critics and interpreters may also render ourselves more complex. We may add dimensions to the identity of Hebrew as a language: an identity that is not founded on a dichotomy between Hebrew and other foreign sounds but on their verbal intercourse. The interpreter, like the psychoanalyst, has to listen to the narrative with an intuitive third ear, not only to understand it better, but also to liberate from silence those forces of longing and desire, which no longer need remain mute.

Notes

1. Yoel Hoffman, *Bernhard,* trans. Alan Treister, with Eddie Levenston (New York: New Directions, 1998), section # 34 [original Hebrew publication: Jerusalem: Keter, 1989]; *A Christ of Fish,* trans. Eddie Levenston (New York: New Directions, 1999) [original Hebrew publication: *Christus Shel Dagim* (Jerusalem: Keter, 1991)]; *Ketschen and The Book of Joseph,* trans. Eddie Levenston and Alan Treister (New York: New Directions, 1998) [original Hebrew publication: *Sefer Yosef* (Jerusalem: Keter, 1988)].

2. The otolaryngolist Alfred Tomatis was the first to argue that the fetus hears—*L'oreille et le Langue* in 1963: published in English as *The Ear and Language* (Canada: Moulin Publication, 1996). See also Paul Madaule, *When Listening Comes Alive: A Guide to Effective Learning and Communication* (Canada: Moulin Publishing, 1993) and C. A. J. Mehler, "Language in the Infant's Mind," *Philosophical Transactions of the Royal Society of London, series B: Biological Sciences* 346 (1315) (October 29, 1994, LSCP, CNRS-EHESS, Paris, France), pp. 13-20.

3. William P. Fifer and Christine M. Moon, "The Role of the Mother's Voice in the Organization of Brain Function in the New Born," *Acta Paediatrica,* Supplement 397 (June 1994): 86-93.

4. Thomas R. Verny, *The Secret Life of the Unborn Child* (New York: Summit Books, 1981), p. 23.

5. Jacqueline Amati-Mehler, Simona Argentieri and Jorge Canestri, *The Babel of the Unconscious : Mother Tongue and Foreign Languages in the Psychoanalytic Dimension,* trans. Whitelaw Cucco (Madison, Conn.: International University Press, 1993).

6. Amalia Kahana-Carmon, "She Writes Nicely, But Only About That Which is Marginal Concerning that Which You have Blessed," *Yedioth Aharonoth,* 25.1.88. [Hebrew]

7. Gershon Shaked, *HaSipporeth Haivrith, 1880-1980* [Modern Hebrew Fiction, 1880-1980] (Jerusalem: Keter and Tel Aviv: Kibbutz Hameuchad, 1988), vol. 3, pp. 81-89. [Hebrew]

8. Yoel Hoffman, *Where Did the Sounds Go: Zen Stories and Haiku Poems* (Masada, 1980) [Hebrew] and *The Sounds of Earth: Selections from Chuang Tzu* (Masada, 1977) [Hebrew].

9. "*Katschen,*" in *The Book of Joseph,* trans. David Kriss (New York: New Directions, 1998), pp. 97-161, quoted on pp. 131–132. *Mutti* means "Mama" in German.

10. Ibid., p. 124; the German translates as "with me."

11. *B'Februar K'dday Liknot Pilim* [It's a good idea to buy elephants in February] (Jerusalem: Keter, 1998). The story has been translated into German by Anne Birkenhauer, forthcoming.

12. *"Katschen,"* pp. 153–154; the German translates as: "Father, why don't you speak Hebrew?"

13. The story first appeared in Hoffmann's *Igrah* (Jerusalem: Keter, 1984), pp. 149-90 [Hebrew], later in *The Book of Joseph.*

14. *Yekke* is the common Hebrew term used for German immigrants to Israel and denotes a tendency toward pedantry.

15. Nili Gold, "Interview with Yoel Hoffman," summer 1994, 1996: not published.

16. *A Christ of Fish,* # 42.

17. Ibid.

18. "A Christ of Fish," in *Conjunctions: Critical Mass,* trans. Eddie Levenston (Annondale on Hudson, New York: Bard College, 1995), pp. 18-19. In Hebrew *sinusitis* is pronounced *sinussitis;* in the original Hoffmann spelled it *simozitis* in order to imitate the Yekke pronunciation.

19. Natan Zach, "To Be Sincere," in *Because I'm Around* (Tel Aviv: Hakibbutz Hameuchad Publishing House, 1996), p. 53. [Hebrew]

20. Dan Pagis, *Kol Hashirim* [Collected Poems and FATHER Prose Selections] (Tel Aviv: Kibbutz Hameuchad and Jerusalem: Mossad Bialik, 1991) [Hebrew] All references to Pagis's poetry are to this book unless otherwise noted. Translations from *Points of Departure,* trans. Stephen Mitchell (Philadelphia: Jewish Publication Society, 1995). Ada Pagis, *Lev Pitomi* [Sudden Heart] (Tel Aviv: Am Oved Publishers, 1995). [Hebrew] Translation per conversation with Anne Birkenhauer, spring 1997. Eleazar Benyoetz was a friend of Pagis and even corresponded with him (Eleazar Benyoetz, *The Edges of Darkness* [Hakibbutz Hameuchad, 1989]). [Hebrew] In a private conversation in the summer of 1996, Benyoetz told me of Pagis's intention to write in German: "Pagis would have started to write in German if he were still alive. I know it!"

Please note, in this context, the development of Appelfeld's work, which, as Yigal Schwartz has shown, followed a more complex pattern. Even Appelfeld, however, moved from obscuring his tracks to greater self-awareness and openness. *Individual Lament and Tribal Eternity: Aharon Appelfeld: The Picture of His World* (Jerusalem: Keter, 1996). [Hebrew]

21. "Epilogue to Robinson Crusoe," in *Variable Directions: The Selected Poetry of Dan Pagis,* trans. Stephen Mitchell (San Francisco: North Point Press, 1989), p. 131. "Alarms" might also be translated as "alarm clocks" or "ringing."

22. "Diagnosis," *Collected Poems,* p. 227.

23. Pagis, *Ben Kol ve-Bat Kol* (Tel Aviv Foundation for Literature and Art, December 1991). The manuscript can be found in the "Genazim" archive, no. 27018. The piece was first played on the radio in March 1973. In May of

1973, it was performed by the Philharmonic Orchestra under the name "Journey into the Present."

24. From an untranslated work.

25. Mitchell, *Points of Departure,* p. 89. One line quoted here from this poem ("without a translator for myself, unfinished") was omitted in Mitchell's version. Because of its importance, I have supplied my own literal rendering of that line.

26. Ibid., pp. 28-37.

27. A *kerovah* is a "piyyut" or "poem" with which ancient cantors introduced the weekly Torah reading. *Rabbi Yannai: Piyyutim for the Torah and Holidays,* ed. and commentary, Zvi Meir Rabinovitch (Jerusalem: Mossad Bialik and Tel Aviv: University of Tel Aviv, 1985).

28. Michael Riffaterre uses the term *interpretant* to mean a "doublesign" that directs the reader to a punlike reading: *Semiotics of Poetry* (Bloomington and London, 1978), p. 86.

29. Ada Pagis, *Sudden Heart,* pp. 83 and 28.

30. Sidra Dekoven Ezrahi, "Seeking the Meridian: The Reconstitution of Space and Audience in the Poetry of Paul Celan and Dan Pagis," in *Religion and the Authority of the Past,* ed. Tobin Siebers (Ann Arbor: University of Michigan Press).

31. Pagis, *Sudden Heart,* p. 28.

32. Ibid., p. 48.

33. Tuvia Rübner, "Ludwig Straus—Biographische Skizzen," in *Ludwig Strauss 1982–1992,* ed. Hans Otto Horch (Tübingen, Germany: Sonderdruck, 1995), p. 52. Ruebner writes: "I met Ludwig Straus in 1944 . . . at the time I still wrote in German . . . I was young, in a country that was still strange, German was the mother tongue in which I still lived. . . ." In 1996 I met Rübner on Kibbutz Merchavia. He told me that when he first met Pagis upon his arrival at the kibbutz, in 1946, Rübner himself still wrote in German.

34. Shaked, "The Boy Who Gave Up," in *Literature Here and Now* (Tel Aviv: Zmora Bitan, 1993), pp. 285–301 [Hebrew]; and Ariel Hirschfeld, "On the Poetry of Dan Pagis," Afterword to Pagis, *Sudden Heart,* pp. 150–168.

35. Anna Birkenhauer, "Dan Pagis übersetzen," in *Jüdischer Almanach* (Frankfurt am Main, Germany: Leo Bäeck Institute *Jüdischer Verlag,* 1995). Birkenhauer's translations appeared in bilingual translation in *Dan Pagis: Die Krone der Schöplung* (Tübingen, Germany: Staelener Manuskript 10, 1990).

36. Mitchell, *Points of Departure,* p. 26.

37. Pagis, *Collected Poems,* p. 11.

38. "One Moment," *Shirim Shonim* [Different Poems] (Tel Aviv: Kibbutz Hameuchad, 1982), p. 23.

39. Zach, "In the Fields of Then Perhaps," p. 20.

40. See Nili Gold, "Soul Poems," *Modern Hebrew Literature* 18 (spring/summer 1997): 42–44.

41. "What Is Going to Be," in *Because I'm Around,* p. 58.

42. "The Jug," in ibid. p. 82.

43. "To Be Sincere," in ibid., p. 53.

44. *Yehuda Amichai: A Life of Poetry, 1948–1994,* selected and translated by Benjamin and Barbara Harshav (New York: Harper Collins, 1994), p. 169.

45. A general tone of harmony is more characteristic of Amichai. See my book *Lo Kabrosh* [Not Like a Cypress: Transformations of Images and Structures in Amichai's Poetry] (Jerusalem and Tel Aviv: Schocken, 1994), pp. 16, 58, 187, and 191. See also Boaz Arpali, *Haprachim V'Haagartal* [The Flowers and the Vase, Amichai's Poetry 1948–1968] (Kibbutz Hameuchad, 1986), especially his chapter on Amichai's worldview, pp. 206–210. [Hebrew]

46. See Gold, "The 'Feminine' in Yehuda Amichai's Poetics," in *The Experienced Soul: Studies in Amichai,* ed. Glenda Abramson (Westview Press, 1997), pp. 77-92.

47. *Yehuda Amichai,* p. 428.

48. Private interview with Amichai, summer 1996.

49. *Shte Brechot BeYa'ar* [Two Pools in the Wood: Hebrew Poetry and the European Tradition] (Tel Aviv: Tel Aviv University, Hakibbutz Hameuchad Publishing House, 1976. [Hebrew]

50. Amichai, *Lo Me'Achshav Lo Mikan* [Not of This Time, Not of This Place] (Tel Aviv: Schocken, 1964), p. 126 [Hebrew]; unless otherwise indicated translations by the author. The novel was subsequently translated as *Not of This Time, Not of This Place,* trans. Shlomo Katz (New York and Evanston: Harper, 1968). Translations from this edition will be so identified.

51. Tel Aviv: Am Oved Publishers, 1985. [Hebrew] See also an interview with Sandback in *Ha'aretz* (May 1996).

52. Conversation with Amichai, winter 1996; with Miron, summer 1997. He claimed that the original manuscript containing the German passages was lost.

53. Amichai, *Not of This Time,* p. 106.

54. Ibid., p. 95.

55. Ibid., p. 331. [Hebrew]

56. Ibid., p. 322. [Hebrew]

57. Ibid., p. 267. [Hebrew]

58. See Eliezer Schweid's chapter in this book.

59. N. Abraham and M. Torok, *The Shell and the Kernel,* trans. N. Rand (Chicago: University of Chicago Press, 1992), vol. 1. Abraham and Torok described a linguistic mechanism connected to mourning, which they called "designification." The recovery of significance, which is the work of the analyst, they called "cryptonymic analysis." And they also describe a phenomenon they call "hiding in language." The work of the literary critic seems similar to that described by Abraham and Torok as the work of the analyst, who must overcome resistance to meaning that hides in language.

CHAPTER THIRTEEN

German Jewish Writers during the Decline
of the Hapsburg Monarchy:
Assessing the Assessment of Gershon Shaked

Wolfgang Iser

Gershon Shaked is not only one of the founding fathers of Hebrew literary criticism, but his dilemma as a postwar scholar of Jewish literature reflects as well those of the writers whom he discusses and of the tradition he helps to found, both in Israel and abroad. His experience and his example go to the heart of contemporary Jewish identity. Indeed, they bring into focus the double-consciousness that is, perhaps, the signal feature of Jewish modernism, perhaps of modernism itself.

Which of Gershon Shaked's achievements as scholar and critic are most likely to last? It seems to me that the answer is twofold. Both parts are illustrative of his singular, and yet representative, position. Shaked has advanced a unique concept of history, and he has provided an equally illuminating approach to the connection between literature and life. In his masterly and massively erudite work on modern Hebrew literature, he unfolds a concept of history that is scarcely matched by any such concept in the West.[1] Faced by writers trying to create literature in a language with no literary tradition, writers who had started writing outside Israel, and were addressing a people not yet united in a nation-state, though striving to maintain a ramified heritage that was to be transplanted into *Eretz Yisrael,* Shaked, wanting to plumb the meaning of it all, was confronted with a formidable challenge. The need to reconcile such diverse elements could not be fulfilled by imposing a pattern from outside. The multifarious connections between the religious traditions, and their transposition into a present that was bound to affect them, required a notion of history that would be neither a linear advance to an imagined goal nor the realization of a preordained telos.

History, then, as Gershon Shaked conceives of it, is a kaleidoscopically changing intertextuality by means of which all of the manifested facets of writers' texts are given a different slant when taken up in subsequent allusions. Thus modern Hebrew literature is presented as a mobile network in which the interlinkage between the heritage, the contemporary challenge, the flavor of localities, aims, and even utopian fantasies is continually processed. What Shaked allows us to see is that history is something that happens, and one might be inclined to maintain that modern Hebrew literature—at least for someone like myself looking at it from outside—provides a vivid picture of history as something in the making. This is the concept of history to which Shaked has given shape.

Shaked's idea of history, portrayed through modern Hebrew literature, would require further elaboration in order to reveal its potential for explaining change and transformation, but I should like to focus on his other achievement: his concept of literature as an adumbration of what lies buried in life. There is no doubt that this approach figures prominently in his interpretation of modern Hebrew literature; however, it can best be laid bare in what I am inclined to call the "deep structure" of the works of two Jewish authors who wrote in German at the eve of the decline and subsequent collapse of the Austro-Hungarian Empire: Franz Kafka (1883–1924) and Joseph Roth (1894–1939).

In discussing this aspect of Shaked's work, I am not only on much safer ground than I would be with Hebrew literature, but I also sense a close affinity between himself and these two writers, who appear to have more than just literary significance for him. I should not like to judge which of the two aspects of Shaked's work is of greater import, but I have no hesitation in saying that his penetrating insights into Kafka and Roth are the most innovative I have ever come across.

Of course, it is hard—especially for an outsider like myself—to account for the impetus that made it possible for Shaked to open up the works of Kafka and Roth in such an original and illuminating manner. There are, however, certain indications to be found in his essay on Saul Friedländer, which is permeated by his own autobiographical reflections.[2] He talks of a pre-Holocaust experience shared by at least some Israelis of his generation, and such an experience, he continues, is at certain moments overwhelmingly present; it does not obscure the monstrousness of the Holocaust, and yet there is a prevailing consciousness that one does not want to be freed from such an experience.[3]

Though the past is irrecoverable, it overshadows the present which, in turn, throws light on the past. It is in such a situation—as Shaked writes—that the survivor feels driven to find a place among the fragments of his mutilated self that will allow him to ponder whether there is any relationship at all between him as a victim and the identity imposed on him by his situation.[4] As such a relationship is impossible to grasp, reflecting on it translates into a heightened sensibility for what it is like to dwell among the ruins of one's self. The trauma of the past can never be eradicated, and so there is no reconciliation with the countries of Europe that turned their backs on their erstwhile Jewish citizens. And Shaked concludes his essay on Friedländer by saying: "I too have lost the foundation of my existence, and hence there is no return to this once and forever destroyed basis."[5]

I am inclined to point out that although Shaked indeed did not return to where he started out from, he did focus on a not unfamiliar past, represented by writers like Kafka and Roth, whose work had fathomed the *condition juive* in the diaspora.[6] Fiction is a mode of writing that allows one to be transported into otherwise inaccessible situations, but this is not Shaked's concern. Instead, he understands fictionality as a surface structure in which a mutilated life finds expression, though simultaneously without any hope of the catharsis that a manifestation of suffering seems to promise. Thus, the life of the past is present in the fictionality of these writers, the exposition of which—so lucidly done by Shaked—makes it possible to explore the shifting scenes between literature and life.

Before trying to detail this original approach, let me say a few words about the situation in which these German-speaking Jewish writers found themselves when the Austro-Hungarian Empire was on the wane. The Jews, as Hannah Arendt once remarked, were the "state people" (Staatsvolk) par excellence in Austria.[7] "They did not constitute a nationality," as Carl Schorske has quite rightly observed, not even a so-called unhistoric nationality like

> the Slovaks or the Ukrainians. Their civic and economic existence depended not on their participation in a national community, such as the German or the Czech, but, on the contrary, on not acquiring such a status. Even if they became assimilated completely to the

culture of a given nationality, they could not outgrow the status
of "converts to that nationality." Neither allegiance to the emperor
nor allegiance to liberalism as a political system posed such
difficulties. The emperor and the liberal system offered status to
the Jews without demanding nationality; they became a supra-
national people of the multi-national state. Their fortunes rose
and fell with those of the liberal, cosmopolitan state. . . . Thus, to
the degree to which the nationalists tried to weaken the central
power of the monarchy in their interest, the Jews were attacked
in the name of every nation. . . . If the emperor was supra-national,
the Jews were subnational, the omnipresent folk substance of the
Empire, whose representatives could be found in every national . . .
grouping. In whatever group they functioned, the Jews never strove
to dismember the Empire. That is why they became the victims of
every centrifugal force, as soon as, and only as long as, that force
aimed to subvert the Empire.[8]

This basic situation in which the Jews found themselves within
the monarchy was overshadowed by a growing pessimism. As early
as 1866, Emperor Franz Joseph had written to his mother: "One
just has to resist as long as possible, do one's duty to the last, and
finally perish with honour."[9] At that time the emperor was only
thirty-six years of age, to quote one authority in the field:

In his will he made arrangements in case "the crown should no
longer remain with our House,"and he advised his daughter, Gisela
[then living in Bavaria] to claim her fortune on his death, since
"it would be safer in Germany than in Vienna." Likewise, Arch-
duke Rudolf [the crown prince of the empire] before committing
suicide at Mayerling, wrote to his sister Maria Valerie, advising
her to leave Austria "when Papa passes away" since, as he put it,
"only I know what will happen then."

This pessimism, however concerning "the future of the Monarchy from the 1890s onward can be linked . . . with the great cultural effervescence that was taking place there at the same time.
This was the period after all of Schnitzler and von Hofmannsthal
in literature; Freud in psychoanalysis; Mahler and Schönberg in
music; Klimt and Schiele in painting; and Kraus in satire. Carl
Schorske has suggested that the connection is to be found in a
flight into art and aesthetics as a reaction to the political sterility
of the times, while others have stressed the darker side of this
cultural climax itself: the obsession with the ego, with sensuality,
with ideology, and with death. . . . Karl Kraus, it will be recalled,

saw the intellectual ferment of his day as a sign of cultural decay or mental hysteria in an Empire that he damned as the 'research laboratory for world destruction'."[10]

We need not continue painting this picture of the declining Austro-Hungarian Empire; what has to be kept in mind, though, from this brief survey is the position of the Jews as the actual "state people" of the monarchy, who did not belong to any nationality but did not form one themselves, as well as the modernity that arose out of the declining empire and that—to an overwhelming extent—was the work of assimilated Jews. What Shaked allows us to perceive through his interpretation of Kafka and Roth are basic features of the *condition juive* in such a situation, and the extent to which the assimilated Jews not only brought about modernity, but simultaneously diagnosed it.

The *condition juive* was marked by a dual identity, which Kafka once described in a letter to Brod as follows: "With their hind legs the Jews are fastened to the Jewish tradition of the fathers, and with their forelegs they get no ground under their feet. The despair thus ensuing translates into inspiration."[11] Such a self-characterization, which Shaked quotes in full, is all the more remarkable as Kafka's writings show no trace whatsoever of his Jewish heritage, although in his diaries and letters he reveals a searching curiosity about European Jewry. In actual fact, shortly before his first book came out in 1912, he wrote to Felice Bauer, his one-time fiancée, that he would like to go with her to Palestine.[12]

This split between Kafka's private attitude and his work is Shaked's starting point for delineating what dual identity may entail. Kafka does not suppress his Jewish heritage, but transfigures it to such an extent that the deep structure of what it means to be a Jew in the diaspora is tellingly revealed. Shaked provides a phenomenology of this dual identity, which applies not only to Kafka but to Roth as well. Such an assessment distinguishes his approach from the great many allegorical readings to which Kafka has been so frequently subjected. Almost all of Kafka's novels and short stories are devoid of any temporal frame and spatial location. There are no references to either history or nationality. Within such timelessness, however, his characters face nonacceptance within a society that makes them into outsiders; they are in perpetual flight, driven from one place to another, accused without knowing what crime they are supposed to have committed, and thus made to feel guilty because they do not know what they have done.

Nonacceptance, persecution, and exile are made all the more oppressive by the thin air of abstraction that characterizes the world in which this humiliation occurs. There are no reasons to be ascertained for this debasement, and no redemption is foreshadowed in this guiltless suffering. Stripping his narratives of all these references, Kafka penetratingly drives home the situation of the diaspora Jew, and the implications of dual identity. If he had introduced into his stories local, social, and historical references, it would have been easy to blame these for his characters' sufferings. But by barring them, he bars all sociological explanations of what it is like to be without a nationality and without all the other attributes necessary for acceptance in a society that gains its stability not least by what it excludes.

Shaked concludes that Kafka transformed the *condition juive* into a new form of art by converting the fate of being outside history into an "absolute virtue," which is open to manifold interpretations.[13] I am inclined to add that none of the interpretations provoked by this "absolute virtue"—which I take to be a cipher for what remains unspeakable—can ever exhaust its inherent unspeakability. Nevertheless, Shaked has provided us with a key to this cipher by highlighting dual identity as the hallmark of Kafka's writings. Dual identity means first and foremost that one has none at all, as it is a contradiction in itself to have two identities at the same time. Whoever is driven to a dual identity hangs in an in-between position, and thus experiences what is unattainable. Shaked offers two main explanations for such a situation.

One might say that the *condition juive* was marked by an external and an internal predicament on the eve of the decline of the Austro-Hungarian Empire. On the one hand there was the pressure for assimilation to which Jews felt exposed because they did not belong to any nationality within this multinational realm, although, as Hannah Arendt has rightly claimed, they were the "state people" par excellence, and thus as supranational as the emperor himself. (One must add that such a qualification applied first and foremost to the Jewish elite.) On the other hand, the urgent need to become assimilated meant, as Kafka put it so succinctly, cutting oneself loose from the Jewish heritage without getting sufficient ground under one's feet.

Being exiled within the society in which they lived, and simultaneously responding to this nonacceptance by exiling themselves from their own heritage, the Jews found themselves in a dilemma when the empire was on the verge of collapse. Thus dual identity, according to Shaked, entailed living in limbo, since two identities are mutually exclusive. As Kafka himself remarked, living in limbo led to despair, and yet this very despair was the source of his inspiration. This brings us back to Shaked's statement that Kafka transformed the Jewish situation into a new form of art. What is implied here is that Kafka does not confine himself to merely imitating the *condition juive* in the diaspora, but that he fathoms the very nature of duality as the mainspring of "inspiration." Being in limbo is a state that cannot be sustained in day-to-day living, and what is mutually exclusive, namely having two identities at once, can never be balanced within the demands of everyday life. And yet the very impossibility of living a dual identity created an urgent need to grasp the multifarious implications of such a situation. Kafka's fiction, therefore, is an enactment of what it is like to live in limbo; he explores all the potential ramifications, more often than not breaking off the very enactment by fragmenting the stories, thus intimating that there are no escape hatches.

There is a faint ring of Dante's *Inferno* in these stories, which is made all the more telling by the eclipse of all hope, let alone solution. What could be the "absolute virtue" of this new form of art, which quite rightly is perceived in Kafka's writings? One might answer this question by saying that fiction as an extension of human beings allows us to figure out what is beyond conceivability, such as the manifold defeats of living in limbo, and thus fictionality may turn into an artistic triumph, because it lures into presence what otherwise would remain ungraspable. This triumph would be Kafka's "virtue," in Shaked's terms. But in what way is it "absolute"? A tentative answer could be that it redeems an irredeemable situation by conjuring it up as an image. The image that Kafka has created of dual identity as life in limbo teems with suggestions that each reader is tempted to work out for him- or herself, only to learn that the references brought to bear cause a vast intangibility to collapse into a mere allegory, which has to be dismantled again in order to reincorporate features excluded from the explanatory pattern that readers fashion for themselves.

Shaked himself has demonstrated how such an experience is engendered in his reading of Kafka's novel *Amerika*. He likens the life of the hero to the myth of Sisyphus, though this does not imply that Kafka's narrative is just a recurrence of an ancient myth. Instead, the story functions, according to Shaked, as a means of spelling out the inconceivable implications of failed repetition.[14] Each chapter has a unity of its own, yet their sequence does not move forward, let alone point to what is to come. There is nothing but unending repetitive failures. Such a pattern of discontinuity, strictly observed in the composition of the novel, turns into a challenge for the reader. This becomes all the more compelling, as the surface structure of the text has a great many social references, tempting the reader to look for something underneath that may tie them together. But whenever the reader does try to provide missing links between the chapters, the bridges built have to be demolished again in view of the new information that is now to be accommodated.

Thus the established patterns must continuously be discarded. As this goes on to the "end" of the novel which—in actual fact, peters out into open-endedness—the reader is turned involuntarily into a Sisyphus, and is thus made to experience what it means never to get ground under one's feet.[15] As the reader is driven to a cyclic repetition of failed meanings, the Sisyphus syndrome highlights an underlying pattern of the modern world, which realizes itself by continually invalidating any kind of reality. Consequently, a nightmarish unreality keeps growing, which makes the incidents perceived into palpable manifestations of an inescapable labyrinth, in which the reader is left to wander in a hopeless state of disorientation. It is interesting to note that Kafka, in a letter to Felice, described his ideal way of life as being locked away with his pen in a spacious vault, allowing him to delve into the innermost recesses of himself, tearing out into the open what is impermeable.[16]

Shaked's analysis of Kafka's *Amerika* becomes all the more intriguing when viewed in relation to the American Jewish authors to whom he devotes a great deal of his attention.[17] If Kafka's *Amerika* is—as Shaked makes us see it—a panorama of flickering shapes that arise out of an inescapable labyrinth, it is diametrically opposite to the world of the American Jewish writers insofar as they exchange Kafka's labyrinth for mythological or literary patterns that structure their stories. Be it a Jewish Schlemihl in Malamud, a Caliban or a Don Quixote in Saul Bellow, characters from Fyodor Dostoyevsky or Leo Tolstoi in Lelchuk, or structures taken either from Boccaccio or the commedia dell' arte in Philip Roth—in all these instances, traditional European patterns serve the American writers concerned to explore social conflicts, to level criticism at the American way of life, or to meet the challenges of social Darwinism in the new world by trying to uphold moral standards inherited from their past. It is one of Shaked's most piercing insights that he has brought out the deep-seated difference between Kafka and the

American Jewish writers, not least by choosing for such a demonstration Kafka's *Amerika,* which allows him to drive home the predicament of dual identity. Execution would be a redemption for Kafka's hero, but perennial persecution is the only form of execution open to him. The setting of the New World thus serves only to make the dilemma more oppressive by canceling out the promises that the land of unlimited opportunity had seemed to hold in store.

Shaked's insight into dual identity as life in limbo, the salient features of which he has so masterfully delineated by contrasting Kafka's *Amerika* with the American Jewish writers, has yet another side to it, for it explains the tremendous fascination Kafka exercised after the Second World War. Although Shaked does not deal directly with the veritable explosion of interest that elevated Kafka to the pinnacle of modernity, he nevertheless provides a key to this unprecedented impact on contemporary consciousness. To what extent, then, is dual identity, demonstrated by Shaked so persuasively as a manifestation of the *condition juive,* also a pointer to the situation of subjectivity in the modern world?

Dual identity implies being grounded in neither identity, and such a situation squares almost exactly with what modern subjectivity is exposed to. It is the hallmark of the latter that any ground it might have, is withheld from it. This may be one of the reasons why ideologies have been so rampant in our century. They are concoctions devised to compensate for what remains unavailable. Unavailability of origins is the stigma of modernity that inscribes itself even into its compensations. Lack of access to any base is a nagging presence in the conscious life of the modern subject, whose decentered position makes it not only into a subject without self, but also into a vortex of ever-changing shapes. Such a duality is double-edged: on the one hand it may cause paralysis, but on the other it energizes the drive to cope with it.

Thus inaccessibility turns into the matrix of an experimental creativity, which is both the epitome and the predicament of modernity. Being wedged between dualities entails that, in Kafka's frightening terminology, there is no ground under one's feet. Simultaneously, it is impossible to keep alive in limbo, just as it is impossible to exist on the tip of a pin as Søren Kierkegaard, another forerunner of modernity, put it. This insoluble duality is at the heart of creation, as was sensed most keenly by the Jewish intellectuals of the declining Austro-Hungarian Empire in consequence of the paradoxical experience of dual identity to which this "state people" of the monarchy found itself condemned. It was the attempt to overcome such imposed self-alienation that made the Jewish intellectuals of the empire into the spearhead of modernity.

There are similar traces also to be spotted in the work of Joseph Roth, to whom Shaked has devoted several important essays that are both enlightening and moving. Roth was Kafka's junior by eleven years, which makes all the difference between them in view of the historic changes Roth witnessed and was subjected to. Interestingly enough, Shaked does not deal with Roth's yearnings for the vanished monarchy, which Roth considered his *Vaterland* (fatherland)—a word that has its peculiar ring in German only. The Austro-Hungarian Empire was, as he solemnly avowed, his fatherland because it allowed him to be both a patriot and a citizen of the world, both an Austrian and a German among the many nationalities of the monarchy.[18] Roth has built a monument to the perished empire in his masterpiece *Radetzkymarsch,* published in 1932, two years after his first really great novel *Hiob* had appeared. If the former is a lament for an irretrievable past, the latter describes the exodus from the shtetl. And it is to *Hiob* that Shaked has devoted his attention, not least perhaps as Roth's nostalgia for the empire remains on the surface of Jewish life, whereas Shaked wants to get down to its roots. Therefore he looks for traces of "Jewishness" in this German-Jewish novel on Job which, by common consent, is one of Roth's peak achievements. This search makes him explore the deep structure of Roth's narrative, just as he had done in his penetrating analysis of Kafka's work.

However, in Roth's case it is another form of duality that Shaked focuses on: that between different languages.[19] Roth's hero, Mendel Singer, does not speak German, and so his language has to be transposed into an alien idiom. This becomes all the more intrusive when Jewish terms such as *melamed, schlemasel, matzo, tefilim,* or even German-sounding words like *kosak* have to be rendered in German, for whatever equivalent is given, the two designations never have the same meaning. This, as Shaked maintains, brings out a sociosemiotic duality.[20] Different cultural codes are coupled with one another, thereby throwing light on their respective specificity, and simultaneously adumbrating what cannot be fathomed and thus defies translatability. Hence we arrive at a paradoxical situation: what is represented in Roth's novel proves to be a state of affairs that does not exist in the very language through which it is presented.[21]

Again there is a palpable split that in turn brings out the quandary of assimilation. The heritage has to be defamiliarized in order to be preserved, but it can only be preserved in a state of disfigurement. Simultaneously, Roth tries to make up for these sacrifices by what has been described as the intertextual patterns of the novel, which are programmatically indicated by the title of the narrative.[22] The title foreshadows what is to come: namely a network of multilayered relationships between the Bible and a welter of texts from the Jewish canon, religious observances, myths, and legends, all of which are intertwined with, and shade into, one another. Such an intertextual pattern, in which the Jewish heritage as well as the life of the shtetl in all its facets is assembled, figures as cultural memory, thus overshadowing the process of assimilation that destroys Mendel Singer's family and turns him into a modern Job.

Cultural memory is collective memory, which cannot be genetically transmitted, and thus has to find its own form. Intertextuality is the epitome of cultural memory, through which forgetting and remembering, the feed forward of the storage, the representation of the absent, and the compensation for loss are given salient features. When cultural memory recalls the absent into presence, when it remembers what has been forgotten, and when it mourns what is irretrievably lost, a duality emerges, intertwining that which is ineluctably separate. Again a duality of a different sort looms large, and what it shows is the graduated sequence of ever-changing dualities into which the basic split of dual identity issues. Instead of a solution to the initially imposed self-division, this very split generates multiple dualities, each of which is marked by the effort to overcome what has caused it. There is a final duality in Roth's Hiob to which Shaked draws our attention. Emigration leads to catastrophe, and yet Menuchim, the son of Mendel, becomes an acclaimed artist, thus redeeming his social group through the recognition earned. Shaked explains this final duality as a parallel between a negative and a positive paradigm of assimilation.[23] Only the artist appears to be able to achieve reconciliation of the dual existence foisted upon him by the world in which he wants to assert himself.

Such a reconciliation was certainly Roth's own longed-for option, borne out not least by his correspondence with Stefan Zweig, whom he admired, as Zweig seemed to have found security in a paradise regained, whereas he, Joseph Roth, considered himself an outcast, cut off from where he wanted to belong.[24] Shaked conceives of this correspondence as an epistolary novel, which he reads as if an intended reader were implied.[25] It is only such an assumed reader who can experience the exchange between Roth and Zweig as the inherent drama between the deracinated Eastern and the assimilated Western Jew. Never to be able to take roots again after having left the shtetl caused Roth to elevate Zweig into his super-ego, an adored stepfather, and a deeply revered prison guard. Shaked makes us feel how the split of dual identity cuts to the quick—a pain that Roth wanted to alleviate, if not to undo by an exaggerated devotion to Zweig, who featured for him as a role model, since he seemed to have overcome the stigma under which Roth labored all his life.

Reconciliation, however, is not an ultimate goal for Roth, in spite of his desire to achieve as an artist what his dual identity denied him. Nevertheless, fathoming the unfathomable made him, like his Jewish contemporaries, into a pioneer of modernity. Becoming an artist in order to redeem a bisected life has a hidden dimension to it that Roth explored in his short story "Leviathan," which Shaked has selected as the basis for his assessment of Roth as an artist.[26] The duality that Shaked spotlights in this story—published in its entirety only one year after Roth's death (1940)—reveals the deep structure that underlies dual identity, and simultaneously allows us to perceive the mainspring of artistic creation. The hero, Nissen Piczenick, is a peddler, dealing in corals that come out of the ocean in whose depths resides Leviathan, symbolizing both fecundity and destruction. The hero is drawn to this ambivalent symbol, and his craze for corals arises out of their doubleness, as these petrified creatures indicate for him the transference of life from water to land.[27] Thus the corals and Leviathan form a link between the unbounded space of the sea and the quotidian life of the shtetl. Piczenik has a deep emotional bond to corals, which for him are much more than just merchandise; the life of the shtetl, however, grows more and more unbearable for him.[28] Emigration becomes his burning desire, and it draws him more and more toward plunging into the ocean, in order to shed the identity by which he feels hedged in, and find another in the boundlessness of the sea. However, at the bottom of the ocean reigns Leviathan, whose duality is duplicitous, as he symbolizes fecundity and destruction. Thus the ocean represents paradise and hell at the same time. The exodus from the shtetl, subconsciously motivated by establishing contact with the ocean, ends in disaster: Piczenick is drowned. Death by water, according to Shaked, has a dual implication: emigration as the last act of assimilation means heading for death; and the desire to get to one's roots by delving into the unconscious means death by dissolution.[29]

One final aspect of this duality deserves attention. Roth himself characterizes his hero as an "oceanic Nissen Piczenick," a human being who "has been turned from inside out," and Roth leaves no doubt that he unreservedly approves of his hero's actions.[30] "Oceanic," of course, has a Freudian ring; and Leviathan, according to Roth, is boundless, infinite, and thus transcending all limitations. The corals, on the other hand, have almost artistically wrought shapes. It is not difficult to read such a pairing as interplay between the primary and secondary process, or in the words of another brilliant, though unjustly forgotten Viennese Jew, Anton Ehrenzweig:

> [the] creative ego rhythm [must] be able to suspend the boundaries between self and not-self in order to become more at home in the world of reality where the objects and self are clearly held apart. The ego rhythm of differentiation and dedifferentiation constantly swings between these two poles and between the inside and the outside world. . . . Temporary dedifferentiation if it is extreme, as in oceanic states, implies a paralysis of surface functions and so can act very disruptively. But the ego could not function at all without its rhythm oscillating between its different levels.[31]

Ehrenzweig concludes by saying that the "minimum content of art, then, may be the representation of the creative process in the ego."[32] What is represented is not something given, but something that does not yet exist. This is exactly what Roth has achieved. Through his hero he has illuminated the precariousness out of which art arises, and has transmuted his own ineluctable duality into a vivid perception of the creative matrix.

Shaked's sociosemiotic approach has the priceless quality that it allows for multiple readings of the authors concerned. Even if he does not exhaust the potential readings that offer themselves— impossible in a book, let alone in an essay—he does unfold a whole range of implications inherent in dual identity. The sociosemiotic approach shows how different cultural codes have to be read, and points to what emerges from the clashes between and the couplings of these codes. Since a basic drive of European modernity originated in the dual identity of the Jewish intellectuals of the Austro-Hungarian Empire, Shaked's assessment of what is mutually exclusive unfolds itself as a trailblazing means of reading culture.

Notes

1. Gershon Shaked, *Geschichte der Modernen Hebräischen Literatur. Prosa von 1880–1980* (Frankfurt am Main: Jüdischer Verlag, 1996), which is an abridged version of the five-volume edition *Hassiporet Haivrit* (Jerusalem and Tel Aviv, 1977–1993).

2. "Kein anderer Ort: Über Saul Friedländer," in Shaked, *Die Macht der Identität. Essays über jüdische Schriftsteller* (Königstein: Jüdischer Verlag bei Athenaeum, 1986), pp. 181–191.

3. Ibid., p. 182.

4. Ibid.

5. Ibid., p. 190.

6. See "Kafka: Jüdisches Erbe und hebräische Literatur," in Shaked, *Die Macht der Identität,* p. 23.

7. Hannah Arendt, *The Origins of Totalitarianism* (New York: Meridian Books, 1958), especially chap. 2.

8. Carl Schorske, *Fin-de-Siècle Vienna: Politics and Culture* (New York: Knopf, 1980), pp. 129ff.

9. Alan Sked, *The Decline and Fall of the Habsburg Empire 1815–1918* (London and New York, 1994), p. 229.

10. Ibid., p. 230.

11. Quoted by Shaked in "Kafka: Jüdisches Erbe und hebräische Literatur," *Macht der Identität,* p. 18. All translations, if not otherwise indicated, are mine.

12. See Elias Canetti, *Das Gewissen der Worte* (München: Hanser, 1983), p. 77.

13. "Kafka: Jüdisches Erbe und hebräische Literatur," in Shaked, *Macht der Identität,* p. 30.

14. See "Der ewige Jude in Kafkas 'Amerika'," in ibid., p. 37.

15. See ibid., p. 40.

16. See Canetti, *Das Gewissen der Worte,* pp. 97 ff.

17. See his essays on Bernard Malamud, Saul Bellow, Philip Roth, and Allen Lelchuk, in Shaked, *Macht der Identität,* pp. 115–180.

18. See David Bronson, *Joseph Roth. Eine Biographie* (Köln: Kiepenheurer & Witsch, 1974), pp. 400–402, who quotes at length Roth's preface to the prepublication of *Radetzkymarsch* in the *Frankfurter Zeitung* of April 17, 1932, in which Roth expressed his deep devotion to the vanished *Vaterland.*

19. "Wie jüdisch ist ein jüdisch-deutscher Roman? Über Joseph Roths 'Hiob'," in Shaked, *Macht der Identität*, p. 82.

20. Ibid., p. 83.

21. Ibid., pp. 92ff.

22. See ibid., p. 88.

23. Ibid., pp. 90ff.

24. See "Die Gnade der Vernunft und die des Unglücks. Zum Briefwechsel zwischen Zweig und Roth," in Shaked, ibid., p. 71.

25. Ibid., pp. 60 and 62.

26. Shaked, "Kulturangst und Sehnsucht nach dem Tode. Joseph Roths 'Der Leviathan'—die intertextuelle Mythisierung der Kleinstadtgeschichte," in *Joseph Roth. Interpretation—Kritik—Rezeption*, eds. Michael Kessler and Fritz Hackert (Tübingen: Stauffenburg Verlag, 1990), pp. 279–298.

27. See ibid., p. 282.

28. Ibid., p. 284.

29. Ibid., pp. 285 and 289.

30. Joseph Roth, *Werke III*, ed. Hermann Kesten (Köln 1976), p. 276.

31. Anton Ehrenzweig, *The Hidden Order of Art: A Study in the Psychology of Artistic Expression* (Berkeley and Los Angeles, 1971), p. 121.

32. Ibid., p. 174.

Contributors

Emily Miller Budick, The Hebrew University
Budick is the Ann and Joseph Edelman Professor of American Studies and chair of the department. Her primary field of expertise is American Literature, having published such studies as *Emily Dickinson and the Life of Language* (1985), *Fiction and Historical Consciousness* (1989), *Engendering Romance* (1994), *Nineteenth-Century American Romance* (1996), and *Blacks and Jews in Literary Conversation* (1998). Recently she edited the English translation of Gershon Shaked's *Modern Hebrew Fiction.*

H. M. Daleski, The Hebrew University
Daleski is a professor emeritus of the English Department. He earned his mark as a literary critic with groundbreaking studies of British fiction, including *The Forked Flame* (1965), *Dickens and the Art of Analogy* (1970), *Joseph Conrad, The Way of Dispossession* (1977), *The Divided Heroine* (1984), and *Thomas Hardy and Paradoxes of Love* (1997). He's a member of the Israeli Academy of Arts and Sciences, and a recipient of the Israel Prize. Recently he was elected to the American Academy of Arts and Sciences.

Morris Dickstein, Graduate Center, City College of New York
Dickstein is a well-known scholar of American thought and culture, who has published on such subjects as *Keats and His Poetry* (1971) and *Double Agent: The Critic and Society* (1992). Recently, he has turned his attention to the project of American Jewish literature and identity. The chapter in this book is part of his current research.

Nili Rachel Scharf Gold, The University of Pennsylvania
Gold teaches Hebrew literature in the Department of Asian and Middle Eastern Studies. Her publications include *Lo Kabrosh* [Not like a Cypress] on the poet Yehuda Amichai and essays on Amichai, Lea Goldberg, and Aharon Appefeld.

Wolfgang Iser, University of California, Irvine and University of Konstanz
Professor emeritus of English Literature, Iser is a literary theorist, primarily known for his theory of reader-response criticism and for his pioneering studies in the field of literary anthropology. Some of his major publications include *The Implied Reader* (1974), *The Act of Reading* (1978), *Prospecting* (1989), and *The Fictive and the Imaginary* (1993).

Michael P. Kramer, Bar-Ilan University
Although Kramer started his career as a specialist in early American literature, he now teaches and writes on ethnic fiction, in particular Jewish American writing. He has edited *New Essays on Seize the Day* and is now involved in a larger project on Jewish American writing and culture. His book *Imagining Language in America* appeared in 1992.

Yitzhak Laor, Tel Aviv University
Laor teaches literature and has published many books of poetry and fiction. He also writes for *Ha'aretz* on both political and cultural affairs.

David G. Roskies, Jewish Theological Seminary of New York
Roskies, who is coeditor of the journal *Prooftexts,* is one of the foremost Yiddishists in the United States today. He has published extensively on Jewish writing, both in Yiddish and in Hebrew, and has been in charge of several translation projects dealing with the recovery of Yiddish texts. His publications include *Against Apocalypse* (1984), *The Literature of Destruction* (1989), and *The Jewish Search for a Usable Past* (1999).

Eliezer Schweid, The Hebrew University
Schweid is a professor emeritus in the Department of Jewish Philosophy. He is a widely published scholar, many of whose books and articles in the field of Jewish thought have been translated from Hebrew to English. He has also written extensively in the field of Hebrew literature, and is a popular commentator on current events, in particular concerning tensions between Jewish orthodoxy and secularism. Among the English translations of his works are *Israel at the Crossroads* (1973) and *Wrestling Until Day-Break: Searching for Meaning in the Thinking on the Holocaust* (1994).

Gershon Shaked, The Hebrew University
Shaked is Israel's foremost scholar of Hebrew literature. He is a professor emeritus in the Hebrew Literature department, who has published and lectured widely abroad, his works appearing not only in the original Hebrew but in many translations as well. He has just published the fifth volume of his comprehensive history of Hebrew fiction from 1881 to the present, part of which is excerpted in a one-volume English abridgment. Other English translations of his work include *The Shadows Within* (1987) and *Shmuel Yosef Agnon* (1989).

Hana Wirth-Nesher, Tel-Aviv University
Wirth-Nesher teaches in the English Department. She holds the Samuel L. and Perry Haber Chair on the Study of the Jewish Experience in the United States. She has edited *What Is Jewish Literature* (1997) and *New Essays on Call It Sleep* (1996). Her book *City Codes* appeared in 1996.

Ruth Wisse, Harvard University
Wisse is a professor of Yiddish and Comparative Literature. In addition to publishing widely in the field of Yiddish literature, and editing and translating many works of Yiddish writing, she has dealt as well with issues of Jewish identity, in particular in relation to contemporary American Jewish and Israeli politics. Her books include *The Schleimiel as Modern Hero* (1980), *I. L. Peretz and the Making of Modern Culture* (1991), and, most recently, *The Modern Jewish Canon* (2000).

A. B. Yehoshua, University of Haifa
Yehoshua teaches literary criticism and is one of Israel's most well-known authors, who has been translated extensively into most European languages as well as into English. Of the Israeli authors read abroad he is one of the most popular, in particular in the United States, where his *Mr. Mani* was a huge success several years ago. Other novels include *A Late Divorce* and most recently *Journey to the End of the Millennium.* He has been a general commentator on Israeli culture and politics throughout his career.

Index